Bouncing off Guardrails

Bouncing off Guardrails

Somewhere in Life Between Victorious Triumph and Horrific Annihilation

Axe

of
Y Chrome Customs LLC
www.ychrome.com

A person can't ever appreciate the real high highs without enduring the real low lows. At that time I understood what he was saying, but I had no idea of the roller coaster that lay ahead of me. —**Axe**

NEW YORK

Bouncing off Guardrails

Somewhere in Life Between Victorious Triumph and Horrific Annihilation

ISBN 978-1-61448-255-0 paperback
ISBN 978-1-61448-256-7 eBook
Library of Congress Control Number: 2012933818

Morgan James Publishing
The Entrepreneurial Publisher
5 Penn Plaza, 23rd Floor,
New York City, New York 10001
(212) 655-5470 office • (516) 908-4496 fax
www.MorganJamesPublishing.com

Front cover photograph by:
AJ Witt Photography

Back cover photograph by:
Travis Daniels Photography

Cover Design by:
Rachel Lopez
www.r2cdesign.com

Interior Design by:
Bonnie Bushman
bonnie@caboodlegraphics.com

In an effort to support local communities, raise awareness and funds, Morgan James Publishing donates a percentage of all book sales for the life of each book to Habitat for Humanity Peninsula and Greater Williamsburg.

Get involved today, visit
www.MorganJamesBuilds.com.

Habitat
for Humanity®
Peninsula and
Greater Williamsburg
Building Partner

Table of Contents

v

Part I
Der Alte

Chapter 1

Acceptance

Wed 29 Oct 08

Who the hell is waking me up by ringing my fucking doorbell at 2:30 am? It must be Sunshine, but why doesn't she just use her key? Wait a minute; she's lying next to me. I can feel her arm over there across the king mattress. If she's lying here already, who the hell's at the door? As I blink my eyes and try to adjust my pupils to the dark, I grab the Smith & Wesson .44 mag from under the bed. It's always loaded, so I never have to wonder at times like this. Guns are like rubbers and airbags; I'd rather have one and not need it than vice versa.

I walk quietly toward the door, biasing my weight toward the toes instead of my usual heel-heavy stomp. It's a good thing I live in a little one-bedroom shoebox, so it's a short walk for me as I follow the ridiculously long 8" blued barrel toward the entrance to the cave. The red front site is right behind the door as I slowly open it and peek both ways down the breezeway. No one is out there. I know I'm a light sleeper, but it's not that I just woke up and thought it was because of the doorbell. I'd swear on my left nut, even if it is the blown one, that I heard that damn doorbell.

As I close the door and lower the heavy revolver to my side, I think about what day it is and realize it's Wednesday. I die one week from today. My overactive brain pictures the grim reaper standing out there in a ragged black cloak with his rusty scythe slung over one shoulder. The image in my half-asleep mind isn't a comical reaper like Death from "Family Guy." Instead, menacing red eyes peer out from beneath his hood while a bony finger rings the doorbell, representative of the symbolic "death knocking at my door." Maybe whoever's in charge of quotes and clichés should get with the times and change it to "death ringing my doorbell" or "death texting me" something like, "u di n 1 wk."

With the image of the reaper standing outside ringing my doorbell and my already fucked up sleep pattern, I know I won't be able to go back to sleep before I have to get up for work. I tell Sunshine I need to go for a drive to clear my head, and point the Goat straight toward YCC. There shouldn't be many JSO's out at this time, and a 45 mph speed limit is way too low for the open sections of Southside, but I better still keep it under 60 mph. All I need is a fucking ticket right now, although I could have a damn good excuse for not paying it soon, depending on how things go next week.

Fortunately Sunshine's a very understanding girl, and accepts the fact that I'm not exactly normal to begin with. Normal people wouldn't picture an agent of death in black standing outside their shoebox apartment in the middle of the night. They wouldn't be sitting in their motorcycle shop in a crack neighborhood at 4 am listening to the Sixx AM cd noting the irony of the lyrics somewhat paralleling their own life. Someone normal wouldn't be staring at a lopsided desk barely stable enough to hold the .40 cal, Crackberry, wallet, keys, and computer screen that's slowly filling with words pieced together from a completely frazzled brain.

I type fast, but I can't keep up with all this shit whirring around between my ears. I stop and look around the shop's office at the Terminator movie poster, a Josey Wales picture, and faded pictures of faded memories in years past on a chopper, getting hammered with my buddies at the first dry VEISHEA, and on my old General with a bottle of whiskey tipped up wearing a shirt that says, "Born on a mountain, raised in a cave, biking and fucking is all I crave." Time has taken a toll on the guys in all those pictures from Arnie to Clint to me. I crack a smirk at my sign that says, "Alcohol, it's my anti-drug." Below it are pinned a hospital bracelet from when I binged my way into the emergency room and the fingerprints from my stunt in Illinois. Yeah, this is far from fucking normal.

I never have been, nor had the desire to be, normal though. Normal is just average, and average is boring. It's the top of the bell curve, the half-way point between extremes. I'm without a doubt an extremist. I tried to explain to the Doc once that most people coast down the road of life on cruise, steering and braking as necessary to keep it between the lines. I've lived more like I wrapped up the engine, dumped the clutch, and have been bouncing from one guardrail to the other ever since. Workaholic, laziness, sobriety, alcoholic, conservatism, bankrupt, abstinence, promiscuity, commitment, starvation, and gluttony are all extremes I've experienced over the years. Like Sixx just said, "When you've tasted excess, everything else is bland." That's the fucking truth, and I always have loved the taste of excess.

The possibility of my death being permanent generates questions in my mind such as how I'd be remembered if I end up worm food. If I had to look back and describe my life for Mom, a probation officer, or a potential employer, I could write it in third person like a resume.

He grew up with his family in the Midwest excelling at art, and completing Algebra in two weeks at a talented and gifted program at ISU during the summer before eighth grade. High school was spent waking up at 4:30 am to deliver papers for his two routes, followed by cooking or unloading groceries at the local store. After school he'd go back to work, but he'd still make time for a workout before going to bed. Study time was unnecessary for him to graduate as class salutorian. He went to church and youth group every week, had cd's, savings, stocks, and mutual funds, and abstained from temptations of the flesh such as alcohol, tobacco, drugs, and sex.

By the time he graduated from ISU with a 3.65 GPA, he had almost two years of work experience through his two co-ops, had two research assistantships under his belt, played guitar, and was almost 200 lbs with less than 6% body fat from daily workouts. He went to work 50-100 hours per week at the Institute and established himself as an expert in his field with secret clearance and access to military bases across the country.

He then moved his new bride across the country and opened up a business. He'd get up between two and five in the morning for his day job as a project manager and work at the business on the nights and weekends. Then he died.

I could also write my obituary citing other fun-filled facts and paint a much different picture.

After spending most of his time drunk and blacking out four to five nights per week, he got a job and pissed away an average of $1400 per month on booze and strippers, while tearing around the city sideways in one of his Porsches or on his Harley.

Eventually he was drinking a Texas fifth of whiskey before he'd even go to the bars. His failed marriage lasted barely over a year of absolute misery and ended the week after he got terminated from his job. He moved to a crack neighborhood with no car or job, and was waking up from benders in ditches and backs of pickups. He lived on one or two ravioli cups or soup cups a day and lost thirty pounds almost instantly.

After wrecking the first car he'd owned in two years and becoming financially ruined, he crushed his leg between his bike and a truck on the way to the bar one night. Soon after, he got so hammered while out of town for a wedding that he fell in a river and broke into a doctor's office for warmth to survive. This resulted in jail, felony charges, probation, and bills he could never pay. He finally bankrupted his business, and got a new job where he struggled to pay off his debt and make ends meet. Then he died.

There are a lot of ways to describe my life up to this point. A lot of people would say my life was a lot of different things, but I don't think anyone that's known me would call it boring, average, or normal. No matter how you describe the story, the ending of each will be the same one week from today. Then perhaps I'll get to see if there's more to the story or if that really is the end.

I'm calmer about the whole thing than I was a few weeks ago. Instead of worrying about the outcome, I've accepted that all I know is what happens between now and next Wednesday when I close my eyes. After my eyes shut, someone is going to crack my chest open, deactivate my heart, perform repairs, and hopefully bring me back to life. The whole thing is completely out of my control, so I'm not worrying about it anymore. Hopefully my eyes will open again, and I'll be new and improved, but there are no guarantees in life but death. When I close my eyes, I'll look back at all the experiences I enjoyed and endured, knowing that I lived more in my thirty-four years than most people do in a lifetime. The truth is I'm not really bothered by my pending flat line, which fortunately won't be documented on a Darwin Award email or follow the words, "Hey, check this shit out!" The only time I'm bothered by it is picturing my parents, sisters, and Sunshine at the funeral. I'm sure it'll upset them at the time, but I also know they'll all move on with their lives and be fine. There is a sense of peace that comes with knowing that they're all doing well and will continue to do so whether I'm around or not.

If my eyes don't open again, then I had the luxury of advance notice that people almost never receive. I'm thinking about going to confession and receiving the final sacrament, Anointing of the Sick. I haven't been to a church since Fatman's burial when I ended up in jail. I guess I should say, "wedding," not "burial." At least at a funeral the suffering is over and not just beginning. The previous time I'd been in a church was at my own wedding. Both experiences cost me a year of misery, highly restricted living, and a lot of time and money I'll never get back. I think the real reason besides logistics that I won't pursue absolution is that I would feel like a hypocrite for asking forgiveness now. I feel like God would look down at me and say, "Sure, asshole, ignore me for years and be a complete prick, but now you want help? Now you want forgiveness? Fuck you." I can't say I'd blame him. It's what I'd say to someone that called me for the first time in years and asked a huge favor. I'd say, "Fuck you" too. I'm sure Mother Dear will do enough praying for both of us.

I suppose I should email Tracer about last weekend. I'm not sure how he'll respond, as we're both like sharks and often attack at the sight of blood. Having learned that fact about him over the years I've known him, I try not to ask much of him, but I think current circumstances allow it. I email him a request to go easy on the dead me jokes in front of Sunshine. I've accepted what's happening, so his continued stabs about me pushing up daisies don't necessarily entertain me, but I don't let them bother me either. However, seeing Sunshine cry as we left Sundog last Sunday after a few of his comments warrants that I at least ask him as a favor that he go easy on the jokes around her. I tell him I don't care if I do bite it and he wants to make jokes to our mutual friends, but I ask that he refrains from making any tasteless comments to my family or Sunshine from here on. I point out that it's fine for him and me to rake on the idiots we encounter in the world, but my family and Sunshine are good people and don't deserve to be antagonized during an already difficult time.

While I've got his attention, I might as well leave my last wishes with him, as it would probably upset Sunshine or my family to tell them. I'm asking him that if this is the end of the ride, I be cremated and my ashes be put in the original gas tank from the Hardass. I see it still sitting out there in my display case, and I still love that sunset orange pearl paint, candy orange flames, and granite-style YCC axe logo at the base. I'm almost glad the customer wanted a bigger tank, as the tank from the first chopper I built when I moved to Florida would make a fitting final resting place. It's only a little peanut tank, which never held much gas, but it should hold a few ashes. Images come to mind of the character that Bosworth kills in "Stone Cold" when they sit the corpse on his bike, light it on fire, and say something like, "Let's send this sonofabitch to Valhalla!" That would probably be a little graphic for my own funeral attendees, so I'll stick to my ashes in a gas tank. It's getting early, X. I better get home, shower, make my loser sandwich for lunch, and head to work.

Sunshine is disappointed that we won't be able to go out for Halloween together this weekend since she'll be in New York and I'll be in Colorado. She shows up with a red dress and asks me to cut it short for a slutty Little Red Riding Hood costume. Unfortunately my tailor skills are lacking, I cut too short, and I can almost see the beaver peaking out from behind the dam. I guess beaver is a little out of date. Maybe I should say Chihuahua or hairless rabbit, but old habits die hard. After some more modifications, she's got her costume more appropriate and is ready to go enjoy what will be our last night together for a while. Hopefully "for a while" is accurate terminology.

I'm wearing the purple suit and tie and green vest that Sunshine dyed earlier. I have on my white makeup, black eye makeup, green hair spray, and blood-red lipstick. Heath Ledger did an amazing job in Batman's "The Dark Knight" as the Joker, but I don't buy the theory that the role was somehow the reason for his death.

It's a fitting look for me, although maybe a little too synonymous with certain aspects of my own twisted sense of humor. The Joker and I both exhibit a sense of social curiosity combined with a high level of schadenfreude. As much as I don't like the idea of text tattoos, being German and having my sense of humor, "schadenfreude" might make an appropriate tattoo. Maybe I'll get another Porsche some day and I can paint that across the hood. It might look tacky, but I can repaint a hood easier than I can remove a tattoo.

We're at Timeout, and I see Tracer and his friends. He and Ms. Texas are the only ones I really recognize. It seems like I remember that redhead with the nice rack and her husband from Urban Flats one night when we were all there for some charity event Ms. Texas was planning. The dogcatcher is working tonight. I have to admit I liked her hair a lot better when it was longer. She's still cute though, and reminds me of a cross between Sandra Bullock and Eva Mendez. Hopefully this won't be awkward. It shouldn't be, but this is the first time I think I've even seen her since I met Sunshine.

I never dated her anyway; we just hung out a couple times. There was the one night when she was hammered and kissed me at MacCool's. I was pretty stoked with that until some douchebag got in between us. I asked, "What the fuck?" and her friend told me it was her boyfriend. I couldn't help but laugh at how awesome he must feel to walk up and see that. He turned toward me to walk her out of the bar, looked up at me, and said, "I'm mad at her, not you." I stepped aside without being a dick, since he was actually being mature and not a Jimmy T about it. Tracer and I left shortly after, and it was great for a laugh for us to watch him yelling at her all the way down the block. The only time she and I really went out on anything close to a date was just to Casa and the Ritz one Wednesday night. She got blitzed, and I ended up chasing her fucking neighbor's dog all over the beach until 3 am. She told me I could stay if I wanted to, but I had to explain that I had to go straight home, shower, and go to work with no sleep. Two things were evident at that point. A) I was getting too fucking old to date girls in their early twenties who don't have to get up the next day and B) That work schedule was having a major detrimental effect on my social life.

Unlike a couple times when she called me an asshole for no apparent reason other than her alcohol intake, she's cool about things, says, "hi," and is polite without throwing any salt on the evening. It's still early when Sunshine and I leave Timeout, so we go to Sundog and grab a drink before calling it a night. There's not much of a crowd, but Sundog and Ragtime are often for the milder and often older crowd. Every now and then there will be younger groups in them, but it's really hit or miss at this end of the beach. Neither of us feels like dealing with the twenty-one year old tough guys in Affliction shirts at Ritz or the bimbos rejecting them, so Sundog will be fine for the last drink of the night before heading back to the shoebox.

Thu 30 Oct 08

I just dropped off Sunshine at the airport so she can fly to New York for the art show. It's definitely different saying, "goodbye" to her compared to our usual adios. Instead of the sparkle in her eye and bright smile, it's more of a shine from a forming tear and a very restrained sadness on her face. Neither of us will say that it could be the last time we see each other, but we're both thinking it.

As I predicted, management at the Office waits until the last minute to scramble and try to decide what to do with my work while I'm gone. Despite my warnings weeks ago, yesterday they called a meeting to try to divide the twelve projects I currently have open. Today I'm letting customers know to contact my management in my absence, getting out a proposal, and showing a few people where information is on my desk. As I explain how to use my hospital marketing tools, VP1 tells me that he hopes within two weeks he's able to call me on my cell. With an estimated six-week recovery time, I'm shocked he asks it, but I shouldn't be anymore. I'm sure I'd be able to physically answer phones in a couple weeks, but I really don't know how the stress will affect recovery. Considering I only have one heart, I better err on the side of caution. He should realize that. It almost sounds like a joke, and I'd ask if he's serious, but I know he is. I explain to him I probably won't even look at a phone for a month, as it's going to be critical that I relax. He states that he doesn't want to involve me, but wants me to be able to answer questions. How is that different? Fuck it, I'm not going to worry about it. Usually when I leave here, I'm already thinking about what I have to do the next day. Usually I wake up at stupid-thirty am, already stressing about what I have to do at work. This is completely different. Today when I walk out that door, this place gets tucked into the farthest corner of my mind so I can focus on my primary goal of extending my life, or at least enjoying the last few days of it.

The whole department drops in and hands me a card with a sizable check in it. I have to admit, regardless of how aggravated

I get with the operations of this place, I couldn't ask for a better bunch of people. I wish I could fix everything that I think is fucked up, give myself and the other people a big raise, and make it a great place to work like it could be. I don't know what pisses me off more between the decisions that get made and the decisions that never get made here. I have to believe the potential is here for success that just seems to elude us. There's not much more I can do about it from the bottom of the pile, and even less I'll be able to do after today for quite a while.

I haven't been out with T-Bag for a while. He shows up with no costume, so I loan him my power ranger pants and jacket so it looks like he at least made an effort. I'm the Joker again now that I'm beginning to master the makeup application. Here we are at Tailgators watching the slutty-dressed, barely legal bar wenches with Stabby and Cam. At least T-Bag hasn't asked any of the waitresses how much money they need to let him film me fucking them tonight. I thought I was impaired in the smoothness department, but he's had some shining moments too.

It's a little chilly on the Ape tonight with no power ranger gear. Heaven forbid I fuck up the makeup with a helmet. I survived fifteen years without wearing one, tonight should be fine. Scratch that. Tonight should be fine if I can keep myself from getting completely annihilated and seeing how fast I can make it home on this Tupperware torpedo.

We're at Brix, which is clearly more energy-conscious since it's not as well-lit inside as the Ritz. The bars are full of saline twins, bleached blonde hair, and makeup that makes Tammy Baker look au natural. They're extremely superficial, great scenery, and painful conversationalists. They often fail to realize that the sun, smoke, and coke are destroying that which they value most and the only thing a lot of the girls have going for them, their looks. Nonetheless they can provide some level of entertainment unlike the douchebags that show up on payday, nursing their two or three drinks, popping the collar on their pink shirts, and hoping to bang one of the unsuspecting hotties.

Now that we've had a few Bull vodka's and Jager Bombs, I am just starting to feel the warm monster in my stomach begin to growl and want more. It wants all of it, and it wants it now. I attempt to switch to water, but T-Bag is determined that we need to get fucked up now. The bad thing is that half of me is agreeing with him, as this could be the last night in town. This could be the last night for a lot of things actually. I'm sure some would see the need to bang one of the bimbos if it could be the last chance to do so. I've never cheated in my life though, and it's probably not good to do something at this point that will ensure my denial at the pearly gates if they exist, just in case I still have a chance at not riding a red-hot pitchfork for eternity.

The booze is just teasing me now. Not only do I have the stomach warmth, but the mouth is just right. What I've had so far has barely filled the cracks in my tongue to just that point of tasting the sweetness of the Bull, the burn from the alcohol, and the slight dryness as it evaporates from the taste buds. Fuck I want to drink more now. I want that next Jager Bomb, to slam it back, and to feel it drip down the chin. I want that next Bull vodka to wind me up like a liquid speed ball. Then after a Jack & Coke or four, I want to start drinking the cheapest, rot-gut whiskey they have here with a splash of 7-up at the top as fast and as many as I can before they close this place for the night.

I know this feeling, as I've felt it hundreds of nights before. It's the time when things start getting sick, and I miss it. I feel like I'm twenty-one again, or even thirty-one again. I'm having fun with good company, the music's blasting, we're surrounding by beautiful young girls, and I've got that drive to take it to the next level. It's my last night in Jacksonville for now, so why not? Jail in Illinois, hospital in Texas, and numerous other clusterfucks are why, jackass. I need to get the fuck out of here, as it's obviously a threatening environment. I don't know why the demon alcohol pulls so strong, but I need to leave. I bid farewell to T-Bag, fire up the Ape, and head west back toward the shoebox before this night takes a turn for the worse under the influence of the booze, the bar, T-Bag, and most of all, myself.

As I bank hard at the right turn off A1A to get on JTB and kick it past three digits across the bridge, I know I left none too soon. I love intoxication, I love speed, and I love mixing the two.

Fri 31 Oct 08

I'm dressed up like the Joker for the third day in a row, but I'll wait with the makeup, as I don't feel like getting a full body cavity search at airport security over a Halloween costume. It's a good thing I left when I did last night. I would have made it home safe, but I'm more worried that I would've got pulled over and they would've nailed me to a cross for how drunk I could've been as I shot over the JTB bridge at 120 mph with no helmet.

Now that I've landed in Denver, it's straight to the bathroom to finish the costume with makeup and wait outside for Ronan the Beerbarian. Here he is in the silver truck, which he's surprisingly only wrecked drunk once since he got it. At least it's surviving better than the Cheroghini he had to scrap. He has to inform me that he is in fact wearing a costume and is dressed as the main character in "King of Queens." Sure enough he is a ringer for Kevin James and has on a delivery costume as worn in the show. He even has a cardboard package with pictures of the real "King of Queens."

From the airport, we head straight to Diamond Dolls for the buffet of course. The last time we were here, Cousin Reno was with us, and we were unavoidably detained causing us to be late for Organisis's wedding rehearsal. I remember Dad calling to see where the hell we were that day. Unfortunately Ronan got lost when we stopped for a 12-pack on the way to the rehearsal via the wrong route too. I could tell Dad was proud when we finally arrived.

Good strip clubs can be a blast, serve delicious food, have beautiful scenery, and give me a sense of warmth knowing that I've helped those poor girls buy more clothes and pay for their expensive surgeries. It's about as close as I come to charity. For someone that just wants to watch the animals in the zoo, it's better. People wanting to actually hunt need to go to the wild like sports bars or dance clubs. I used to believe that guys had zero chance at actually scoring a stripper, who was there to flirt just enough to get our money. I always believed that until Fatman gave my number to V at the Palace one night, and she actually called me. Unfortunately I was dating the ex at the time, and even got V's message in front of her. Awesome timing. I can remember making out with a girl I'd just met at Tazzles one night, watching her stop and turn around, and seeing Fatman on his knees licking her ass. As soon as I get a girlfriend though, he gives V my number. Dick. It must've been at least a couple years later when V came and sat at our table at Sugar's when the ex was in New Orleans for New Year's Eve. V flat out asked if I'd fuck her, and I had to tell her I was taken and couldn't cheat. I can still picture V on that stage shaking that fake rack, compliments of one of her customers, and rubbing that quarter-bouncing ass up against me trying to talk me into going back to her place later. I am Will Powers sometimes. V had a kid, and she only lived a few blocks away, which eventually would've blown up in my face anyway. She was fucking hot though and would have been fun for a while until the headaches and pains in the ass outweighed the head and tail. I don't wish I would've cheated; I just wish I would've realized what kind of mistake I was making sooner and wouldn't have had to deny myself that pleasure.

One of the ballet dancers comes by to chat. Tattoos and a face piercing are good indications she'd be a fun girl. All the members of the show have costumes from dirty police girls to slutty teachers to naughty nurses, and I smirk at the fact that I've fucked police girls, teachers, and nurses. After a very enjoyable lunch that includes a few Jack & Cokes, we head to some outdoor area near a mall. This way we can set up camp along the outside fence of the bar at a table and harass people on the way by, as well as watch the show from our side with drinks in hand. It's hard to say which side of the fence is for the spectators and which side is for the animals, but we enjoy ourselves and that's what counts. This also lets Ronan call his twenty-three year-old girl and tell her we are somewhere other than the strip club. I guess Sporty Spice isn't a fan of the pole-dancing dollar-snatchers.

Eventually we take our elevated BAC levels to his girlfriend's house. Sporty Spice and her family are decorating the entire yard for the trick-or-treaters. It looks like Clarke Griswold has done Halloween at the house, but I applaud their enthusiasm. Her attempt at caramel apples is sitting on the counter, but somehow all the caramel has melted off the apples. Ronan and I head to the local Hops for a few Flying Squirrel Ales. Much to my disappointment, the cool Flying Squirrel logo in the menu resembling Bullwinkle's buddy, Rocky, isn't sold on any shirts, cups, or anything else I can buy.

As we head toward the liquor store, I realize that my late nights and early morning have compounded with the time change and removed the wind from my sails. I get asked to leave the liquor store, as no makeup is allowed inside. Another rule set up for good reason without common sense execution, much like speed limits and Government assistance programs. That's a good indication that I should just stay in the truck and snooze while Ronan and Sporty Spice go into the party for a while.

They're done with the party, Ronan is in Stage II or so, and I'm awake and ready to go to the bar. I've had a little rest and should be able to enjoy the night. With a couple Bull vodkas, I'm coming back to life. I laugh like the Joker at people walking by us. When anyone gives me a funny look, the simple response in that slow menacing voice is, "Why so serious?" I talk to a couple girls near our table and they ask me why I'm in town. I tell them I'm having open heart surgery next week. Once they realize I'm serious, I almost feel guilty as their smiles melt. I tell them not to worry. I've enjoyed my life to the hilt, and things will probably be just fine. I wonder why they care. They didn't know me before tonight, they won't know me tomorrow, and they won't know whether I even survive or not. I'm just some joker who's getting cracked open next week. I guess I could just appreciate their concern instead of questioning it, but I do get a kick out of trying to understand human nature. There's really no need to worry about anything except having a good time and enjoying the night. The place is jammed with lots of eye candy, drinks, cool costumes, and a live rock band. It doesn't get much better than this for a night out on the town. Unfortunately the next two or three drinks rocket Ronan from Stage II all the way to Stage IV. His English is now unrecognizable and he's falling off the barstool where Sporty Spice and I last placed him. It's only 11:30 but we're on our way home. Ronan's still good entertainment, but he's not quite as suitable for the long haul as he used to be. His dwindling alcohol tolerance is getting me back to bed earlier and more sober than I planned, so I shouldn't complain.

It's good to see the Beerbarian again, as he's always a blast, and seeing him reminds me of the fun of the past. I've been drinking on and off with this clown for fifteen years. We had all those blurry years in college in the dorms and bars, and the messy times while he was staying in Jax for work. Between his arrest for pissing on a hot dog stand in front of the cops and his bad influence in general, it made for some great entertainment, but it's probably best for both of us that he's not in Jax anymore. I couldn't believe he didn't even remember being cuffed the next day. When a cop is telling him that the only reason he's being let go is because his sober responsible buddy, yours truly, is taking care of him, it's a bad night for the Beerbarian. Pushing him three miles back to the hotel in a shopping cart after he got us kicked out of Club Christopher's was another one of those memorable nights he can't remember. Captain D wasn't much help either that night. He was asleep in his car and finally called when he couldn't find his car keys, which were hiding in his car door. Good times were had by all as always.

Sat 01 Nov 08

Vermin shows up to haul me to Ft. Collins bright and early. We stop at the Duc dealer on the way, so I can look at the 1098's. They have a demonstration model, and I take the 160 horsepower beast on the blacktop by the shop. This is a seventeen-thousand dollar machine, so I'm not going to bank around the turns too aggressively. If I buy one, I want it to be to ride, not because I wrecked it. I can definitely feel the extra 30 horsepower it has compared to the Ape, and there is no denying the engineering and style appeal of the Duc. Something about it just feels small with regard to the seating position and tank though. I have to admit the Ape feels better, and of course this is all relative since race or sport bikes aren't made to be comfortable in the first place. I've always preferred chopper sitting positions to looking like a monkey fucking a football, although I have grown much fonder of my Ape than I ever expected. It's hard to justify seventeen grand for this 1098, but it's a matter of want, not need. I'll see if I survive my pending flat line first.

Vermin, the guy she's marrying, and I are in Elliot's Martini Bar for a couple drinks while we wait for our table at the Japanese restaurant across the street. The last time I was in this bar, he told me he was planning to propose to Vermin when they went to France. I asked him if he thought he could handle her, as she can be difficult. She's a great kid, but she is my sister and seems like she could really lose her temper at times. Not that I'm a model of self-control, moderation, stability, or any other mature behavior, but I genuinely hope it works out well for them. As Vermin said at Organisis's wedding, "It has to go better than our brother's, mister one-year-and-divorced." That was before I decided to jump in the pool with my tux and froze my ass. I felt pretty bad for Mom the next day. It was bad enough to see her first-born son's tattoo collection while I was puking in the bushes outside of the cabin, but worse to see my sisters' slutty friend come out of the cabin wrapped in a blanket. It's no wonder that so many people have offered their condolences to my poor mother after meeting me.

Looking back at that wedding as an example, Fatman was probably right when he was cussing me out recently about my selfishness at events like weddings that are supposed to be for other people, not me.

My issue with him was that he's always been the first one egging me on to drink more and do more stupid things. Now he wants to look down his nose at me from the pedestal he put himself on for getting married and having kids? He said bluntly that everyone considers me a joke, that my behavior is the reason Hollywood and Sleaze didn't want me at their weddings, and why they and Sambo haven't talked to me much since they got married. Even though I have a job, a small business, and the same girlfriend I've had for months, do they all still view me as that same fuckup? It's not unreasonable to think they do, as they've all gotten married, calmed down, and likely only remember the version of me from years ago. After years of their encouragement and laughing at my self-induced misfortune, are they all pointing out to their girls how bad I am as if they never did anything bad? I'd like to think otherwise, but who knows? I apologized to each of them for my behavior and lack of support of their marriages, but explained it's hard to be happy for someone doing the very thing that became my biggest mistake in life. Now that I've tried to grow up a little, there's nothing else I can do except accept that our friendships may have changed terms and conditions over the years. They're not any more interested in my oil changes than I am in their diaper changes. They've grown one way, and I've grown another, but there's of course still middle ground for remaining friends.

After forty minutes and a few drinks at Elliot's, the three of us trot across the street and the waitress leads us to our table. As we enter the seated area, I look and see that everyone is sitting at one-foot high tables. I'm cringing at the thought of trying to cram myself with my cast iron-flexibility under that table. Fortunately we soon see that each table has a hole under it for our legs, so I can actually enjoy my meal and not end up a sake-soaked contortionist.

Now it's off to Trailhead, which isn't my favorite place. My hair is long for me, but hasn't been down to my shoulders since I graduated high school. I don't have a beard, a stupid hat, or a vest that makes me look like a drunken boatman lost at sea. I'm not sure when dressing like a complete slob and not taking the time to bother shaving became attractive to girls, but the last thing I plan on doing tonight is diagramming the intellect of a human in its early twenties. I'll put it on my list of things to figure out while I'm recovering from the big cut. Fortunately we don't stay very long and soon head back to the engaged couple's place to crash.

Sun 02 Nov 08

I guess this long hair I grew out for Halloween doesn't have to look good for the next month or two. I've thought about growing it out until I go back to work, but it'll be so much easier to deal with if it's short. I bought clippers with Ronan in Denver Saturday morning, so I might as well use them now. I'm not even using a guard, so it's as short as I can make it. With the extremely short hair and the 5 o'clock shadow, I can almost see where Crowley got his notion that I look a little like Vin Diesel. I actually remind myself more of the beginning of "Full Metal Jacket" and picture myself sitting in the barber chair at the beginning of the movie hearing, "Goodbye, darling. Hello, Vietnam." I guess I can't make fun of Nutzack anymore for looking like Private Pyle with his clipped head, although it's funny how much his build, expressions, and hair are all very similar to Leonard's. Wow, that's a pile of hair, but I won't need it where I'm going.

This Boxster is a blast to drive through the mountain curves, though I'm surprised Vermin let me drive it knowing my excessive taste for speed. She's ridden with me in my Porsches enough to know I moderate my speed about as well as I moderate my drinking, eating, or anything else in life. I'd love to have one of those Duc's or my Ape up here cutting through these roads. Vermin and I try to go up to Estes Park, but at the Dam Store I notice she's caught a nail and has a flat tire. It's not a big deal as I should have plenty of time to come back up here after surgery. The doctor told me I'd be walking the day after surgery and out of the hospital in five days. It probably won't be a breeze by any stretch, but it sounds less crippling than that fucking hernia surgery when I was twenty. Nothing like having someone tear open your crotch, rip out the eight inches of intestines hanging in your right nut, then staple them shut. I looked like Frankencrotch with those fourteen staples down there. It hurt like a sonofabitch all summer too, plus my crotch itched since they had to shave it for surgery. It was like having blue balls and crabs at the same time with a come-a-long cranked between my right nut and sternum. Hopefully heart surgery won't be as bad with the whiz-bang technology available today.

The air seems to be holding in her tire for now; so on the way back we stop by a guitar store or two. I shipped a box of clothes out here before I left, but didn't want to dick around shipping guitars, especially since Organisis has a guitar. I'll probably play that to entertain myself and relax while I recover on her couch for the next few weeks. She also has a piano, which was a wedding present from Dad. The girls were both very good at the piano once Mom got them interested, whereas I lost interest after two weeks of playing "Johnny Hallelujah." In comparison, the first song I learned on that old Peavey guitar I repossessed from Fred was "Kickstart my Heart," so I took an instant liking to the axe as a preferred instrument. Hearing that the axe-man was the guy that played guitar, I'd thought "Axe" would be a cool name. I remember sitting at a party my first week in college drinking a Jack & Coke and using that name. The name stuck and the cartoon character began as I started the transition from a disciplined, saintly high-schooler to the monster I'd later become. I'd already assigned "Hollywood" due to his Ken-doll looks, and "Sambo" for his resemblance to Sam Kinison. I know it's a little ridiculous to assign your own alias, but we all had our alter-ego's separate from the version of us that sat in class studying for a future, and people just remember colorful names better than average ones. In addition, no one can look up a nickname in a phone book.

No stores have the Sixx AM guitar music or Kid Rock's *Rock and Roll Jesus* book, so I guess I'll have to play what I can from memory after

I get out of the hospital. As we stop at a book store in the mall as a last try, there's no music, but there's a book called "The Heroin Diaries." Apparently the book is about Nikki's ordeals with heroin and coincides with the Sixx AM cd I've been listening to constantly for the last few weeks. Excellent. I'll be forced to polish a couch with my ass for a while, so I might as well be reading something that has a better than average chance of keeping my interest.

Tue 04 Nov 08

Organisis drops me off at the heart center for the pre-surgery appointment. A lot of this is the staff telling me what to expect, showing me a video, and asking a few questions. Basic tests are all they do since most of the information from the testing back home is already in their hands. Lauri is just as nice in person as she's been over the phone. I am extremely impressed with not only the facility, but the fact that everyone who works here is knowledgeable and helpful. This is amazing in a world where customer service is all but extinct. I haven't been anything but disappointed by almost every organization I've encountered for years. I guess if I had to choose people to impress me, I'd rather it be the ones cracking my chest open than the ones fucking up my fatburger and fries.

I meet the surgeon who will be cutting me, and fortunately he impresses me as much as the rest of the staff. He understands how important it is for me to have a repair and assures me he'll do his best to repair the native valve, with a tissue valve-replacement as Plan B. I make it crystal clear that the artificial valve is not an option, based on what I'd heard from other doctors back home and the Doc. Even though the Doc was a demanding pain in the ass to date toward the end, she was helpful in that she pointed out that my heart was fucked just by listening to it, and she was right. She also warned me that an artificial valve in theory lasts as long as I will, but would require coumadin for the rest of my life so blood doesn't coagulate on the valve. Since the blood gets thinner on coumadin, a patient has to avoid activities that could cause bleeding, like riding motorcycles and working with sharp metal and tools. Fuck that. I'd rather get ten more years of real living than fifty years of boredom. I'd rather jerk off with a cheese grater than have to look forward to golf on Saturdays and Bingo on Sundays for the rest of my life. Fuck that.

I also ask the surgeon and Lauri for a special favor. I would like to have a picture taken of me when I'm lying on the block with my chest cracked open. My preference would be that the picture be taken from my right side so the photo will show all the tattoos. They both look at me somewhat surprised, and maybe a little disgusted, and tell me they'll try to see if they can accommodate the request. I'm not sure why the request seems taboo. All the pictures of my life got left behind after the divorce due to my rushing to get the fuck away from that misery as soon as possible, so I'm not a big picture person. However, most people like to have pictures of vacations, ceremonies, accomplishments, and other notable events of their lives. This will be the most significant event of my life, so I don't think a little memento of the occasion is out of line. I will admit part of the desire for it is shock value when I hang it at the Office and show it to people. I'm predicting it will also be a good reminder to stay calm and not get too frazzled about things.

Given the fact that this could be my last full day on earth, I feel as at-ease as possible, purely because of the professionalism of the staff from the receptionist to the rehabilitation nurse to the surgeon. I need to remember to thank Organisis for suggesting this place. Hopefully she doesn't want a finder's fee. If she does, hopefully it's not percentage-based, because this isn't going to be cheap.

Wed 05 Nov 08

Vermin is taking me to the hospital this morning. The receptionist is cute and bouncy considering how early it is, so I'm pleasantly distracted for now. It must be something in the water out here, as Sunshine is always smiling no matter what time I wake her too. Once I check in, I give Vermin my wallet, while my keys, phone, and anything else of value was left back at Organisis's. I hug Vermin, thank her for the ride, and tell her, "goodbye." Much like dropping Sunshine off at the airport a few days ago, there is again the awkward silence of both of us thinking this could be the last time we see each other, but neither of us say it.

Like other times in life, it feels like I should be more concerned or wound up, but I'm really not. I almost look more at these events as social analysis than crisis, even when I'm the test subject. In theory, this could be the last time I see my little sister. This could be my last morning before the mourning. I don't know if I'm expecting this to be the end, or expecting to wake up in a day or so and be fine. I think I've just disconnected from analyzing the situation at this point, and I'm ready to go take a nap. I accept the possibility that this is the end, and if I do wake up after this, I'll be pleasantly surprised.

If this nap is permanent, I'm looking back right now and it's been a wild fucking ride. I experienced life balls-deep, and those experiences are all I have right now to appreciate, because they're all I can take with me where I'm headed. Everything I brought with me goes into a bag, just like when I went to jail. They put the bag under my bed so it stays with me when I get wheeled down the hall in a little while. That makes sense, as I'd want the carburetor to stay with the engine from which it came if I was performing engine overhauls. After going to the back, I change into the gown and get on the bed. Here comes the anesthesiologist to induce my snooze. I'm rolling down the hallway and beginning to fade. I can hear Axle Rose crooning, "Ain't in fun when you know that you're gonna die young, it's such fun." This isn't so bad. It's actually really peaceful. I'm more at peace right now than I've been since I don't know when. By only having this one concern, I don't have to worry about anything else in the world. Since I have no control over this one thing, there's no reason to worry about it, so for the first time ever I genuinely have no worries at all. It's just the doctors, nurses, and me now. This is the end of something. I don't know what or for how long, but it's definitely the end of something.

Chapter 2

Indestructible

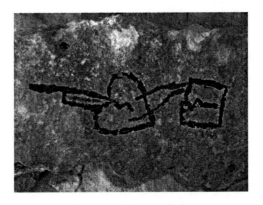

Thu 06 Nov 08

I guess I'm in ICU, as Organisis said I'd be there first. Fuck. Things are so blurry. I could swear Organisis said most people don't remember any of their time in ICU. Am I imagining this? Is this a fucking dream? Maybe I'm actually dead. That'd fucking suck. This feels real and surreal at the same time. No, I know I'm alive, in ICU, numb physically and completely fucking out of it mentally. There's a better than average chance I'm completely whacked out on pain killers, as I can't feel any part of my body. This reminds me of that stupid movie Dad and I watched when I was a kid one Sunday afternoon. What was the fucking name of that movie? The guy dies but is still alive in his brain. He can think and see, but can't move at all. He sees them burying him. I'm not buried, but I really can't feel anything. Are all my limbs ok? I can barely move my head to even look at myself. Why wouldn't they be, dumbass? I'm here for heart surgery, not from a fucking bike wreck or anything. I don't know what time it is or even what fucking day it is. I don't remember any nurses or anything. I'm going back to sleep until I can grasp this pseudo-reality better, as if I had a choice.

Fri 07 Nov 08

I assume I'm still in ICU, as this looks like the same room as before. But all hospital rooms probably look alike. Don't they? I'm apparently alive yet, still fucking groggy, but becoming slightly more conscious of the surroundings. I'm covered with a sheet, but I see some kind of fucking tube coming out from under the sheet. When I cough, the bloody fluid in the tube moves back and forth, so this must be some kind of drain tube to my insides. Tim, the nurse, is as professional as everyone else has been. What time is it? What fucking day is it? It's Friday morning according to Tim, and the hospital wants to get me out of ICU and to the cardiac floor. Tim explains it's time to remove the catheter, which is some tube that is crammed up my piss hole and into my bladder. Because I'm numb everywhere, I didn't even realize I had one of these catheters, but it's about to get yanked. One, two, three, breathe, and yank. It feels strange, but doesn't hurt, as I barely feel any part of my body yet.

I don't remember when the chest tubes were pulled out, but they're gone now too. I do know there was a pain killer injected through some point into my neck that puts me out within ten minutes though. Now I'm being moved to the cardiac floor for a change of scenery. Have I seen my sisters yet? I'm not sure. I don't even know if they repaired my heart valve or replaced it, do I? Regardless, I'm alive, and that's a pleasant surprise I wasn't expecting. Thank fuck. I survived death. Viva la cucaracha.

Sun 09 Nov 08

Something's fucked up. I realize by now that I have all the athletic prowess of a newborn kitten, but I'm having real difficulty just breathing. I don't know what's wrong, but something's fucking wrong. I ring the nurse to tell her. The staff is running more lab tests, and here comes the surgeon. Even though the repair they'd spent eight hours performing, compared to the usual four hours, appeared successful after surgery, it's now gone bad. My heart valve was just too fucked up, and it's going to have to be replaced. He asks again about my request for a tissue valve if a replacement is necessary, even though it's estimated to last only ten years. This means I'll now have a renewable contract with the grim reaper once per decade. Besides the anguish of going through this every ten years, I also know there are only so many times you can rebuild an engine before the cases crack. Ten years is better than nothing by a long stretch though. He offers a second option, the artificial valve once more, and I respond with, "no fucking way!" It feels like I'm yelling, but it sounds like I'm whispering. Having to take blood thinners the rest of my life is bad enough, but having to avoid any activity that could make me bleed is just not going to happen. If I have to give up riding bikes and working with metal, I'll lose the point of going through all this very fast. Like I wrote on my final legal documents when I did my will a couple weeks ago, "Quality of life is more important than life."

The first surgery was approached from my eyes calmly and gently. As soon as they realize I need this second surgery, I get an oxygen hose down the throat. I'm laying here wondering if my already weakened body will actually survive another surgery so soon after the first. There's no use worrying about it, as it's out of my control anyway, but I'm not feeling the same serenity I did before the first surgery. I'm getting rolled down the hallway to the operating room, but for some reason it feels like I'm being wheeled through a playground, or at least outside. Did they already give me more drugs that are fucking with my head again? I'm inside the operating room watching the staff get their tools ready to cut me open again, waiting to see one of them sharpening a butcher knife on a steel like I used to do at the meat market in high school. Now I know what a slab of meat used to feel like when I'd throw it on the butcher's block, except the slab didn't have this fucking oxygen tube rammed down its throat. Finally someone removes the tube. It's about fucking time.

I hear someone's voice bark to the others to throw me on the chill plate. Four people pick up the sheet under me and slide me onto a cold stainless steel plate. Now that I have the meat slab perspective, I get to see what a scoop of ice cream feels like being thrown on the marble slab or cold stone depending on your preference. Hopefully no one will try crushing my nuts or mixing gumdrops in me on this thing. It's freaking me the fuck out to feel that cold steel pulling every bit of heat out of my back and even bones, knowing that the purpose of the chill plate is to cool your heart down to a flat line so the team can work on it. Effectively, I'm lying on the device that temporarily kills me. I'm hoping for "temporarily" anyway. I realize that I am conscious of a whole lot more of the process this time than last time, and I fear that they perhaps got distracted and forgot to knock me out. I call to one of the staff and ask her, "You're going to shut me the fuck down before you start cutting me, right?" She assures me they will and shortly thereafter the anesthesiologist comes in and puts me to sleep. I don't feel good about this at all. I made it through last time, but this time something's really fucking wrong. Fuck. This nap might be permanent. Fuck. Double or nothing. Fuck.

Mon 10 Nov 08

It looks like 12:00 on the clock on the wall, and must be midnight since everything's dark yet. This must be ICU again, but it feels completely different than the ICU room before. The walls all look like they're dirty. Is that fucking crayon-scribbling all over them? Did they put me in a different hospital because something went wrong? Maybe they really did roll me through some kind of outdoor area for surgery. But wasn't that on an upper floor? Do they have play areas on outdoor patios or some shit? I have no fucking idea what day it is, where I'm at, or what my condition might be. I'm still alive though, and that's a welcome surprise I wasn't sure would happen this time. Fucking A.

My nurse looks a little like a Pam Anderson-type with heavy makeup and a healthy rack. My first thought is that she reminds me of girls I've met in the past with that look that are stuck on themselves and shallow as the average mud puddle. However, she is every bit as great as everyone else at the hospital, and I feel guilty for pre-judging her solely on her looks. I'm not sure why she's telling me about her recent divorce and concern with her kids and what to do, but I feel even worse now for thinking less of her. It's a quick lesson that similar looks to past acquaintances aside, this girl is just as nice as could be, and we all have our own struggles we deal with in our own way. Tragedy plays no favorites, and "deserves have nothing to do with it" as William Munny said in "The Unforgiven." What an incredible fucking movie. "Don't you be cutting up or otherwise harming no whores, or I'll come back and kill every one of you sonsabitches." That was the movie I watched in the hospital when they fixed my nuts. It was some shitty channel and fuzzy, but still a good movie. Clint's still a fucking badass. How old is he now? It's wild how young he looked in Dirty Harry. Of course Stallone and Arnie are pretty fucking built for their ages too. Stallone was thirty when he made the first Rocky. I wonder what I'll look like when I get out of here. I guess I shouldn't change that much. I sure miss being an alcohol-fueled demi-god in college. Fuck I was in good shape then, despite the fact that I was constantly trying to poison myself with mass quantities of whiskey. It's surprising how much abuse a body can take. I was getting straight A's, working as a research assistant, in honor societies, 190 lbs with 6% body fat, benching over 300 lbs, squatting

over 400 lbs, doing dips with 180 lbs hanging between my legs, and
blacking out from stupid amounts of whiskey at least four nights a
week. Spring breaks were a fucking blast. College was like training
and spring break was the annual event where I applied that training.
It was vacation with your buddies some place warm and sunny on a
beach with the ocean. We were surrounded by beautiful girls in bikinis
and skimpy dresses that were just there to have a good time like us.
Padre Island, Cancun twice, Padre again, Daytona, and Miami were
all balls-to-the-wall sickness. Fuck I used to love spring breaks. That
battle royal in Padre sure hurt between the sunburn and getting cut
from falling on all the crushed beer cans. Puking in the sand after the
tug-of-war wasn't the highlight of that day, but that's what happens
when you mix excessive drinking with excessive effort. I wonder what
ever happened to those people that found me in the sand dune that
evening. I wonder if DWI with the pierced clit hood took her sweet ass
back to her boyfriend and told her about the good time she and I had
together. Where'd those girls from west of San Antonio end up? Robin
was the tall one, and what was the other's name? Kim, that's it. They
were both cuties, but I never heard from them again. Cancun had such
gorgeous beaches. I was fucking terrified when the policia were going to
take me to jail. She's the one that had her shirt off. Why did I have to
get arrested? Times like that I'm so fucking glad I don't take drugs or I'd
still be in a Mexican jail. Drugs must fuck a person up. I don't even like
this shit they're putting in me. I feel like it's fucking me all up.

My new nurse is a brunette who reminds me of Amy, a friend of
one of Hollywood's girlfriends in college who resisted my alcohol-
fueled charm once. The last time I saw her she was at that party with
Hollywood, his luggage, and me. It seems like someone got tired or
sick and wanted to go. I guess I was ignoring her, which is probably
why she never called me back. That's the night I was hitting on Pipe's
ex, Wild Sonja. I vaguely remember walking through the grass from
that party with my arm around her. She warned me about the ground
saying, "Watch out. There's a hole down here." I told her, "Of course.

Why do you think I'm talking to you?" I have to laugh at some of the smartass comments I used to come up with. The key was to offer the option without coming out and asking. Implied sales is always more effective. Wild Sonja gave me a ride home from Tazzles on the first night back to school one year. I invited her in to watch a movie, even though the electronics weren't even set up. She told Pipes later about it, even though he was already banging someone else. She said she wouldn't watch a movie sober with me on a Tuesday at noon. I got her back with the Schlong Island Ice Tea though. Fuck that was funny for Sambo and I to see her drinking that Long Island I'd just stirred with my prick. It was kind of like a blowjob by proxy I guess. I was kind of a dick, but all in good fun. It was part of my charm. Cat used to say I'd get away with things that would get his ass kicked if he tried them. That night at Park Place I dropped my shorts to show some girl where the ex had bitten me on the ass with a cop just around the corner. Then after acting like a jackass doing karaoke to some rock song, some dude that looked like Stone Cold Steve Austin came up to me. He told me it was a good show, introduced himself as someone from Dallas, and held out his hand to shake. I pulled out my nuts and said, "Well I'm Axe and this is how we say, "hi" in San Antonio, mother fucker!" He started laughing and walked away, while Cat stood there in amazement. It's all on delivery. Say anything; just say it with a smile. I'm getting tired.

Wait a minute. Was there just a shift change, or did I move rooms? Where is the crayon-scribbling on the wall? Was that all just more drug-induced illusions? The nurse gives me the pain killer I had last time in ICU in the neck IV again, but I don't even notice a change in how I feel this time. Last time I'd be asleep within ten fucking minutes of receiving it, but I could be so numb from everything else that I can't tell I've even been given anything. I always built up a strong tolerance to alcohol when I was drinking heavy, so maybe my body just builds fast tolerance to chemicals. Who fucking knows? I'm not a doctor, I just used to fuck one while she watched TV.

I'm back on the cardiac floor and going through the same catheter removal, chest drain tube removal, and neck IV removal as last time. Vermin's here now and is going to stay the night on the couch. The nurse gives me Norco or Vicodin, and then asks me what day it is. I have no fucking idea as I've lost all sense of information from clocks or calendars by this point, and my notebook, although only a few feet away, might as well be on another planet right now as incapacitated as I feel. Now that I think about it, I really don't care what fucking day it is. She then asks me what month it is as an easy starter question. I'm staring blankly at her and Vermin and realize that I don't even know that. I tell the nurse it's some time between October and December, but I can't tell her what fucking month it is. Next she asks me if I am hot or cold. I know what those words mean, and I'm searching for some temperature indication from some part of my body, but all I can do is stare at her and tell her I don't know. I do know I sound as stupid as I think I do by the way both the nurse and Vermin are looking at me. What was this shit? How did it make me so stupid so quickly? I've drank enough to kill small villages and still known what fucking day it is.

Before bedtime the nurse gives me Percoset, since the Vicodin had crippled my thought processing ability. I have never felt the effect of any fucking thing like this. It's not causing what I'd call hallucinations, as I'm not seeing things that aren't really here when my eyes are open like before. I could have sworn a couple days ago that Organisis arranged to have Nikki Sixx stop by, and have memories of seeing him standing at the foot of my bed with his circular-lens sunglasses he wore in the "Decade of Decadence" tape. I obviously know that didn't happen. This is harder to describe. I can't say it's causing bizarre dreams, as I'm still awake. It is causing me to see the wildest, most colorful fucking images I've ever seen when I close my eyes though. Every time I close them, I watch the back of my eyelids for the next image until I open them again. Vermin is asking me about the details as I tell her I can see red-stained wooden chairs on a felt multi-tier green. I see overviews of medieval battle scenes, hillsides in Asia with people farming, workstations in Africa of children making bowls out of clay, which are things of which I have no prior exposure and have never seen.

Most of these images contain such vivid color and clarity, but there are even incredible black and white visions of a late '60's Mustang parked under a street light and close up images of stones and wrought iron chairs as well. Motion in these visions is slow, smooth, and calculated like computer-generated animations morphing from shape to shape. Others are like still frames with one small part moving in a quick rabbit-fucking motion, or one part of every creature in the image moving at once. These remind me of a Marilyn Manson or NIN video, which can only lead me to believe that those videos were potentially inspired by drug use.

The feelings of the images are the most sensational and real I've ever seen or felt. One consists of Organisis's ankle-biter, dressed in a dragon costume, running up to me, and hugging me. I move to hug him back, and I can feel him in my arms. What the fuck? No fucking way. These drugs not only make me see weird shit but feel it? How in the fuck is that possible? I finally realize that what I feel is the pillow I have on my chest to hold if I cough or sneeze. Some images are very sensual. I see a beautiful girl floating toward me with full sleeves of tattoos. As she nears me and her head moves past mine, I smile when I notice the same YCC tattoo on her left shoulder blade that I have on my right shoulder. I feel almost guilty over my attraction to this imagined beauty, when I have Sunshine back in Florida. The image then morphs into a hollow tree trunk rotating as I looked at the inside of it. As it rotates I see Sunshine's face on the inside of the trunk as beautiful as ever. It's as if that were really her golden eyes right there looking at me hovering on the wooden canvas above her shining smile. A branch on the side of the trunk slowly transforms into her arm as the vision fades. I reach again for the disappearing image and am brought back to reality by Vermin's voice as my eyes open to see the dark room again. Vermin asks if I know I'm tracing and reaching for images in the air and tells me she's been watching my hand reach into the open space above my hospital bed. These drugs are really fucking with my brain, but I can't help but be intrigued by the images I'm seeing.

I wish it were possible to capture the images, but these notes will be the only trace of them when I get out of here. I'd like AJ to be able to see them, as they could inspire his photography perhaps. Maybe he could arrange to have some hottie in a giant hot dog bun with chili and cheese topping her. We could get a girl to lay in a giant bowl and cover her with giant scoops of ice cream, chocolate syrup, nuts, and topped with a cherry, something the girl probably won't be able to remember having or losing.

These pictures in my mind are incredible and make me wonder if the drugs cause me to see what I am, or if they just relax the mind enough that I am able to enjoy and appreciate things I hadn't before. Do drugs offer some clarity that normal life does not? Are so many great works of art in every type of media inspired by drug use, or at least appreciated more by those who are in an altered state? Now I'm seeing more images of the sea of arms pounding in the air like a Manson or NIN video. They're pounding faster and they won't stop. It feels like this whole image is getting too intense and going to spiral out of control. This is starting to fucking get to me. I can't control the images, and they're there whenever I shut my eyes, but I can't sleep with my eyes open either. This shit is really fucking with me now. I feel like those fists all pounding in every direction are going to make my brain explode. Fuck. Try to calm down. Think of calmer images. Hang with me, brain. Close your eyes. Sleep.

Tue 11 Nov 08

What the hell is that? It looks like a shower drain, so I must be standing in a shower. Wait a minute, I can't fucking stand by myself, and I sure as hell can't take a shower by myself. Yet there is a drain at my feet. This must be another image, so I close my eyes to reset my vision to the actual room. I open my eyes again, but the shower drain is still there. What the fuck? Finally I realize that's the TV on the wall past the foot of my bed. How the hell did I think that was a shower drain? The combination of the drugs and my lack of contacts is not a good combination at times like this. Tonight when I go to bed, I have to remember to ask the nurse for a sleeping pill and hope it will cancel out the visions.

I haven't had the TV on yet. I don't watch it at home because I always have something better to do. After canceling cable at my first house in Texas, I realized how much more productive I was without it. Besides having cable to reduce arguing points by one with the ex for a while when we moved to Florida, I haven't had cable since then. I really don't have anything that has to be done besides get better here in the hospital, but I've gotten to the point where I just feel lazy watching TV and try to avoid it. That's also partially due to Dad drilling into my head at an early age that watching TV equaled laziness. Movies are somehow okay though. I don't necessarily understand; I just accept it as part of both his and now my belief system.

My brain is still oatmeal, but I might as well start reading "The Heroin Diaries" since I can't do anything else. Maybe I'll get some literary ideas as I write my own memoirs, or at least gain some sort of intellectual stimulation. It's hard not to notice a lot of the similarities between his story and mine. We both have a passion for the intensity that hard rock provides, and indulged our taste for excess living the "Kickstart my Heart" video with fast cars, bikes, booze, and women. Our addictions at some extent have held back the achievements we could have made with our combined creativity and intelligence, but we've lived more experiences in our lives than most people even imagine. After the last couple weeks, we even both temporarily died twice, and doctors had to kickstart our hearts. We're both extremists that have to abstain to survive since we never could learn to temper our self-destructive nature.

As I look at the water cup I use here in the hospital that says, "Valley Health System," I can hear Sixx AM singing, "I don't want to die out here in the valley, waiting for my luck to change." "Life is Beautiful" is definitely my favorite track, and the lyrics are so true and so fitting for my fucked up life to date. Mom will continue to "Pray for Me," and Sunshine is my "Girl with Golden Eyes." Maybe when I get back and am still incapacitated, I'll do a painting or something like what I did with Danzig's "Mother" where I did a pencil sketch of the goat's skull in the background and the lyrics in calligraphy with ink on top. I could even make it bigger and put excerpts from other Crue songs on it as well. "Primal Scream," "Hooligan's Holiday," "Wild Side," "Too Fast for Love," "Live Wire," and "Girls, Girls, Girls" all have very relative lyrics to my own past adventures.

Despite some similarities between people like Nikki Sixx and me, I'm not a rock star. I never main-lined Jack Daniels, although I did snort it. I totaled an Intrepid and a Scrotus, not a Pantera like Vince Neil, and I was sober both times. I drank enough to forget what state I was visiting, and had ten cops in West Des Moines pointing guns at me one night, but I never holed up in a closet with heroin and a shotgun fearing imaginary enemies. I probably would've made a great rock star, considering how much of that lifestyle I've been able to enjoy as a career engineer. Even if I had the ability to be a rock star, I doubt I would've taken the chance. I don't play the lottery, and I wouldn't base my whole future on those kinds of odds.

Motley Crue might look at me as a boring pussy that wouldn't take the risks or have the experiences they did. I look at the typical Jason with his high school sweetheart, Jennifer, little Eric and Erica, and their home on 210 with the white picket fence and think the same thing. All things are relative and perception is personal reality. Jason probably looks at me with the same balanced combination of buried envy and disrespect for my life choices as I do looking at the Crue. The difference is I'm more honest about being jealous of the excitement. Jason just cites me as a bad example to Jennifer in order to make himself look better, when he hasn't told her about the hooker he fucked in Vegas. In contrast I will openly admit that as much as I should identify a lesson of what not to do in the Crue, I can't help but read about them and want to drink a fifth of Jack, ride the Hawg at full throttle, and snort coke off some stripper's ass before I drill her into the nearest piece of furniture.

Here come the cute little walker girls again to brighten my day. I still can't get over how friendly and nice everyone is here. It's pretty humiliating to need help from two girls to help me go for a short walk, but there's no room for pride or stubbornness here. Whatever the hospital employees tell me is exactly what I do. I've got nowhere to be except right here doing what they tell me and getting better. As they get ready to take me for my walk, Jeanie leans over and I can't help but smirk as I see her thong rise out of the back of her pants. My weakened brain struggles to formulate the words, "Aww, Jeanie, you wore a thong for me? I'm flattered, but I have a girlfriend." My mouth opens, but fortunately the internal monologue stops the words from rolling off my tongue. I don't want to add a slap print on my face to my list of issues right now.

Wed 12 Nov 08

How in the fuck am I going to coordinate among Ducati, the exhaust manufacturer, and the salesman? I can't make all three of these people happy, and why the fuck am I dealing with this anyway? Here I am in a fucking hospital bed, and I have a ton of emails to deal with on this project now. If I'm in a hospital bed, how the fuck can I get emails? I haven't looked at an email since I got here. I couldn't access it if I wanted, so everything I'm thinking about is the result of some ridiculous dream. The sleeping pill they gave me last night eliminated the distraction of the images, but they were replaced by my overactive mind's creations. I am awake enough now to know that I'm here for surgery and recovery, not for any kind of project or even communication with the outside world. An active brain is a great tool to have, but it can get the best of me if I begin to lose control of it. It's time to go back to sleep.

Organisis's here to visit with Junior again, who's now mastered the art of shitting his diaper within an hour of arrival in my room. The stomach situation is bad enough without that smell, but Organisis always changes it as soon as she realizes it like a good mother and sister. Once she arrives, she says there is a surprise, and in walks Sunshine.

I'd told Sunshine and Mom I didn't want visitors until I was better. It's bad enough being miserable without an audience. It wasn't necessarily easy to tell either of them I don't want them around, and I know they both have the best intentions, but the most important thing right now is for me to get better. I've gotten through every bad experience in my life by myself, and I'm not going to use a scenario like this for an experiment. So as much as I just wanted to relax with minimal external stimulus, it's very nice to see her smile brighten the room in her short gray dress, and knee-high boots, looking like a high class go-go dancer. That's sort of a dichotomy like a hooker with a heart of gold, but it's only a saying and only an image, and what every guy really wants. Her choice of cold weather clothes makes me laugh. Knee-high boots somehow keep her warm while wearing a short dress in November in Colorado. It's a good fucking thing I'm a guy.

Thu 13 Nov 08

What the hell is wrong with me? I can't blame this fucked up sleep pattern on the drugs. Since I was a kid, I've had the unfortunate habit of confusing dream with reality and becoming obsessed with some ridiculous task with no bearing on anything. Right now I'm beating my head against the bed rail to understand the dreamed requirements I've made up. It's 2 am, but I won't be able to sleep so I might as well attempt a shower. I ask the nurse to crank up the finicky climate controls in hopes of avoiding ballsicles after the shower.

After giving the heat time to warm up the room, it's time to hobble to the bathroom to rinse off. The nurses are a little surprised as to why I'm up at this time doing this, as it's not normal I'm sure. They do seem to appreciate the fact that it spreads out shower assistance-duty to the slower hours. It's so fucking hard to get the breathing right, even with this oxygen tube in my nose, as I sit on the chair under the water cranked up as hot as it will go, which is around 115 degrees according to the readout on the shower. I have a digital temperature gage on my shower water, but not on the room temperature. Weird.

The coughing is becoming a terrible inconvenience at best. I've been coughing violently for an hour, clutching my chest pillow to prevent reopening of the chest, while Sunshine stands by and watches helplessly. There is nothing either of us can do except hope the chest doesn't tear or crack open, but hope in one hand and shit in the other, and I know which fills up first. The nurse finally gives me glorified cough syrup, which seemed to slow down the cough at least. I notice the bandages on my chest are wet. I must've spilled some water on them.

The dietician is asking why I haven't been drinking my meal-substitute shakes. I explain to her that absolutely nothing sounds good, and I try to eat what I can, but I have to force myself to do that. If I get down one or two bites of food per meal, it's an accomplishment for me. She suggests a couple different things that sound bad and make me almost sick. Then Sunshine suggests rice and beans for some unknown reason. I have to tell both of them to just shut up and not mention any more foods, as I'll eat what I can when I can. I know I sound rude and they're just trying to help, but I have no desire to add nausea to my other list of fun feelings right now. My appetite is so far fucked right now. I'm starting to question whether I'll ever eat again before I am off the medications. I can't believe it's been since November 4th since I had a full meal. It's amazing when I consider I'd eat two to three meals for lunch quite often prior to surgery. Despite how little I'm eating, my overweight 223 pounds I brought out here is still 230 pounds due to the fluid retention from surgery. Unfortunately, unlike a girl, I can't look at a calendar or the moon, think about my cycle, and determine when the fluid retention and bloating will release and my mood will return to normal. Since this is a medical condition and not PMS, I'm stuck with it until it's done.

I almost got paroled today except for this damn cough. The fluid on my bandages is actually leaking chest fluid. The cough is more under control with the cough syrup, but my bandages still get soaked frequently. I guess the fluids in the chest have to go somewhere, but I could do without the stench of death as the nurse cleans my wound and applies fresh bandages. "Underworld" is on, so I'm breaking my no-TV rule besides catching "Family Guy" a few times. I chuckle at the irony in watching the main werewolf pull the ninja star weapons out of one of his henchmen and throw them in a bloody bowl as the nurse simultaneously cleans blood off a ten inch cut on my chest. She probably just thinks I'm fucked up for finding humor in the bloody mess, but she wouldn't be the first person to think that and I don't feel like explaining myself.

Fri 14 Nov 08

The doctor is talking like I might be leaving tomorrow. I just need to walk a little more and keep the chest from leaking. I can't believe how humbling this is. I've been through a few challenging experiences in life to say the least, but never one like this. Hernia surgery was physically humbling, it's mentally humbling to be black-out drunk and pissing on yourself or someone else, but neither of those is a pimple on the ass of this ordeal. I realize this as I sit in the shower with no bandages covering the wound. When I cough, a stream of bloody fluid sprays about two feet out of the hole at the bottom of the incision on my chest. Disturbed to say the least, I yell at my sister to get the fucking nurse in here. I show Whitney my magic trick, but she doesn't seem concerned and just bandages it after the shower.

Not that I was shy before, but modesty has no place here in a hospital, and only makes things less efficient. There is only room for one priority, my recovery. I may have taken it to an extreme by freely roaming the hallways with the walker girls and the back of my gown open. I've got bigger problems than worrying about showing my ass right now though.

Sat 15 Nov 08

Two weeks ago today I was waking up on Ronan's couch in Denver. Here I sit now excited that I actually got a long night's sleep, over ten hours, which is likely the longest I've slept in one night since I was a kid. Before this surgery I was averaging about five hours a night, and a couple years ago I was running about two to three hours of sleep a night working long days and playing long nights at the bars. This is a big accomplishment for me. I wonder if for the first time in years I don't have enough worries running through my head to keep me from getting a good night's sleep. Realistically I'm looking at this as I'm still alive, and the rest is just details. I attempt to determine which memories from last night were dreams and which were reality. The nurse loads me back up on pain killers and cough syrup, as well as makes me a cup of hot tea to help soothe my throat. It's really come to this. I have to ask someone to make me a cup of tea. It's not a seven-course meal, it's just a cup of hot water with a bag dipped in it. Like I said though, I'm alive, and these are just details. Maybe this is payback for the girls' drinks I've tea-bagged over the years.

It looks like the wound didn't leak overnight as the gown is still dry on the chest. I weigh in at a lean 225 pounds this morning, so maybe the hole in my chest is actually letting some of that fluid out. As long as I'm up, I might as well watch the "Bourne Supremacy" on the hospital movie channel. I'm trying to take a couple sips of orange juice, but like everything, it has the same nauseating effect. Yuck. Pain killers have to be the best appetite suppressant I've ever encountered.

My body must love this hospital, because it's fucking up every time I get close to leaving. My heart rhythm went into atrial fibulation again last night, whatever the hell that means. My oxygen levels dropped drastically, while my blood pressure skyrocketed. For fuck's sake, I've already been here ten days, twice as much as originally estimated. The people who work in this hospital are outstanding, and I couldn't ask for better support, but I just can't believe how aggravating this really is. Details, but with all the complications at this age, will I even survive this ordeal in ten years when my renewable contract with Death comes due? I guess I'll find out eventually.

Sun 16 Nov 08

Why are all the nurses waking me up to ask if I'm okay? I feel as good as I did yesterday as far as I can tell. They tell me that my heart rhythm went back to atrial fibulation again. I've been off the oxygen, but they put me right back on it and drug me. The heart rhythm is now in junctional, and even sinus rhythm for a while, which is normal rhythm. The doctor tells me I need twenty-four hours of steady heart rhythm in either the junctional or sinus range before I can leave. I guess in this unique case, normal would be preferred, as it'd get me the fuck out of here. I'm still waiting to hear if the culture the hospital took from the hole in my chest shows infection or not. My understanding is that the infection result is the last thing keeping me here, or was the last thing keeping me here.

I can't believe my body is surviving on such a minimal caloric intake. I doubt I've consumed a pound of food total in the two weeks I've been here. It looks like I need to clip my nails too, as they've gotten extremely long in the time here. As I look at my fingernails, the tips of my fingers are almost purple. It's not plum crazy purple, but instead the purple that makeup artists apply to people in movies that are dead. This isn't exactly encouraging.

This book is badass and helps pass the time, plus it's interesting that I started my own memoirs right before starting to read Nikki's diary. Sunshine had said that AJ had bought the book too and gave it to her back in Jax to give to me as a gift. She didn't tell him I'd already bought it, as she didn't want him to feel unappreciated. It was a nice gesture of him. I don't condone dishonesty at all, but in this case I guess not telling him the fact that I already bought the book was okay.

What the hell? My vision on the right side just went out, almost like the upper right corner of my right eye just lost its signal. Is it because I've been reading for quite a while? I slowly crawl from the chair to the bed and ring the nurse. They do some tests and ask questions, but can't seem to find anything wrong. The idea of losing my sight scares the hell out of me, but after a while of lying with my eyes closed, the vision seems normal again. I guess it's just something else to watch.

Mon 17 Nov 08

Several nurses are waking me up again asking if I'm okay. I was sound asleep until they woke me up, and still feel fine. They are telling me that my heart quit beating for 3.9 seconds. I could've gone from 0-60 mph in a new 911 Turbo in the time my heart stopped. Wild. When fluids spraying out of a hole in my chest don't excite the nurses, it makes me very concerned when several of them rush in worrying.

My heart continues to find new ways to keep me trapped here. After great progress on my walks, today I have about half the ability I had yesterday, and am close to where I was after surgery again. I've been optimistic about my progress up to this point, but it is beyond discouraging to lose that much ground during an already snail's pace recovery. Even Joanetta's bubbly outlook isn't working today. I'm told there is fluid on my right lung, that I'll be given a diuretic, and that the fluid will have to be drained tomorrow if the diuretic fails to alleviate the problem. That sounds like it should be a fucking blast.

Organisis brought in the nail clippers so I could trim my nails before I just chewed them off like I do way too often. It's a disgusting habit, but not as serious as crack or bestiality. Vermin attempts to cut my hair with the barber's clippers I'd bought and used at her place a couple weeks ago. Somehow she manages to miss a couple patches, but I really don't care. This is no modeling audition. I figure it's worth cutting the hair off the arms and chest as well to minimize the discomfort of the hair removal I've undergone with every removed Band-Aid and drape.

Tue 18 Nov 08

I feel refreshed after a great night's sleep, and my first night on oxycontin. I've heard a lot of bad things about this often-abused pain killer and that people get addicted to it after having it prescribed. I'm not sure what the appeal to these substances is, as I definitely enjoyed abusing alcohol a hell of a lot more than these pain killers. Perhaps I actually enjoyed the environment for my alcohol abuse more than the scenario for pain killers. Being weak in a hospital bed on pain killers doesn't quite compare to being in my prime, in a club, drunk with my buddies, and enjoying the scenery. There's no question about which sounds more fun.

The diuretics the nurses gave me yesterday to help with the fluid on the lung are working. I'm ringing them every few minutes to empty my port-a-john. I didn't think it was possible for my mouth to get any dryer, but it definitely is thanks to yet another drug, whose sole purpose is to remove fluid from my body. I lost eight pounds of fluid overnight, and we're waiting for the results from the latest chest x-ray to see if the target fluid around the lung disappeared, or if I just pissed out all my remaining hydration.

Unfortunately the fluid on the lung is still in place, so now I have to get a drain tube stuck in my back. Marvelous. Since the doctor uses a local anesthetic, it doesn't hurt too badly. He's done. I would expect a vial or two of fluid is what he removed, but the guy pulled two liters of fluid off the right lung. I can't believe a lung is even two liters in total volume, but I see the fluid sitting there in jars. Hopefully this is a big step in the right direction for recovery and I can escape these walls soon. Even Organisis is surprised at how much fluid came off that lung. I'm surprised Junior behaved for her as long as he has, but it's time for her to take him home for his nap now. I think he shit himself within ten minutes of arrival today. I wonder if he's doing it on purpose just to fuck with me? He's not even two years old, so probably not.

Now that the fluid is drained, the cough seems different, but still bad. Apparently as my right lung tries to expand, it's rubbing on the walls around it where there used to be fluid. I can't even talk without worrying about coughing, which still hurts like hell on the tender chest. Until this chest heals, I'll be carrying this pillow around like Linus with his fucking blanket. Lying in the bed only leads to more coughing. I can't talk or I'll cough again, but I need Vermin to help arrange the wheeled cart next to my bed by the chair, so I can sleep sitting up with my head on the table leaning forward. I'll draw a picture and see if she gets it. Fortunately she understands and helps, as this seems to be the only sleeping position I can imagine that keeps the cough at bay.

Wed 19 Nov 08

I've been sitting in this chair since yesterday afternoon to minimize coughing. The doctor said I may have pericarditis now. That's the bad news. The worse news is that the infection may have spread to the lining of the lungs too. When was it that I had pericarditis the first time? It must have been 2002 when I got that infection in the lining of the heart after my ten-day bender that landed me in the ER. I vaguely remember the last day of that binge starting in Sugar's, giving King a ride around the neighborhood in the Turbo, going to Bennigan's, riding with a couple military kids back to Sugar's, and the last memory of the night was cleaning glasses behind the bar at Jewel's until Nicole told me I had to leave. It seems like I called Uncle Slim as I stumbled home from Jewel's struggling to keep the sandals from falling off my uncoordinated feet. When I woke up two days later, it felt like Fatman was sitting on my chest. The doctors kept asking if I'd done any coke, and I told them I'd never touched a drug in my life, but had been drinking for the last week and a half. "Binge drinking?" he asked. I told him that was putting it mildly. They finally determined it to be pericarditis and the next day told me I'd be kept in the hospital for one more night. I told the doctor, "Fuck no, I'm leaving now," and started ripping off the electrodes. All the more reason I'm surprised I'm able to sit here in this hospital as calm as I've been, as if I have a choice.

The doctor and nurse insist I try to sleep lying down tonight, as my lower legs have swelled like a college kid's prick at a sorority party from sitting upright in this chair for too long. Surprisingly, I'm able to lay in the bed without going into a coughing frenzy. "The Last Boy Scout" is on, and I haven't seen it since college. My favorite line is his mockery of his friend's casual apology about fucking his wife. "Oh, so you were walking down the street when you tripped and fell and your dick landed in my wife…Head or gut." I'll watch that and zonk out.

Thu 20 Nov 08

I can't believe Thanksgiving is only a week away and I'm still sitting here. I've got about as good of a chance of going back to Florida with Sunshine on the 30th as scheduled as a one-legged man in an ass-kicking contest. The sternum that's been sawed in half and wired together twice is healing alright according to the doctors. When I first got out of surgery, the nurses and walkers were extremely stern about motion of the arms and chest, as they should be. When I'd move my arm, I could actually feel the two halves of the sternum grinding together. It was one of those feelings that make your teeth hurt. Now it feels a little more solid, as it's had a couple weeks of recovery. The lung capacity appears to be on the right path now that I have both lungs operational as well. The heart is just recovering slowly, but like Organisis explained, it endured a tremendous amount of trauma. The first surgery took twice as long as it normally would, and the second surgery was only four days later.

This walk didn't go as well as the earlier walk this morning. My oxygen levels have been dipping a little low, so this trot was somewhat taxing. Now for my tough decision of the day; do I shower or snooze?

Fri 21 Nov 08

I think I may have finally figured out why nothing tastes right. Last night I took a taste of water and it tasted slightly like ocean water. I'm continually bombed with saline solution prior to every injection or any other use of the IV's, which may cause everything to taste like salt. Whatever the reason, I'm still here and still barely able to eat half of an apple sauce cup with a glass of tea. I'm trying to remember to brush my teeth as they feel like they're growing hair and rotting, and dental care isn't going to be an option for quite a while. It sounds like even after I leave here, I have to check my blood pressure, heart rate, and other parameters and call nurses to adjust medication levels. I'm told I'll probably have to sleep with oxygen for a while. They also recommend twelve weeks of cardiac rehab, so this experience is not even close to done yet.

Jeanie comes by to give me the physical therapy information and give some pointers for when I get released. She goes through the packet, and then I ask her how long before I can fuck again. She flinches ever so slightly, but she's a cute, athletic young girl and probably isn't as surprised to hear me ask as some people might be. She recommends letting the girl do the work. It's a good thing I have Sunshine, or I'd probably ask Jeanie if she'd be so kind as to continue my therapy through that exercise as well. There's one slap I risked and another slap I avoided.

I just found out I'm leaving today. After three weeks since I was sitting at Diamond Dolls dressed like the Joker slamming Jack &

Cokes with the Beerbarian, I'm going to re-enter the world. I suspected today was the day since some girl stopped by my room to fill out my paperwork for home oxygen equipment, and a guy stopped to talk about the balance and payment for the hospital. It was very gracious of him to offer the ten-dollar discount if I paid the eleven-hundred dollar balance on the spot, but I told him I'd go ahead and wait until I got back to Florida and was able to go through all my bills. I'll have to figure out how to miracle five grand when I get back to pay for all this work. The cardiac rehab would extend several months into the next year, so I'm guessing I'll try to squeeze in a few appointments with them until the year's end before the annual insurance cap resets. I know how to exercise by this point in life, as I've been doing it religiously since junior high, but perhaps they have special goals and items to note that I can learn.

I guess now that I'm starting to slowly come around health-wise, I'll have time to start focusing more on future-planning. Obviously my primary concern is getting healthy, but as I improve I'll be thinking more about paying bills, being productive in the shop, and figuring out what to do with the job. All of this has to be done with minimum stress, as there's no need to expedite my return for the next round of chest-cracking. It seems ridiculous to think about going back to a lifestyle like I lived before that not only causes stress all day at work, but stress at home trying to determine how to pay bills. Granted stress and every other emotion is generated internally and in theory can be controlled, but our job is basically to deal with every problem that comes up on our projects. I've tried to tell Stabby and the Hare that we need to care without worrying, to do the best we can, but accept the limits of our control when we hit them. In addition being paid significantly lower than what appears fair based on local salary.com information and even within our own division gives a significant level of stress when managing personal financials. I hate to say it, but it might be time to hunt for something better, and time is too precious to waste as I've learned this month.

I'm going to try not to worry about the job or anything else though anymore, but instead to understand the situations, make educated decisions on things within my control, and accept things out of my control. Now comes the time for me to learn how to relax and manage stress. Since I'm getting out today, this chapter is closed, and my recovery at Organisis's home is about to begin. Organisis just got here to pick me up, and Whitney has grabbed a couple warm blankets for me to take outside. It feels so different to be in street clothes again after spending seventeen days with my bare ass hanging out the back of a hospital gown. It's time to get into the wheelchair, load up the oxygen tank, bundle up, and get wheeled outside. I'll miss Whitney, the walker girls, Joanetta's cheer, the Susans and surgeons checking on me, April hanging out on the night shift, and even the dietician trying to make me drink those shakes and the nursing students stabbing at me to find veins. I hope John has fun with his family at Disney, Jeanie does well in her triathlon, and Kristen has a healthy kid. These people were some of the most important in my life over the past few weeks, and are the reason I'm still alive. It may not have been fun here, but these incredible people all made it the best it could be, and I'll never forget them or what they did for me.

Holy fuck it's cold out here. I haven't taken a breath of fresh air for two and a half weeks, and I'm having flashbacks from Iowa in this weather. Organisis is parked right at the door and has the heat cranked in the old Taurus wagon. However, I have lost thirty pounds of insulation, have lived in warm southern climates for the last decade, and am on narcotics. This is the coldest I've been since I stood next to that river in Illinois soaking wet in 40 degree air. Dammit.

Now that we're back at Organisis's house, I'm stumbling into the living room and assuming the position in the reclining part of the couch that I imagine I'll be maintaining for the next couple weeks. Matic gets home from work shortly after we get settled. The Office has sent a big box, so we let Junior open that. It's a very thoughtful care package filled with cards, magazines, cd's, dvd's, and books. I appreciate the gesture by everyone, and it is a clear reminder of how great my co-workers really are. It's too bad the high level aspects of the job can't be more accommodating sometimes, but it sure is an incredible team of friends.

Chapter 3

Mountain Mending

Sat 22 Nov 08

This is my first full day out of the hospital. I woke up and had to piss last night, but without my port-a-john I have to get up and walk twenty feet to the bathroom, which is significantly difficult after being sound asleep. It's so hard to believe I spent seventeen days of lying on my sides in that hospital. If it weren't for being able to look back through these notes, I wouldn't believe it was that long. It's strange looking back and slowly remembering forgotten details as I read what I've written over those two and a half weeks. When compared to the days I used to drink until I'd black out, at least this experience has left me with my own notes to jog the memory instead of blurred testimonials from fellow consumers of spirits and libations.

Sun 23 Nov 08

Organisis and Junior are at the store getting supplies for the chili tonight. Organisis told me that Sunshine's preggers sister, Rooster, is coming up from Boulder to watch Junior around 3 o'clock so she can go do some Christmas shopping. Then we'll all enjoy the chili before Vermin and Organisis expand their minds by watching "Desperate Housewives."

Since I'm home by myself for the first time, Organisis located my cell phone and left it with me just in case I need it. I turn it on just long enough to text Sunshine and Tracer to say, "hi." There are seventeen voice mails, but no missed text messages. I have to assume whatever texts were sent in that time were lost in phone world. Sunshine texted right back though, so the phone appears to work. I'd turned on the work Crackberry yesterday just long enough to get Cartmanini's mailing address so I could send a thank you card per Organisis's direction for the card and relaxation book he'd sent. The Crackberry was too low on power to get a signal, so fortunately I didn't have to see how many emails I'd missed. Well, maybe "missed" isn't as accurate as "unread."

There were over a hundred unread emails after the first couple days out of the Office, so I really don't want to know how many are there, and I'm sure as shit not going to worry about it right now. When you're concerned about breathing, work emails fall slightly lower on the priority list. KL had said that he expected he'd be able to call me on my Crackberry or personal cell with any work questions within a couple weeks of leaving the Office, but little did I know at that time how ruined I'd still be. Two weeks from that statement I was still in the hospital, fucked up on pain killers, and had fluid spraying out of the hole in my chest. I know I'll eventually have to start dealing with work again, but not just yet. I'm not sure how to gage when the ticker will be ready to deal with stress again. Exercise level abilities measure ability to handle physical exertion, but I have no idea how to estimate stress-effect resilience. Regardless I'm going to have to learn how to keep stress levels at a minimum, whether it's from work or anything else.

Mon 24 Nov 08

It's obvious I won't be flying home on November 30th as planned, so I better change my flight and look at bills. I call JEA, the landlord, and the post office for both the shop and apartment, as well as the insurance company and Heart Center in Jacksonville. What a pain in the ass it is dealing with the people that answer the phones to help with special considerations. It's ironic when they answer the phone as "customer service." At least most of these issues are resolved until mid-December when I should be back home. Sunshine will be out here for her thirtieth birthday, so I'll plan on returning with her on December 12th. That gives me a few weeks to get well enough to travel.

Wed 26 Nov 08

Mother Dear and Dad just arrived at Organisis's after a long drive here from Iowa. It's always great to see them, but I always notice that they're getting older, which reminds me that I'm getting older. They're both very mobile and healthy for their age thankfully. In fact this time they're getting around way better than I am. They may be nearly thirty years older, but I'm the one that's walking around slow and hunched over in a bathrobe and tube socks with an oxygen hose feeding my nose because I can't even breathe for myself. I love calling her Mother Dear. I'm referencing the Bloodhound Gang song when one guy calls his mom "Mother Dear" before he tells her he's trying to think of words that rhyme with vagina. I get a laugh and Mom thinks I'm being nice. Win, win.

Naturally it doesn't take long for Mom and Dad to greet Organisis and me before they transition from parents to grandparents and turn their attention to Junior, their only grandchild. I'm really glad Organisis got married and had Junior. Not only does she seem happy, but Organisis and Vermin's good lives in the mountains have drawn a lot of attention away from my fucked up world in Florida when I needed a good distraction.

Having barely lasted fourteen months in my own marriage hell, I admire my parents for staying together this long through the highs and lows. They both grew up in Iowa, both value family and integrity over material goods, and are good people who believe in sticking to your word and not in divorce. That's really the only thing it takes is for both to decide to stick together I guess. Two people can be polar opposites who disagree on everything, but accept the other person for who they are and be perfectly happy together. Two other people can have almost identical personalities, but end up divorced because one squeezes the toothpaste in the middle and one squeezes it at the end.

Notwithstanding the similarities in values, they are two very different people. I'm almost amazed they ever got together in the first place. Mom was raised in a large Catholic family on the farm, went to church on Sundays, and lived in their farmhouse outside of a very small town sheltered from the evils of the world. She lived in the big city of Des Moines for a while, and it seems she spent some time in Jersey too. Grandpa moved with Grandma into his parents' house, so he lived there since the early 1900's. I remember walking out to the grove with Grandma so she could show me where she made soap. Every year I'd watch Mom and Grandma pick vegetables from the garden and can or freeze them. Grandma made rhubarb into everything from bars and pies to jam and sauce. It was like Bubba with his fifty ways to make shrimp. Every year we'd go out to see the baby chickens running around in the hay under the heat lamp out in the barn. The wildest thing on that old farm was the first time I saw Grandpa tie a chicken in a noose against the tree and chop his head off with the axe. I remember staring in amazement at that headless chicken running around the yard behind the milk house, just baffled as to how this animal could still move with no head. I thought the brain controlled everything and wondered how it was possible. The wings flapped as the blood splattered the once clean white feathers until the executed bird finally fell to rest. Then Grandma butchered it while Grandpa grabbed the next unlucky bird. That kid of Organisis's gets to watch wheat grass grow on the window sill, but will probably never see a real farm like that. How many kids these days would ever see that?

Dad on the other hand grew up pretty rough. They'd hunt and fish or even steal chickens for food to survive. In his teens Dad hitchhiked to California, without bothering to inform his mom. The police took his guns away on his way back, but the officer that took them sent them back to his home. You'd never see that happen today. I wish those pricks in West Des Moines would send my old .44 mag back to me. I don't remember much about Grandpa, besides the one time he made me wait in the car while he went into the liquor store. He told me they didn't like little kids in there. He died on Thanksgiving in '77 or '78 I think. I guess it's fitting I was give his name for my middle name. Uncle Slim saw me pull a bottle of whiskey out of the freezer one morning and warned me that the only other person he'd ever seen do that was Grandpa. Aunt Kat also warned me against ending up like him if I wasn't careful. It sounds like Dad still respected Grandpa as his father, even though most of the other siblings didn't. That's why Grandpa would stay with us when he did visit. I heard that when he died, the kids called each other and said, "Good news or bad news, the old man died." They bickered with the funeral director to try to get as cheap of a burial package as they could. At a time when most people are so distraught by sorrow, this family was more worried about a bargain.

I know Mom and Dad haven't had it easy. Dad lost his parents years ago. The first born son of every family right down the line died in drunk-driving wrecks, three for three, before any of Dad's generation even passed. Since those wrecks he's lost three brothers to self-induced demises too. It's no secret where I get my masochistic tendencies. Mom's gone through plenty too between losing both of her parents, who were a lot closer to her than Dad's were to him. For such a close Catholic family, it sure seemed like none of them got along for shit when her parents passed. That whole clusterfuck with Mom getting saddled with the retarded sister was just plain fucked up too.

Sometimes I've felt sorry for them over the years, as they've sacrificed a lot for us kids. Right now I'm happy for them though. Here they are gray-haired and both over sixty years old, but still together and enjoying their grandkid. I don't exactly understand the whole thing, as I still feel like this experience of my sister having a kid is very foreign to me, but it makes me happy to see them happy.

Thu 27 Nov 08

Tonight is the first night I've left this couch since I got to Organisis's. She helps me get a couple portable oxygen tanks in place so we can take them over to Vermin's and Dionysus's house for dinner. Vermin is making a turkey on the grill, but unfortunately realizes she's run out of gas at some point in the cooking process. The turkey is only slightly later than planned, but still comes out well.

The whole family is here including Mom and Dad, Vermin, Organisis, me, and all three of our significant others. It's the first time our family has sat around a holiday meal since probably my first Christmas in San Antonio when they came to visit and their car got stolen out of my driveway. Was that the weekend Stu was in town? That's right. He was with Sambo and me at the Riverwalk. I'd been kicked off the stage at Howl at the Moon, kicked out of PolyEster's for abusing the Marcia Brady cardboard cutout, and passed out before the family got there around 3 am. At 8 am Dad was pounding down my bedroom door and freaking out because his car was gone. Fuck he was pissed. Merry Christmas, Dad, how do you like my new home so far?

It's been so many years since I've been at a large family event like holidays at Grandma's and Grandpa's as a kid, that even this little group is taking some adjustment on my part. I know and like everyone here, but for some reason I almost get un-nerved in something that feels like a family environment. I'm better than I was a year ago though. Last October we all came out for Organisis's thirtieth birthday and I saw Junior for the first time. Sitting around Organisis's table was completely surreal. My little sister was there with her house, husband, child, and yellow lab. The white picket fence was all that was missing. My other sister, now Aunt Vermin was playing with Junior. Mom and Dad were now Grandma and Grandpa. It was a totally bizarre experience in which I felt as if I was watching the whole thing on TV. There was no way it could be real, but it was.

When we go around the table telling for what we're thankful, Organisis announces she's corked up with the second ankle-biter. She's happy so I'm happy. I'm also happy it's her that's expecting and not me. That's probably not what I need to minimize my stress and recover. My answer is simply, "I'm alive." A couple years ago I went to Cousin Reno's for Thanksgiving after my Illinois stunt. When asked the same question, my response was, "I'm not in jail, I'm not in a hospital, and I'm not in a ghetto anymore." The other couple they'd invited looked at me like I was Damien, but it was true and sincere. As I used to tell myself as a kid, "Never feel guilty for telling the truth." Yes, I'm thankful I'm fucking alive. Everything else is just details.

Sun 30 Nov 08

I hear Organisis yelling for Emma, the family yellow lab, since Emma didn't come back to the door and must've gotten distracted. Organisis asks me to watch Junior while she drives to find Emma. I hear Junior whimpering in his room, so I walk in there and crouch down at his level. At least he's already out of his crib, as he exceeds my five-pound lifting restriction. He leans up against me and I put the blanket around him, which seems to put him at ease. I guess after just waking all he needs is someone to let him know he's not alone in the house.

I hear Organisis come in the door, but when I see her come into the living room, she's crying, "She's dead. I found her on the sidewalk, and she's dead, and I had to leave her there because I couldn't carry her." I hug her and tell her I'm sorry because I can't think of anything else to say. The doctor may have torn my chest open and ripped into my heart, but this hurts worse and it feels like that's what's happened again to see Organisis crying like this. After all that my sister has done for me, I owe my life to her. I feel so helpless, as here I stand not able to do a fucking thing to make her feel better. I can't even go get the dog for her. All I can do is call animal control and ask them to go pick up the body. She just wants it removed instead of going through seeing and burying the family pet.

I'm saddened to know Emma died, as I've grown fond of her since I've been living around her. What tore me up was to see Organisis that upset. In comparing it to my own recent temporary departure, I was never that bothered with the idea of dying. It was only the thought of the people I would've left behind being upset that disturbed me. Maybe it's because I accept that dying is part of life. When a creature perishes, the suffering for that being is over, but the people left behind are still alive and will still hurt.

I try to put my own pills in line for the first time and not bother Organisis with breakfast or anything. She cries when Matic gets home from work and a little when Vermin comes over with flowers. Other than that I don't hear her cry or say anything more about Emma. I have to admit how impressed I am with Organisis's ability to cope. Not only can she keep smiling amidst Junior's dirty diapers, crying, and messes, but she became apparently immune to the loss of

Emma within a very short time after being extremely upset when she originally found her. That's a strength you don't learn from a book or get in the gym. That's internal strength, and I have to admire her for that.

Fri 05 Dec 08

Snow? What's this shit? I left Iowa ten years ago to avoid this. I made a promise to myself that I would never complain about the heat as long as I never had to see that white shit again. When I left for Texas after college, Mom asked if I'd ever move back to Iowa. I told her the only snow I ever wanted to see is what goes up a stripper's nose. By coincidence I called Mom after my first week in San Antonio and told her I saw snow in Texas. I'd met some stripper at a bar and gone to a party with her where her friends were doing coke. I assured Mother Dear that I immediately left the premises and maintained my status as having never touched a drug. I could tell she was proud.

Matic is getting a little stir-crazy today since he is trapped in the house. Finally he and I decide to go for a drive to Hawg Wild. When we visited Fort Collins almost twenty years ago, Cousin Eddie had taken us to this place. It had a showroom full of custom and classic bikes, and I recall one bike having a piece of cardboard under it to catch the oil drip when the beast marked its territory. The T-shirt I bought that day is still in my closet, but it's torn and full of holes from grinding, welding sparks, and two decades of abuse. The Hawg Wild logo is on the back and the front has an eagle with muscular arms holding a sledge hammer. The bottom of the shirt says, "Japanese Motorcycle Repair Man. Call 1-800-TRASH-IT." The shop is still there, but now only a couple bikes are on the floor hiding among the shelves and racks of a vast selection of parts. There are rows of heads and cylinders, brand-new factory brake calipers, clutch cables, and front ends from thirty years ago. Unfortunately they don't have any shirts like the one I'd bought last time, so this visit is free.

Matic takes me to the store so I can buy a few groceries, since I told them I'd make chili for dinner tonight. Organisis insisted on chili beans, which are actually pinto beans, instead of the kidney beans I generally use. She also asked us to get stewed tomatoes for it, but I know Matic doesn't care for those and to be honest, I can do without them too, so we conveniently forget to buy those. Once home I pull a stool up to the kitchen counter and stove, and successfully cook my first meal since my reincarnation as a skinny, humble me.

Sat 06 Dec 08

I wake up and see Junior zoom past my couch/bed toward the Christmas tree and back again. The next time I open my eyes, I see Organisis sitting with him by the tree, a silhouette with lights shining from it, which she's just plugged in. She's trying to show Junior how to put the hanging balls on the tree. He's gotten very good at removing them and scattering them throughout the house, but needs direction putting them back on the tree. I'm curious what thoughts are passing through his twenty-two month-old brain. I watch him absorb Organisis placing the ball on the tree, start to mimic her, then get distracted and begin banging the decorative metal popcorn container like a drum.

As I look at Junior, it's hard to imagine remembering anything from his age, but I do. I was less than two years old when Uncle Slim wrecked a motorcycle and broke his leg, and I remember crawling under his bed when we visited him in the hospital. Obviously I didn't learn anything about motorcycles being dangerous at that point. I was about that age when Mom had her leg surgery and Dad took me to the store to rent a carpet cleaner. He wanted to have everything nice and clean when Mom got home from the hospital. I'm surprised I remember that, but not the whole bed thing Mom explained to me many years after it'd happened. Mom told me that when we all got home from picking her up at the hospital, I ran to where my bed used to be, but it was still at Grandma's house where I'd been staying. Mom said I just stared at the empty space confused and disappointed. She still blames herself for my overly independent nature being caused by that night. Before that happened I always had to have Mom and Dad put me to bed. She said after that I went to bed when I was ready regardless of whether Mom or Dad knew it or not, and haven't trusted anyone since.

I wonder if someday Junior will grow up and his earliest memory will be sitting in the hospital playing with a blood pressure machine or an image of his skinny uncle sitting on the couch at his house. I'll have to remember to ask him in a few years and see.

The temperature is warming up significantly. Thank fuck. From my spot on the couch I can see the water drizzling off the roof from the melting snow. I question whether this oxycontin is doing any good for the pain at this point and need to quit taking it before I need to drive. Organisis told me I'd need to wean off of it, so today I'll take two half pills instead of two whole pills and see if I can tell any difference in pain.

Sun 07 Dec 08

I really don't notice any pain difference from the reduced dosage of oxycontin, so today I'll just quit taking it altogether and see what happens. I'm down to 186 pounds this morning. I can't believe I've lost almost forty pounds in five weeks. I slowly maneuver out of my clothes and glance in the mirror before I climb into the shower. Wow. Have I not looked in the mirror at all since I got here or has this happened just recently? My stomach fat is still in place, but the muscle I worked so hard to build in my chest and arms has completely disappeared. I haven't looked this weak since early high school. I didn't lose forty pounds of fat; I lost forty pounds of muscle. Why did the body choose to lose muscle instead of fat? Hopefully quitting these fucking drugs will allow me to start eating a little more before I lose any more muscle than I already have.

Mon 08 Dec 08

Why am I so cold? I feel like I'm wet and the cold air is freezing my skin. The only reason I'd be wet is if I was sweating though. I did use that extra blanket last night, but did that cause me to sweat so badly? I've only been asleep for a few hours, but what are the chances I'll fall asleep again? My spinning mind seems to think there's a necessary order to how my body should warm itself. Eventually I wake enough to realize this notion is ridiculous and get past it.

I still can't fall back asleep and instead stare at the dark living room and the stuffed St. Bernard sitting on the other half of the couch, almost like he is staring at me and angry that I am lying on his couch. For whatever reason, the Unicorn prances into my head. I haven't thought about her in a long time, probably almost since I met Sunshine, yet I find myself replaying an executive summary of the three months with her. Like many past relationships, I don't wish I was still with the girl so much as I try to understand what went wrong so I can learn from it.

When I met Unicorn, it was the first time I ever really flipped for a girl. She was waiting tables at Casa in her tight black pants and skimpy top, and I told Tracer, "That's what I want." Eventually we started dating and she was a vast improvement over the drugs, booze, and all night partying that finally drove me away from the bartender I'd been dating. I had a new job, new apartment, and new girl. Unicorn was an absolute doll, always seemed happy, and we really clicked. Being with her almost erased the memories of all girls prior to her. There were of course some great girls before her, like Nicole the cheerleader. I had to go to spring break in Daytona Beach to meet a cute little blonde from Iowa. It's too bad she smoked, and too bad she lived in Iowa when I lived in Texas. It was hard to swallow the fact that I told her I couldn't continue a long distance attempt, because I'd met the ex, and it wasn't fair to either of them. If they'd both lived in San Antonio, I would've chosen the cheerleader, but I couldn't ask her to uproot, move to Texas, and hope things would work out. If they didn't work out, I'd have the guilt of having derailed her life for a guy that wasn't right for her. I could drive myself crazier thinking about all the what-ifs, but it's all in the past, can't be changed, and can only serve as lessons so as not to repeat mistakes. Her sister emailed me a few years ago and said Nicole was married and pregnant. I'm genuinely happy for her, as she was a sweet girl and got what she wanted. Nurse Nicole from Austin was a sweetheart too with blond hair and blue skies, but she wanted me to grow up before I was ready. I'm sure she's not the only quality girl I put aside before she interfered with my rock-and-roll lifestyle. I guess it takes not only compatibility, but timing for things to work, and Unicorn was the first time that really happened.

Several weeks into dating, Unicorn came over and told me she decided she didn't want to seriously date anyone, and then moved in with me a week or two later since she had issues with her roommate. There just wasn't enough room for the two of us in the one-bedroom shoebox apartment. The cheerful girl I'd enjoyed became cold and unhappy. She moved in with her friend eventually, texted me some chicken-shit breakup the next Wednesday, and I never saw her again. It was really disappointing to know the girl I'd respected so much took such a cowardly out. I heard Unicorn got married several months later and moved to North Carolina. As much as I was disappointed with how she parted ways, she was still a sweet girl too, and I'm glad she also ended up with someone she really wanted. Reality is that she could be divorced already too, but hopefully she grew a little and learned to let her guard down enough to stay happy with someone.

Who knows exactly why she left? She was in her early twenties and still trying to figure out life. I wonder if it's because the sex wasn't as good as she wanted? She seemed like such a princess, that I always got nervous about wanting things to be perfect with her. I felt almost guilty about being too aggressive with her, when that's probably what she wanted. I had started to drink a little again with her, and that didn't help things. The booze and the bum heart valve didn't make for the best drilling, but I can't help but notice I've got a diamond cutter right now. This is the first time I've had a hard-on since surgery. It feels more intense than I can remember for years. I wondered if the hardness factor would improve when I got surgery, and it looks like that's an affirmative yes. Outstanding. You better watch out St. Bernard. If you don't quit giving me dirty looks, you're going to be a dry-hump victim.

While I was dating Unicorn, that hot trashy Hooters waitress told me I was fucking hot one day at lunch and gave me her number. I left her alone since I was already occupied, but called her when I had an opening. Unfortunately once Unicorn was gone, so was the trashy waitress due to lack of attention. I'd also met the Jagette during that time. Besides the hair that was way too short, the Jagette was hot with her fake rack, former cheerleader body, and party girl demeanor. That girl may never win a Nobel Prize, but she sure could fuck. Unfortunately she got that way through practicing with several other dudes at the same time as I found out later. The inside of her crotch must've looked like Spiderman's shooting range.

Months later she cornered me asking why I ignored her in bars. I reminded her that I'd always told her if at some point she wanted to go fuck around to just be honest. Instead she'd lied about everyone else that was pole-vaulting in her grand canyon, and that's why I didn't want to associate with her. I have no problem with promiscuity, but dishonesty is something for which I have no tolerance. When I was single, I acted like it, and no girl ever thought I was going to be her Prince Charming. When I gave my word I would be loyal though, I never broke that word. If I can do it, anyone should be able to do it, but they don't. One thing I did learn from the Jagette is how to fuck. I'd been told before by more than one girl that I was well-built. I've heard, "That's big. That's scary big," and "What do you feed that thing?" I've also been commended on many occasions for my oral skills such as, "I've never come from a guy doing that before," and "I've never even had an orgasm from sex." I guess I was just never with a girl long and sober enough to really sharpen my overall skills. I remember when Mabel and Mabel back at ISU asked me if there was a difference between making love and fucking. I told them, "Girls make love. Guys fuck." After the Jagette and her sex Olympics as she called them, I was a believer in the intensity of sex, and decided from then on I would never leave a girl any question in her mind whether we'd fucked or not. At the end of the day, that's what the girl wants too, and if she doesn't, then I'm not interested in her anyway.

I found myself blinking through girls I'd met, dated, and/or banged over the years. One week I can remember having five dates. I didn't actually screw anyone that week, but I still had a pretty busy social calendar. When I saw Doc's sweet ass leaning over the rail at that piano bar behind Dick's Wings, I thought I'd better have it, and I did for almost nine months. She had a killer body, and I was impressed that she had the intelligence and work ethic to become a doctor. Unfortunately Doc had a knack for interpreting things as negatively as possible and the belief that she deserved more than she was willing to offer.

All relationships, business or personal, require balance and fairness. I explained the ladder theory to her over breakfast one morning and told her that she'd never be happy with anyone. She wanted a guy from the upper rungs that would be handsome, funny, romantic, hard working, wealthy, and honest, but required a guy from the lower rungs with enough flaws and low esteem that he would kiss her ass and expect minimal return. The likeliness of even one rung of overlap in these two types is nearly impossible. She told me she's had great guys before that would do all this stuff for her, and I pointed out she wasn't with any of them anymore either. She's intelligent, but sometimes social ironies and self-criteria need to be pointed out bluntly to have effect.

I'm not sure why my brain is deciding to review sexual and relationship escapades of the past at this particular time. Perhaps it's out of boredom since I can't sleep. Maybe my hormones just woke up, explaining this extra ligament I've got in my shorts, and they're controlling both heads. I've known some beautiful girls, some intelligent girls, some real sweethearts, and unfortunately a lot of raging bitches and trash too. I have some fond memories of most of the girls I have known, whether I ever made sticky messes with them or not, but there's at least one reason for each that I'm not with any of them today. There is one valid conclusion from hours of sleep I've lost replaying all of this in my mind. When I think about Sunshine, it is obvious that after a life of wrong choices, I finally made a good decision when it comes to girls. The fact that I have her now is what really makes the other girls just memories and learning experiences. When I first saw that smile of hers in the art gallery that day, everyone else just melted into the past.

As expected I don't notice any pain difference now that I've quit the oxycontin. It seems like every pain medication they gave me lost its effect after a few days. When I tell Organisis about the sleepless night and cold sweats, she points out that oxycontin is still an opiate and will probably still cause some withdrawal effects. In other words it wasn't giving me any pain relief, but still fucks me up when I quit taking it. That's like getting a hangover from non-alcohol beer or catching crabs from a toilet seat. When I tell her I tried to wean off them by taking half pills, she explains that those were time-released pills. Instead of slowly entering the body through their shell, the ones I cut in half dumped the drug into my body. No wonder I was all fucked up last night. I'd mimicked mainlining heroin the day before. Awesome.

Sunshine's birthday gift from Tiffany's arrived today and is now wrapped and ready. It's a heart-shaped necklace Organisis helped me select online. Sunshine commented shortly after we'd met that she wanted something from Tiffany's by her thirtieth birthday. Her sister was going to buy her a Tiffany's keychain, which they guessed to be the only affordable thing from that store. I obviously don't understand, as I can't drive and enjoy a Ferrari T-shirt, but girls and guys have clearly different mindsets. I know I violated Dad's advice about never buying a girl clothes or jewelry. He told me that right after Mom exchanged the necklace he'd bought for her for their twenty-fifth anniversary. I'm guessing Sunshine will appreciate the thought more than the actual gift, which is fine as long as she's happy.

Vermin is here tonight so we can finish watching "Into the Wild." As the main character dies alone in the bus, only one word comes to mind. I look at the TV and say, "Idiot!" in the Napoleon Dynamite voice. The movie was incredibly written and had some great points. However, in the end this intelligent young man with the world at his fingers substitutes ideals and stubbornness for intelligence. When boiled down to facts, his extreme behavior becomes his demise no differently than if he were a dead heroin addict. Obviously there is some level of moderation and balance between the extremity of his actions and a role in the materialistic society he was escaping that would've ironically saved his life.

The freedom of the main character, although taken to a fatal extreme, makes me envy a younger version of myself. Years ago my internal reasoning was peppered more with, "So what? If this doesn't work I'll try something else. What's the worse that'll happen? Nothing really bad has happened to me so far." I also find myself jealous of

Yoda. I email him and ask what he's learned in life that allows him to take every day at a time without really worrying. Much of it has to do with financial security of course. I understand that we can become slaves to our material desires, echoing one of the primary themes of the movie. I don't have an extravagant lifestyle though. However, I don't have savings or credit either, and now I'm going to have hospital bills on top of the normal bills. I cannot afford to lose my job. I've been in that gutter in the crack neighborhood living on daily rations of ravioli cups and a few glasses of whiskey a day, and I don't want to fail that badly again in life. From my perspective the Office has me by the balls.

Tue 09 Dec 08

Dad turns sixty-three years old today. I've only been asleep about two to three hours again, so I guess I'll lay here until I call him around 4:30 am Iowa time when he usually wakes up. That will be 3:30 am here in Colorado. If it's hard to believe I've lived to be thirty-four, it's even more difficult to believe Dad's lived to be his age. Uncle Slim told me once as we were getting fucked up in Texas that there is absolutely no reason for Dad to be alive, but yet somehow he's survived the odds. Slim talked about a younger Dad getting impatient, putting his old Sportie on the center line, and riding back from the Keys on Christmas morning as opposed to waiting in traffic. There was also a time he literally slid the bike on its side up to a gas pump while one of the other guys yelled, "Safe!" Fat Slim also noted that it didn't appear there was much reason for me to be alive, but I've somehow survived longer than I should have as well.

I can't talk much yet, so it is a short call, but fulfills my duty as a son to call and wish him a happy birthday. We never did much for his birthday as kids, but Mom usually baked his favorite cake, maple nut with white cream frosting, and bought him something he needed like socks instead of something he may have wanted. In general to Dad, a need is a want. In contrast many people today consider wants as needs. The trick is to be able to identify a need from a want and then prioritize properly.

Yoda emails me back acknowledging that part of his freedom is the byproduct of financial management instilled in him by his wife. He also explains that he moved all of his personal belongings in a box when he started work. He put the empty box under his desk and tells me that if the day comes that he is no longer happy at work, he will pack that box and disappear. He doesn't just mean that he'll leave his job. He also keeps a map on the wall and marks places he'd like to see. If or when the day comes where he feels the need, he'll take that map off the wall, hop on his full dresser, and disappear for however long the trip takes him. Those saddlebags have held enough to allow him three months on the road before, and they may again. Yoda's response lets me know I asked the right man the right question. I feel enlightened by what he's written to me, but I need to apply what he's learned to my own life before I can effectively benefit.

Vermin brings back Dionysus's Durango and parks it in Matic's and Organisis's garage so we can change the thermostat. Vermin and I looked at it yesterday, but by the time we got back from the parts store, we decided it was too cold, late, and dark to start the project. Unfortunately I'm not much help since I can't move or operate tools very well right now, so I'll have to tell her what to do. The transmission slips when it's cold, so we make sure the transmission fluid is at least full and clean, but it obviously needs more attention than what we're able to do now. We get the shop lights adjusted, put the pan under the radiator, and I attempt to use the crawler underneath the truck to show her what she needs to do. I also point out the leak in the refrigerant line and she tells me that the heat and AC haven't worked in a year on the vehicle. She takes one look at the radiator clamp she'd have to remove to drain a little fluid and decides it isn't worth the effort.

Matic stays up a little later than usual enjoying a few beers supporting his employer, Coors. I'm sleeping on the couch, so I can't go to bed until he does, and we sit awake until around midnight shooting the shit. Most of the conversation revolves around machines like the equipment at his job, his old truck project, classic muscle cars, new exotics, and workings of the internal combustion engine. I can't help but smile watching him enjoy his beer and hearing him talk about the things at work, his projects in the garage that may or may not ever get finished, and watching the genuine excitement and child-like curiosity about anything mechanical. Yes, Organisis really did marry a younger version of her father.

Wed 10 Dec 08

I now weigh 185.5 lbs, which is only a half pound less than Sunday, so hopefully the weight loss is starting to subside. I still only eat about as much as Junior, who weighs a whopping twenty-five pounds, but the appetite is slowly improving. Now that I think about it, since quitting the oxycontin I feel entirely better. There were a few nights of restless sleep, but that's closer to my normal fucked up sleep pattern before surgery. I can eat better, shit better, get morning wood again thankfully, and just feel better in general. Can people on heroin even fuck, or do they just not care? I can't believe people get addicted to opiates after seeing how much better I'm doing without them. Then again there are people that can't understand why I'd drink to the point of blacking out and puking. Life's full of mysteries.

It's a little strange being over here at Sunshine's dad's house. He's here with his wife, who used to be best friends with Sunshine's mom, who is also there with her boyfriend of how many years. There's a little awkwardness there, but they all seem to leave their swords in sheathes so Sunshine can enjoy the event. I guess that's what couples do when kids are involved. Uncle Slim found out about Red Sonja's extracurricular activities the morning of Slim's daughter's graduation. They put the drama aside so his daughter could have her graduation party and dealt with it later. I was there that day and didn't know anything about it until later. Slim and his first wife had split and both remarried other police officers. When Slim emailed me saying that he'd found out Red Sonja was fucking another one of the cops, I responded by telling him if he'd find a respectable profession, his coworkers would quit banging his old ladies. I always like to be there for friends and family when they need support. Ironically he's married to another cop now, but he's been with her for quite a few years. The third time's a charm I guess.

I'm sitting by Dionysus at dinner, who appears to be a very upstanding guy. It's just a little foreign to me to imagine having a girlfriend attempting to fix my clearly neglected car as Vermin was attempting to do with his Durango earlier in the week. I mention it to him out of curiosity, and he explains that if he can make a hundred bucks per hour programming, it's not enjoyable or wise for him to waste his time working on the Durango. That's a logical response I can accept. His computer knowledge is way beyond my scope of comprehension, but I learn more about it by listening to him and asking questions.

I realize that Dionysus's interests and priorities are just different than someone like mine or Matic's, but not wrong. He would probably look at my computer at the shop and critique the terrible way I've cared for it over the five years I've owned it. I use a computer to do a task and don't worry about it until it breaks. In the same manner, Dionysus looks at the Durango as something he drives when he has to do so and only worries about it when it breaks. It probably baffles him why I have a car, two bikes, and I'm building a third bike just as much as it baffles me as to why he'd collect wine. Differences in hobbies aside, if he and Vermin are happy, I'm happy.

Thu 11 Dec 08

Sunshine's here pretty early for her. We're taking a drive up to Estes Park, as I haven't been mobile enough to see the area since I got to Organisis's from the hospital. We're only twenty-three miles from Estes and I can barely breathe, as the air has gotten thinner. I let Sunshine know not to expect much conversation from me the rest of the way. It's amazing how much of an effect the change in elevation has when my oxygen levels are so marginal already. I wonder if I'll be able to breathe easier in Florida when I'm back down to sea level.

We stop for breakfast and I finish an egg, hash browns, and toast, which is the most I've eaten since before surgery. I sure don't miss that fucking oxycontin. We stop to get groceries for dinner on the way back. Fortunately I keep her reeled in from buying twice as much food as we need, as her eyes can be bigger than her stomach or wallet sometimes. The food she cooks is always outstanding though.

Tonight Sunshine has been gracious enough to make stuffed chicken breasts for one last dinner with Organisis and Matic, Junior, Vermin and Dionysus, and us. I actually eat a whole meal again surprisingly. Fucking oxycontin. This could be the last meal all of us get to share for a long time. Vermin's and Dionysus's pending nuptials will likely be the next time that happens, though there's no date set yet.

Now that dinner's over we all sit down to play Adult Cranium for a while. Vermin accidentally bought the Spanish version and had to return it because she couldn't read a label. She's always good for a laugh. Between Cranium, Wordsters, and Scattegories, I have played more games in the last month than I have since I was a kid. After plowing through a whole pile of bike, car, and Maxim magazines, I've also read more than I have since high school. It's not like I actually read much in school either. I read "Cujo" in sixth grade, "Kill and Tell" in ninth grade, "Christine" and "Gardens of Stone" at some point, and "Arnold's Encyclopedia to Bodybuilding" as a senior. Since then I've read Marilyn Manson's autobiography, Motley Crue's book "Dirt," and Brock Yates' book about the original Cannonball Run. I guess I just read "Plato and a Platypus Walk into a Bar" before surgery too. Sunshine bought it for me thinking it was a joke book, but it actually used jokes to explain many philosophical principles. I enjoyed it more than if it were just a joke book since I was able to learn something about the strange animals known as humans and how they think, or fail to do, in most cases.

After finishing "The Heroin Diaries," I'm now reading the book Cartmanini sent me on relaxation and stress management. Nikki's book was highly entertaining, and taught me more about life and death than I thought it would. This stress book isn't very exciting, and I don't swallow all of the energy field voodoo like Organisis, but it is still a good book and I need to learn how to tone down the overactive mind activity. One of the most useful things I've learned from it is how to properly breathe deeply. Every day since surgery I've been doing the breath test with that little pressure-measuring device insurance bought me. Between those exercises and the book's instruction on breathing deep into the stomach versus shallow with the chest, maybe I'll develop some actual breathing capacity as my heart improves.

Chapter 4

Back to the Beach

Fri 12 Dec 08

Today I'm learning what it feels like to be handicapped. I need wheelchair service in the airports, am bundled to the hilt trying to stay warm, and still carrying my chest pillow from the hospital. It's very humbling to look at seventy year-old men, envious of their ability to walk unassisted.

We just landed in Jacksonville, and I can feel warmth and breathe oxygen in the air as soon as I walk out of the airplane. This is a world of difference from the cold, thin atmosphere of Colorado. AJ is waiting in the reception area, as he's come to greet us and help with any bags. I'm still moving slow, but I walk all the way to baggage claim without needing to be pushed in a wheelchair. It's amazing how much different if feels to be back in Florida's atmosphere, and how much it affects my breathing capacity.

It feels very weird to be opening the door to my shoebox apartment, feeling as virgin to the quarters as a strange hotel room. It's been six weeks since I've been here, and I'm sure it'll eventually feel familiar again, but right now it feels like I'm moving into a new place for the first time. After resting and eating a fourth of a tuna sub, we call it a night. As much as I've told myself I need to exercise restraint, I've been caging my libido since that first night after quitting the oxycontin. We're finally alone for the first time in a month and a half. I can barely move or breathe, my chest is still sore as hell, but I lay back anyway while she moves down and risks the Cobain, considering how long it's been. After a nap and a reload we go another round, and then we go another round. Holy fuck, literally. I couldn't do this before surgery. I keep waiting for the heart to just stop, but it keeps doing what it should and so do we. Okay, so maybe it's too much too soon, but I never could moderate something I enjoy. The sandman finally enters, and pleased with the post-surgery performance and post-coital survival, I picture Animal Mother saying, "If I'm going to die for a word, that word is poon-tang."

Sat 13 Dec 08

I just spent $250 in groceries? I did have bare cupboards and an empty fridge, but I didn't think I'd need this much stuff. This should be enough food to last me for a month or better considering my minimal current appetite. The Goat starts, and so does the Ape, but I'm not ready to drive either. Just trying to turn the handlebars on the Ape is tough. I'll have to have someone help move it to the front of the garage so I can get the Goat out if I need.

Tracer and Ms. Texas just arrived at the shoebox. All I've had all day is half of that tuna sub, so I might as well eat a bowl of cereal while they're sitting here. Organisis would be so proud as it's organic milk. I figure I don't need any estrogen, plus for whatever reason it doesn't expire as quickly as normal milk.

I'm glad Tracer started dating Ms. Texas about the same time I met Sunshine. We used to have a lot of fun running around to the beach bars on two wheels, and both evolved from being single to having girlfriends within weeks of each other. I'm also glad I met Tracer when I did. We'd both recently gone through divorce and unemployment. I handled it starving in a crack neighborhood and trying to keep a bike shop afloat. He moved in with his parents and walked the beach looking for sharks' teeth until the next job came along. Seeing him celebrating his single life instead of resenting it provided a positive example compared to most people I'd seen who become miserable after divorce. It was a good lesson in making jet fuel out of lemons. We definitely enjoyed our bachelor lifestyle and the characters of our cartoon world for quite a while. Now we both enjoy the girls we found worth keeping and two bikes and a Quicksilver LS-powered car at home in the garage.

Sunshine just showed up, so all four of us are out the door to see the new Bond flick, "Quantum of Solace." The previews show that a new "Fast and Furious" is coming out with Vin and Walker from the original. Yes, I'll admit I'll probably go see that one, after all it does show a Buick Grand National in the trailer.

The Bond movie was excellent, and even better than "Casino Royale." Now Sunshine and I are home, but I'm still wide awake, so I pop in "Bill and Ted's Bogus Journey." Sunshine is asleep shortly into the movie, and I can't say as I blame her. It's mildly entertaining to me, but not exactly Oscar material.

Sun 14 Dec 08

It's sad that a twenty-three minute walk is a great accomplishment, but during the first week in the hospital I could barely walk from the bed to the door. Even doing that took oxygen and assistance, so at least I'm progressing. I've got a hell of a long way to go, but I've improved drastically in the last five weeks. It's just that I started at almost zero.

Cartmanini is here from Orlando and Cousin Reno is here from Deltona. Both are here for Sunshine's surprise birthday get-together tonight, but came early since they both live a couple hours away. Mindless or not, we're watching some of the "Beavis and Butthead" dvd's Reno brought for an early Christmas gift. He also brought a bunch of food for me, including sardines and toothbrushes. That's a stab at me to remind me of the time I called him when I was down on my luck to put it mildly eating sardines with a toothbrush. Touché.

As Sunshine walks in, she is a little surprised to see Reno and Cartmanini as she only knows we're meeting Tracer and Ms. Texas at the Mellow Mushroom at 6:30. Mr. and Mrs. Stabby have already called from the Mushroom and have our name listed for a large table.

AJ and Stretch are also at the Mushroom when we arrive. Sunshine is of course happy to see a bunch of people she didn't expect for her birthday dinner, even though her birthday is technically tomorrow. It's such a nice change to have a girlfriend that's easy to please. Here come Tracer and Ms. Texas so it's time to get our table and eat.

Mon 15 Dec 08

My normal cardiologist is out for December, so I'm seeing a doctor I've never met. Once the nurse takes my list of current medications I'm taking, an EKG, and my blood pressure, I wait a few minutes for the doctor. I have to wait with my shirt off, and it's freezing since I'm by a window. It's still warmer than Colorado was though. The doctor briefly looks over the information Vermin faxed to him, asks me if I'm progressing, and tells me to call him in three months. I'm shocked that after the intense attention received in Colorado, this guy tells me to call that long from now. This confirms that my decision to get everything done in Colorado was the right thing to do.

This guy doesn't impress me, but the girl at the checkout desk says that he's the guy you want working on you, despite his bedside manners, or lack thereof. I'll admit even he's better than the awful manners of the doctor I had in San Antonio when I had that pericarditis. I told him something was still wrong when I went back two weeks after the stay in the hospital. All he told me was that I was fine, that I should never lift weights again, and that I should start taking beta blockers. Obviously I wasn't fine as I just got my heart rebuilt dumb fuck.

Tue 16 Dec 08

This is a new experience, or at least feels new again. I haven't driven a car, let alone a stick, for over a month. Nerve-racking would be a good way to describe driving. Shifting gears, pulling on the steering wheel, and turning my head to look for traffic all cause tension in the tight chest. I'm driving with the hospital pillow under the shoulder seatbelt. It's more comfortable to spread out the load while driving, and if I have to slam on the brakes, maybe it'll help just a little and reduce the likelihood of re-breaking my sternum.

The apartment is starting to become familiar at this point, but now the shop is new to me again. I look out into the work area at all the stuff for customers and me that need attention, and realize I can't touch anything out there. Since I'm incapacitated I might as well go through some finances and emails that have accumulated during my time off. "Self, remember you're way farther than you were a month ago."

Shitty neighborhood or not, this shop is the closest thing to home I have. I remember Cousin Reno helping me move into this place back in December of '03. Damn that seems like a long time ago. Between my boss and wife, this shop gave me something to enjoy in life. After my boss and wife both went back on their word about their respective arrangements with me within days of each other, this shop was all I had. Y Chrome gave me a reason to get up in the morning when nothing else did. It took me a few months after the week of the simultaneous termination and divorce, ironically right around Independence Day, but I remember sitting in the shop that summer, sanding the parts for the Ripper, listening to Pantera's *Cowboys from Hell*, and for the first time in a long time I was happy. My fridge, stomach, and bank were all empty, but finally my soul wasn't. Through all the bullshit of jobs, girls, health, and legal issues, this shop has always been a place I can go and find myself again.

Wed 17 Dec 08

The drive down to Staug last night was still an adjustment, so we'll see how it goes driving to La Belle today to visit Uncle Steven. I'm not sure why he calls everyone he meets Uncle Whatever, but it's funny to hear him say it in his Dutch accent. It must've been about '04 when I met Uncle Steven at that bike show in West Palm Beach, and picked up my frame from him in Lauderdale shortly after for the Ripper, the first bike I built for a customer. Too bad he's not still in Lauderdale, as I always enjoy visiting my birthplace, but it'll be interesting to see a new part of Florida.

Driving on the open road isn't too bad, as there's not much shifting or turning required. It's actually kind of relaxing cruising through the back roads of central Florida amidst the grazing cattle, marsh areas, and of course the scent of the orange orchards. It's funny to drive through Sebring, a world recognized speedway, out here in the middle of nowhere.

Steven and I go through the list of parts for my next shop bike. This may be the last bike I build, so I want to build it for me as something I could sell or I could keep forever. Steven already gave me the frame and wheels for it in trade for an engine and primary drive I'd given him a long time ago. Today I'm getting tires, brake discs, a sprocket, rear brake parts, and wheel hubs and bearings. The plan is to get a front end and be ready to start doing the metal work, as I'll be fabricating the oil and gas tanks from nothing for this bike. I'd prefer to hold off on spending the ten grand for the driveline for this bike for now, so I'll try to use the driveline out of my customer's bike to mock things up while I'm painting and assembling his bike. There's a lot of work to do in that shop, so if I'm going to move any time soon, I need to get better and get my ass to work in there.

Sebring is a quaint little town and I don't feel like driving all the way back to Jax tonight, so we're looking for a hotel here. Sunshine spots a sign for eighty-nine bucks per night at a nice place. Its pool is right by the lake, we get 10% off dinner, and we get two free breakfasts for the morning. Sold. Now that gas is actually below two bucks per gallon, this whole excursion is only about a two-hundred dollar trip. I'd given Steven about a grand some time ago, so the parts were sort of free today, and now my health is the only roadblock between me and getting started on my next chopper.

Thu 18 Dec 08

Breakfast was good and now we're sitting by the pool and watching the birds on the edge of the lake. It's a nice reminder that the weather in Florida is better than most places. I snap a picture of the sunrise over the lake and text it to Fatman, who replies with a picture of snow in Chicago. Fuck that.

Fri 19 Dec 08

I drive straight from Staug to the shop so I can unload the parts from Uncle Steven. This is pure torture. I've got a bike to build for a customer, a bike to build for myself, several customers I need to call on other jobs, and I have to sit on my ass at this computer. I'm happy to be alive, but nobody like's to starve at a feast.

Here are some forms from work I might as well complete and have done. The boss is not only being understanding of the situation, but invites me to his family's home for lunch on Christmas day. Good people like him make me like the Office, but it's so hard to get over the fairness in pay versus responsibility issue. The grass is always greener on the other side as they say, and I may find that what I have right now really is the best situation I have available. I owe it to myself to find out. I'm going to find a better option, or realize this job is the best option. Either way, I no longer have to sit every day feeling like I'm getting fucked. I may only get ten more years on this planet, so I have to make the best of it and look for a job with either the same responsibility and better pay or the same pay and less responsibility. I'm not going to hold my breath for a job with less responsibility and better pay, but it sure would be nice. Who am I kidding? If I'm not challenged by my job, I'll lose interest. Some would say it's a good personal quality like ambition, others would say it's more like masochism. I definitely need to look for something with more responsibility, and a lot more pay.

AJ's picking me up to run some errands and get some fresh air. We stop at a place at the beach so he can buy root beer of all things, and then head toward an old air strip. I told AJ the defunct runway might make a good location to photograph the Ape, since it's a fast bike. I think using Nette, the Hooters girl with the double D's, on the Ape will be better than with the Goat. The shop is supposed be about bikes, so we'll do shots with the Goat later after we get the bikes done. Shel, another Hooters girl can do the Ripper, and Ali, that tattooed cutie with a pin-up girl look, can do my Anarchist. I'd really like to do all the upgrades to the Anarchist before the shots, but we'll see what time allows.

It's a great night to be out for a walk, but it seems like a different traffic pattern than usual at this time. Oh yeah, it's Friday night. These cars are on their way to bars, restaurants, and friends' houses to blow off some steam. This is the night of fifty-dollar millionaires taking their paycheck they just received after putting in their forty hours and spending it like they're rich, only to have to skip several meals before that next check comes. I hear Tejano music from an old Chevy, rap from the SUV, and heavy metal from a PT Cruiser of all things. A little over five years ago I would've been doing the same thing with Rammstein blasting from the ten speakers in the Grauer Geist on the way to the club. Now it all seems so empty. It's not that I have room to criticize these people when my past behavior was likely way worse. Most times I rode with friends or called Alex for a cab ride because I'd already have a fifth of whiskey in me prior to going to the bars and had no business driving anything but a pogo stick. Now it's just so clear that when you don't have your health, nothing else matters.

I admit I have some level of contempt now for young people out drinking and having a good time. This is partially envy because I couldn't handle the booze without letting the monkey out of the cage. Now I have to be extremely careful and try to moderate to keep from heading back down that path of self-destruction. The other part of this is likely some level of contempt for myself in the past. I was a young smartass thinking I knew everything just like these kids. The fact is I didn't know shit, and if I would've, I'd have known not to spend everything I made in an effort to drink all the booze in sight. When I first moved to Texas, I was making good money in a cheap city, had per diem for all the travel, no car payment, and less than six-hundred bucks in monthly rent. After a year and half, Caine got broke into behind XTC, the all-nude strip club. The next day I thought about buying a new Alpine, but didn't want to spend the two-hundred bucks for a new one. Then I thought if I'd stayed home the previous night, I'd still have my stereo and the two-hundred bucks I blew there. I went back and determined that I'd averaged fourteen-hundred dollars per month on booze and strippers since I moved to Texas and almost got sick at the thought. Most people fear that they'll eventually become what they despise. I guess I'm coming to despise what I once was.

Now that I just completed my thirty-minute walk, it's time to relax. I'm ready for the Olympics, Special Olympics maybe. It's Friday night and I'm sitting here at home alone, which I have to admit is rather peaceful. I suppose all things considered I should try to have at least one quiet night a week just to clear the head. I'm rifling through a pile of car and bike magazines from Tracer, and even though it's supposed to be recreational, I get some sort of task-accomplishment satisfaction every time I finish and toss one.

Tue 23 Dec 08

In my efforts to be better about doing what's right, I'm going to put the past aside and email the Doc for her pointing out the severity of my situation. She'd heard my heart and so eloquently stated, "Your heart's fucked!" She'd also done a little research, talked to her mom who'd had similar issues, and gave me a summary of the situation. All mutual frustrations aside, I at least owe her a small gesture of gratitude. I'm going to send a very dry thank you note with no pleasantries, fulfill my perceived obligation, and hope for no response or awkwardness.

Great, now she's calling my cell phone, and again she's calling. No good deed goes unpunished, but caller ID is great for screening calls. Now she's emailing wanting to talk about the situation and offering to help however she can. That's a very nice gesture of course and somewhat surprising to me, as I'd estimated she'd read the email and delete it instantly. Not that I can even talk well on the phone yet, but no good would come from this. I don't need her doing any more cameos in my cartoon world or causing grief with Sunshine. Even if I were single, I don't know that I'd entertain any more contact than I am now. It's nothing personal against the Doc, as she has a lot to offer, and is eager to help, but my heart doesn't need the frustration we caused each other not so long ago. Sunshine had even suggested calling her prior to surgery for advice, but I was adamant about not doing it. I'm writing another email to Doc and explaining that I was in no way trying to bother her for help, but only to thank her for flagging the problem. I also state that it wouldn't be respectful to Sunshine if I was corresponding with her. Surprisingly she's now responding with a simple holiday wish as opposed to the stabs at my behavior that I half-expected from her. Good, this chapter is completely closed. She continues going her way and I continue going mine.

Wed 24 Dec 08

I've been sleeping much better since all this happened, and have probably been getting two to three times the sleep I did prior to surgery. It's only 5:30 am, but I might as well get up and make something to eat. Oatmeal and reheated enchiladas are clearly the breakfast of champions, and the breakfast of me today.

Here it is, 7:22 am on Christmas Eve, a beautiful girl laying in bed back at my apartment, and I'm here in the shop with Marilyn Manson blasting on the stereo, my YCC beanie keeping my hairless head warm, the shop office's half-assed heater on high, and the Glock clipped inside my cargo pants. As I look through some of the medical forms, I find directions to my first day of cardiac rehab scheduled for this morning, about which I'd completely forgotten. That means it's time to head back to the shoebox and get ready for rehab.

The people at cardiac rehab are great, and remind me of the great staff back in Colorado. I explain that my insurance resets at year's end, so I'll get in what I can between now and New Year's Eve. They have an interesting setup with which they can monitor all the patients' heart rhythm on a central computer screen. It's not that I don't have an extensive knowledge of the human body, but I learn different stretching and exercise techniques here more relevant to my current athletic status. One of the therapists ask me if I'm dealing with any depression, anxiety, or feelings of self-pity. I ask her if she's serious, and she confusingly confirms. I say, "If there's ever a time I'm just fucking happy to be alive, it's now. Why in the hell would anyone be depressed at a time like this?" She explains that unfortunately my perspective on the situation is pretty rare, but I just don't see it any other way.

Tonight we are driving to Fernandina Beach to meet the Hare and Robin for a Japanese dinner. Robin's sister, mother, and grandmother are all in town too. I feel, hear, and see traces of flames from the show at the table behind us. Maybe it's because of the last month of dodging the reaper, but instantly images of flames in hell enter my head. Every time the cooks light the oil or food on the grill and I feel the heat of the flames, I immediately scan for a pitchfork wondering, "what if?"

My feelings of the afterlife are pretty mixed between my Catholic upbringing and my scientific mind. I remember Father Gregory pointing out the fact that even if heaven doesn't exist, he'd rather be safe than sorry, just in case. I'm not good at believing something that hasn't been proven to me, however I won't sit and argue a point I can't prove either. If you asked me if I believe in God, a big part of me would say that I don't believe any of it, but I wouldn't probably just denounce him, just in case he does exist. Most Catholics would call me a poor one because I don't go to church, I'm divorced, and I haven't lived the most saintly life. It's not like I pride myself on breaking the Ten

Commandments. I almost never say, "Jesus Christ" or "God-Dammit" as they're taking the name of the Lord in vain. My youth, which lasted up to just a few years ago, was filled with not just giving in to, but aggressively pursuing temptations of the flesh like polluting my body with booze and sport-fucking, but I stayed away from married girls since that would be committing adultery. I might work on Sundays, but I don't lie, cheat, steal, or kill. I guess much like my legal approach to life, I may not be completely innocent, but I've tried to lay a decent pattern of overall good behavior so that if I do stand before the man, I have a case for special consideration. I'll hope for probation over prison and purgatory over hell.

Now we're on the way back to the beach to meet Tracer and Ms. Texas at Casa Marina. They both have on goofy Christmas hats, but it's funny to see Tracy exhibiting some level of Christmas spirit. He looks like some kind of cross between an episode of "Miami Vice" and "The Grinch" with his suit coat and Dr. Seuss-style Christmas hat. Fortunately Casa is empty tonight, so we were able to sit at the bar and not deal with a crowd. It's hard not to remember the Unicorn bouncing through here in her skimpy black top smiling when she worked here. Then I look at Sunshine and see her smile, which is constant and didn't fade after a couple months into an unhappy frown. Any images of the Unicorn melt away.

This blows. The Japanese food tonight contained butter, eggs, and shrimp, all of which I was allergic to as a kid. It also had salt and sugar in it, which I'm not used to eating anymore. My stomach started to hurt after dinner, hurt even more at Casa, and is now in complete knots. It's bad enough that Sunshine has to go to the CVS and get Pepto Bismol and Rolaids for me.

She is sweet enough to get me a dvd set of "Platoon" and "The Thin Red Line" for me for Christmas, so we watch about half of "Platoon." I know it's not her preference for movies, but it is a great movie, and she sits patiently spending her Christmas Eve with a boyfriend with a broken chest and weak heart hunched over in pain from a torrid stomach watching "Platoon." Nothing says, "happy holidays" like watching Sergeant Elias get gunned down by Charlie and die as he struggles toward the helicopter. You can see the restrained joy in Staff Sergeant Barnes's solemn eyes as he sees that no one will ever know there is also lead in Elias from Barnes's M-16. It's like watching the joy in a child's eyes on Christmas morning around the presents under a sparkling pine.

Thu 25 Dec 08

This blows worse. I feel like I barely slept thanks to the stomach knots. I have to puke. Yuck. I guess now that I'm awake, I'll call my parents to say, "Merry Christmas." This is the first time I've talked to either of them since Thanksgiving, except for the brief call to Dad on his birthday. Sunshine is at the store getting Saltine crackers and 7-up which seems to help the stomach. I call Organisis and Vermin as well to convey holiday wishes while Sunshine is getting ready. We pack up the Goat and head south toward Cousin Reno's place in Deltona.

His warden of over eight years comes out of the kitchen to greet us and thank us for coming down. His latest rug rat has grown even more and is now talking pretty clearly. It's actually the first time I've ever heard him talk in person. Sunshine sits down to play Hungry Hippo with him, and he seems to talk to her right away. I guess kids can tell what adults are okay with kids and which ones aren't. There's a huge amount of food as usual from lasagna to turkey and all the potatoes, beans, and desserts in between. They use the wine glasses we gave them for Christmas, Reno opens "Stepbrothers," and Sunshine and I are trying to help the ankle-biter set up the Hot Wheels track we gave him. It didn't seem to work as good as I thought it should, probably as result of being made in China for as cheap as possible with zero regard for quality of the final product.

After eating and watching some of "Lampoon's Christmas Vacation," it is starting to get dark, so we begin the drive back to

Jax. As we'd talked about earlier, we end the night enjoying "Bad Santa," a true Christmas classic.

Fri 26 Dec 08

Rehab is going well this morning. I have to remember to take off these EKG stickers later in the shower. The hot water softens the adhesive and doesn't pull so much hair out of my chest. I keep thinking the heart monitor from Crowley is not right because of how low it reads, but the monitors here show about the same rates, so I guess it's okay and my heart is just beating slow. I am around sixty-five beats per minute sitting between exercises, and in the low fifties during exercise. The rehab staff suspects the Lopressor is actually dropping the heart rate down to questionable levels. Since the local doctor I saw recently is about as much use as a solar-powered flashlight, I'll be calling the Colorado doctors again.

Sat 27 Dec 08

Today is my thirty-fifth birthday. How the hell am I still alive? I don't buy into everything happening for a reason, or any master-planning theories. I'm alive for two basic reasons. The first reason is that somehow the intelligence-backed survival skills and some good luck have just slightly outweighed my self-destructive behavior and bad luck. The second reason is because the medical staff in Colorado saved my ass.

I start my day waking up early and spooning Sunshine, which is a great way to start any day. Eventually we get out of bed and I make an omelet for us, despite her offer to make me breakfast. I explain to her again that today will be my quiet day with the cell phone, shop phone, and any other womb-exit anniversary acknowledgement ignored. The theme of the day is loud music and a quiet mind.

Even though I generally keep to myself and try my best to ignore birthdays anyway, this year I don't even have the option to go do some of the stuff of the past. I can't go to a strip club, drink, get a tattoo, or even ride my bike. Alright, so I could technically do those things, but it would be stupid considering the recent chest-cracking. By this age I should be smarter than that. I said, "should."

Since I can't do those things and the sun is shining, I go outside and wash the Goat, as it's in dire need of a bathing. Even this chore reminds me that the chest is definitely sore, but I accept that washing a car is now strenuous activity. It's still difficult just to reach across the roof or hood of the car. However, I'll chalk this up as the first manual task I've completed since getting sliced. Now that I've completed that, I head back to the apartment to change, grab my heart monitor and MP3 player, and go to the beach for a walk while it's still nice out so I can enjoy the sunshine.

Only in Florida is the beach-access parking lot slammed two days after Christmas. I find one spot no one else took because the slightly flat tire on the oversized pickup parked next to it is over the white line causing a tight fit. There are lots of people at the beach in their swimwear. In contrast Fatman is probably freezing his balls in Chicago right now. In the words of Han Solo and Animal Mother, "Better you than me." There's definitely a broad variety of beach-goers today, including couples aged from kids to Q-tips walking along the water and enjoying the gorgeous day. You have the assortment of drunks and stoners attempting to keep their bicycles upright while riding down the beach. No day at the beach is complete without some overdeveloped jailbait with their bikinis, teenage faces, and twenty year old bodies. They're getting eye-fucked by kids their own age who wouldn't know what to do with them if they caught them, retired perverts who couldn't get a hard-on if they caught them, and everything in between, including yours truly. It's not like I can help but notice, and it's okay to be a dirt bag if I'm honest about it.

I've been walking for about twenty minutes, and forty minutes is about my limit for a continuous walk, so I turn around to walk back to the Goat closer to the water's edge. The cold water rippling along the sand gives the illusion of a moving ground and reminds me to look ahead or I'll lose balance and fall in the muck. In just this much time, the beach has already thinned out, and only a few groups still remain close to the pier. I can't help but laugh at the old guy jogging shirtless with his bright red shoulders and upper chest indicating that he'll be hurting in the morning from his late December sunburn. Now that I think about it, perhaps this guy should be laughing at me because he's in his sixties and jogging topless on the beach, and I'm thirty-five and slowly walking while wearing a T-shirt because I'm too embarrassed about my post-surgery muscle loss and stomach fat retention.

I think this is the last time I'll clip my head to the scalp before I let it grow out again. I have to admit this hairstyle has been very low maintenance, but I probably need to fit back into society again, especially if I'm going to be interviewing at some point.

I forgot how much I enjoy playing the electric guitar. The twelve-string acoustic is great, easier to grab, more neighbor-friendly for an apartment, and generally more relaxing. It's like enjoying both choppers and sport bikes. They're very different animals, but enjoyable in their own respect in very different ways. I haven't played the electric guitar in a while since the strings, action, and knobs are poor at best. I'll put "guitar rebuild' on my endless list of shit I need to do. At least I don't have a house right now. There's no lawn to mow, leaves to rake, repairs or upgrades to do, and most importantly, no anchor keeping me here.

Playing some of the music I used to have memorized is fun, but it's frustrating to learn new songs at this age. When I first started playing years ago, I would spend hours repeating the music precisely until it was memorized. Now I pick it up faster, but the patience to spend the time to memorize the detailed notes has dissipated over the years. Maybe it's not the patience, but the perceived time available to do so.

I feel a little guilty about not calling Sunshine to do something tonight as she offered, but it's supposed to be my day to do what I prefer. I did get to have breakfast with her, and I'll text her a goodnight, but I need a weekly quiet day to clear my head. Most people still insist on wishing a happy birthday, even if they know I prefer to ignore them, because most people want their birthdays to be special and recognized. It's probably because of the big deal parents make over birthdays when their kids are young, which paves the way for those kids to grow up thinking birthdays should be the day the rest of the world stops to celebrate with them.

Sunshine doesn't think that at all, but rather she just appreciated the fact that her family and friends got together on her birthday. That's the right way to approach a birthday. I steer way toward the other end of the spectrum by hiding from the world on mine. Part of it is because I don't like the idea of getting older, which is ironic because if anyone should celebrate surviving another year, it's me. The second part I notice is I don't feel like I deserve a special day and don't like a big deal made over it, special treatment, or anything of that nature. I do like time on my own, and to me a birthday seems like a good day to look back over the last year, analyze, and learn. That especially seems like a good idea after this year.

At least my thirties are half over, as it seems like everything really shitty has happened since I turned thirty. Wow, it's almost depressing thinking about the last five years. In my late twenties I had a good

job, was a respected leader in my field, and lived in a nice house in the suburbs with one or two Porsches and a bike in the garage. I thought I had the world by the balls.

By thirty I had locked horns with my boss and he was slowly winning. I was stuck in an absolute hell called marriage, had sold my last Porsche at a huge loss, and had the house for sale. I ran away from my life of misery to Florida, hoping that maybe somehow, maybe since I was born here, I'd find happiness. My thirtieth birthday was spent hammered and passed out in a rental car in someone's driveway close to the bar. I'd actually pissed in the rental car, and woke up just before sunrise with contacts stuck to my eyes feeling like complete shit. That was just the beginning of my thirties.

The ex moved back to Texas in March for a month leaving me in some transitional suspended level of hell, so I turned to what I really loved. I spent every waking moment outside of my work obligations finishing the Hardass in thirty days flat and drove it proudly to Daytona Beach for Bike Week. If she would've just divorced me then, at least I could have enjoyed my accomplishment and freedom, but the masochist in me continued the torture. Like a stubborn idiot, I convinced her to move back and I agreed to go to counseling. The first doctor told her she was bipolar. Our couples' counselor questioned bipolarism, but admitted she needed some kind of medication. I told him I didn't know about bipolarism either, but I was pretty sure the first two letters were correct.

After weeks of Dr. Touchy-Feely helping us find out how miserable we were, hearing her cry in the tub with the door locked, finding magazines stabbed repeatedly with my switchblade, drunken outbursts while throwing furniture and clothes, and enough sadistic mental torture to drive any mortal insane, something good finally happened in my life. I sold a job that I'd been pursuing for a couple years, and thought it would secure my employment, even if part-time for a while. Unfortunately my boss finally got his way and despite prior agreements I failed to get in writing, I was told to either move back to Texas or be let go. I was completely beside myself. Nowork had lied to me and changed my timesheet to screw me out of vacation when I went to see Uncle Ike when he was diagnosed with cancer. He'd told the receptionist to send me a letter with his wife's positive pregnancy test at work pretending to be a girl I'd banged from the Atrium. That was the day I'd come in at 2 am because I was leaving early to go to Uncle Ike's funeral. Everyone at work had been interviewed and unanimously told upper management the guy couldn't be trusted. I'd just sold a two and a half million-dollar job and I was being let go. Unfuckingbelievable, but no one ever said life was fair.

July 2nd of 2004 was my final day of employment with the Institute, but I had my first order from a customer for a complete hand-made chopper, and that was something that gave me reason to be happy. A week later the final paycheck came, but I was going to put my all into my shop, and whatever I could into my marriage without making myself any more miserable than I already was. I'd financially supported the ex so she could get certified to teach, which helped both matters. We'd gone so far as to pick out insurance plans through her pending job as she prepared to start teaching in the fall. I remember waking up the Sunday after that last paycheck had arrived. I thought I should stay home from the shop and spend it with her to enjoy the day and celebrate the next chapter of our lives. She had similar but different ideas, and told me she was divorcing me. Up to that point I'd really kept trying, but as soon as I heard that word, I completely shut off and threw in the proverbial towel. She left, and I hopped on the Hardass and met AJ and Navy Greg at the Winghouse, which had just opened the day before. We drank there and headed to the beach bars with our American V twins thundering the whole way. It was a blur between Ocean Club, Ritz, and eventually Bourbon Street Station that night. At 1 am I was wrapping out that Hardass's engine all the way home with mixed feelings of bitterness and betrayal combined with relief and a renewed freedom.

I shook the etch a sketch of my life and started turning the two white knobs on a clean display. Every day was spent living for nothing but to build bikes in that shop. I didn't even have a car for two years, was eating nothing, drinking everything, and enjoying the fact that I no longer answered to either of the only two people in the world I'd say I ever really hated in my life. About the time I really understood how much I needed to quit drinking, Fatman had his wedding. After drinking a fifth of my favorite, Hawkeye whiskey, on the way to lunch from the airport, I barely remember the wedding rehearsal, party, or bars. The Axe cam went blank, and the next thing I remember was standing next to a river soaking wet, freezing in the forty-degree air. No one will ever know if I fell into the river or jumped into it, but my phone didn't work, and I had no idea where I was. I couldn't even see the glow of a city over the trees around me. I had to get inside somewhere fast before I froze to death. As much as I hated to do it, I found one building with stained glass windows I identified as a church, and broke the smallest window I could to get inside. I thought, "God forgives, so I'll just pay him back for the window tomorrow." After breaking that little stained glass window, I flipped the deadlock and opened the door to blaring alarms. I saw a fire alarm on the wall thinking of it as an on/off switch. However, when I pulled it to turn off the original alarms, more alarms sounded. I crashed on a couch hoping someone would find me soon and I wouldn't be a victim of hypothermia.

I don't know how long it took, but soon I was awakened by police and some shiny new bracelets. My initial reaction was relief that I'd been found. I apologized calmly and told them I'd be happy to pay for the window I broke. Back at the police station as I sat handcuffed to a bench under a blanket, one officer asked me what I was doing. I explained to him that I was sorry, but I wasn't from Colorado and didn't know the area. I'd love to have a picture of his face as he told me, "Boy, you're in Illinois." I thought for a minute and replied, "Oh yeah, this is Fatman's wedding in Illinois. I was in Colorado a couple months ago for my sister's wedding." Hours later Irv and Newton were graciously bailing me out of county jail to the tune of three grand after I'd been told I was facing one to three years in Illinois State. It turned out that the building was a plastic surgeon's office, not a church. God might forgive, but that guy didn't. He charged me for the window I broke, the door I unlocked, the fire alarm system I turned on, the new floor in the waiting room on which I'd walked, and the reupholstering of all the furniture in that waiting room for the couch on which I'd laid. Ironically this guy had done the boob job on Newton's wife, which I learned while living on their couch for a while when I couldn't leave the state.

I was on probation for criminal damage and completely stopped drinking right then and there. When I finally got back to Florida, even the grass in the ghetto looked greener. At a point in my life when I thought I had nothing left to lose, my stupidity almost cost me the thing I cherish most, my freedom. I swore I was going to turn my fucked up life around. I got a job doing mortgages to try to supplement the shop, but I hated it and didn't make any money there either. I dropped full coverage insurance on the Scrotus I'd bought, and six days later turned left in front of a Dodge Ram coming at me at highway speed. I felt like a Geico commercial. "I just saved thirty dollars a month on my car insurance by switching to liability-only six days before I totaled my car." Since I didn't get anything out of it, some of the other guys with shops near mine and I destroyed it. T-Roy spray painted vandalism all over it. J3 brought over a long, heavy pry bar that we took turns using to spear holes in the car. For the final touch, one of T-Roy's buddies drove his monster truck over the hood of it. Eventually I got a new job, new apartment, new girls, and eventually became a proud graduate of the Illinois Second Chance Program. Even though I eventually had a drink here and there, I pretty much outgrew the heavy boozing. Things were steadily improving, until realizing I needed open heart surgery a few months ago.

Crowley has always used his ten added years over my age to provide some pretty useful insight over the time I've known him. When we were in college working on the ISU robotic project, he told me that some people go through life completely monotone thinking everything is just okay, no matter how good or bad it is. A person can't ever appreciate the real high highs without enduring the real low lows. At that time I understood what he was saying, but I had no idea of the roller coaster that lay ahead of me. Since I've turned thirty, I've experienced failures in legal, relationship, business, health, and financial aspects. I'd made a lot of bad decisions and my luck had run out. I remember Dad saying, "If you'd been more of a fuckup as a kid, you wouldn't be such a disappointment now." These lows have taught me to never think it can't get worse, because it always can. However, they've also taught me that most of the adversities in life aren't worth worrying about. Most importantly I've learned to cherish the highs. Hopefully the last half of my fourth decade on this planet will bring a lot more highs than lows, and I know the only person that can make that happen is me.

Tue 30 Dec 08

I just spoke to a representative from an employee marketing firm with which I've been corresponding. He tells me that everything looks great for marketability and transferable skills. The biggest liability he identifies is that the current title and salary are well below my responsibilities, which might hinder getting a significantly better position as desired. Great. He basically tells me I'm not only getting screwed in the present, but screwed for the future.

Looking for a job is about as much fun is getting a blowjob from Jaws or jerked off by Captain Hook. There are a lot of project manager positions between Austin and San Antonio. Houston has quite a few positions open as well, and I've already been emailed out of the blue by a potential employer in that city. I had a great time partying over there with Fatman when he lived there. I woke up on a sidewalk with fire ants chewing my arms one day after that brunette decided I couldn't stay with her for the night. Another morning I woke up on a floor, noticed blood on the carpet, and then looked down and saw a nipple ring that hadn't been there before. Houston could be a fun place to live I'm sure. I may eventually explore options in Houston or even Dallas, but for now I'll stick with my comfort zone.

I'm applying for two operations manager positions paying a hundred and fifty grand annually, not including bonuses. They're both likely way out of my league, but will be good practice in seeking a job. It's the same principle as easily scoring a date with a nice girl next door after hitting on some materialistic, plastic Barbie doll in Miami to no avail. As a freshman in college, a guy asked me if I'd gotten the number from the cutie I'd been working earlier. When I said, "no" he asked me if I'd asked for it. I said, "no" again and he pulled her number out of his pocket. He told me, "If you don't get rejected, you're not trying hard enough." I've lived by that ever since, and it applies to all aspects of life. I've failed at a lot of things, but I've also tried a hell of a lot more than most people.

Here I am somewhere I never pictured myself. I can't believe I'm in a yoga class. Sarah from cardiac rehab is teaching us Introduction to Yoga. It's not like I have a bunch of girls in their early twenties bending around like pretzels to enjoy either. Six guys in their sixties are here with me. Maybe it's better not to have the distraction of flexible females so I can focus on the yoga. I actually can see a benefit to this like Organisis told me I would. Stretching, some strength exercises, and the calmness are all good for my heart, so I'll just put my stubbornness aside, accept my current situation, and get what I can from it.

As Sarah instructs, it reminds me of the relaxation book from Cartmanini. I know my mind is supposed to be at rest right now, but it suddenly becomes clear why all of this is good for the heart. Focusing on breathing, stretching, walking, running, lifting weights, or any extracurricular activity prevents your brain from focusing on all the things that cause stress. The key is not necessarily benching twice your weight or putting your feet behind your head, but distracting yourself from life's turmoil. Now that I've discovered the underlying theme to all these teachings, I can better apply it to my own life as I recover.

Wed 31 Dec 08

It's New Year's Eve and I'm sober as a judge, which I can say because I've met several of them. Granted it's still early in the morning, but that's progress from some years of the past. Surprisingly I get an email from the placement firm on one of the big money jobs stating that I met the initial requirements, and they are recommending me as a qualified candidate. No shit? This is more proof that it's not the gift, but how you wrap it. I could enjoy living in Texas at a hundred and fifty grand a year. However, I won't get my hopes up, as expectations pave the way to disappointment. For right now I have to assume employment at my current position until I can change that.

I was going to change oil in the Goat and Sunshine's car, but another week will allow me to be stronger and do it myself instead of having to tell her how to do it. She shows up to the shop to try to download some pictures of a painting she wants to sell, but forgot to bring the software cd to do so. Now that I've finished my last couple tasks for job-hunting today, we'll grab lunch at the little sidewalk café across the street from the shoebox.

I prefer going to an actual gym, but it is nice that the apartment complex has a basic workout center. Apartments in this area seem to have pretty nice exercise rooms, which makes it convenient to do something without having to drive outside the complex, accommodating my occasional limitations in time or ambition. I go through all the basic motions of both lower and upper body with minimal weight just to get the muscles accustomed to being used again. The chest press is clearly the most challenging of these. This chest exhibits all the strength of a wet paper bag, and is still tighter than a nun's cunt.

We're just getting back from CVS where I bought a blood pressure indicator. This will be the first New Year's Eve in many years that I stayed in for the night. Even though I didn't drink during probation for the Illinois display of stupidity, I still went out for New Year's. Tonight is amateur night, and a good time to get in a car wreck or shoved by some tough guy with beer muscles. Neither of these would be great for a healing sternum, plus I just don't have the desire to put up with a crowd, especially when most of the people will be drunk and I won't be.

Sunshine is making a ribeye steak dinner with asparagus and sweet potatoes. Other than the nasty-smelling asparagus piss that will follow, the meal is perfect. We each eat about half of our plate and put the rest in the fridge for leftovers. My food budget has definitely decreased now that my appetite is a fraction of what it used to be, which is ideal as I need the money now more than ever. We watch "Deathrace 2000" and "Stepbrothers," then fall asleep to "Napoleon Dynamite." This has got to be another holiday dream coming true for her, but I appreciate her staying in with me. When I see midnight on the clock, I wake her up to wish her a happy new year, turn off the TV, close my eyes, and close the book on a most eventful 2008.

Sat 03 Jan 09

This is the first entry from 2009 and the last entry in these memoirs. I can remember waking up New Year's Day of 2008 with the Doc mad at me about the night before, taking Irv and Boz to some game they wanted to watch, and coming to the shop to work on the Anarchist upgrades I was doing. This year started off much better by waking up next to a happy girl like Sunshine and relaxing for the whole day with her, which is something I wouldn't have done a year ago.

The flip of the calendar finds me at a pivotal point in life. I'm thirty-five years old and the last five years have encompassed some of the highest and undoubtedly the lowest points of my life. I have a job that I perceive as off-balance with responsibilities outweighing the pay by about 25%, but instead of stressing about it, the job will be appreciated until I can make the situation better. Y Chrome Customs has plenty of work ready and waiting for me to attack as soon as I'm physically able. The Goat, Ape, Anarchist, guitars, and guns are all still in my life for me to enjoy and distract me from the insignificant bullshit that really doesn't matter in the big picture of things.

My family is doing well, Organisis and Matic are expecting their second ankle-biter, and Vermin will be marrying Dionysus this year. I have the best girlfriend I could ever hope to have, and a lot of good friends and family across the country. Most importantly, I'm alive and able to experience and enjoy all these things. My health is limiting my ability to do everything I'd like to do right now, but it's improving every day and eventually will be even better than before. Those are the things that really matter, and nothing else really does.

Sleaze called yesterday morning and said he also stayed in for New Year's, as his new wife is a week away from hatching their first loin trophy. Fatman and his wife had dinner and called it a night, considering they have twins almost two years old. I called Foxy, and his twins are on the way in March. Sunshine's sister is due in April I believe, and Organisis's next ankle-biter is due in August. Newton called last night, and his wife is scheduled to produce their first tricycle motor in June. Importantly they all seem very happy about their evolutions from partiers to parents. It's great to be happy, and even better to see people close to you happy.

Newton asked me about the surgery and recovery experience. When I told him it changed my perspectives on a lot of things, he asked me what I learned. It really made me stop and think a little last night in between my attempt at yoga and some reading. I'd already learned quite a bit about life before surgery. My memory has allowed me to remember a lot of information like the fact that Ozzy Osborne has tattooed eyeliner, and so did a hot blonde named Haley from Lubbock that I met at the Library in Austin, who later moved to Austin and worked at Sam's Boat. To me memorization of facts isn't learning. A fact is trivia, but a lesson is something you can use. Learning includes tricks, tips, skills, and application of science to real life. I could use a matchbook cover to set the points on the old General, a sideways stance minimizes the target area for your opponent in a gunfight, and the key to calligraphy is holding the pen edge at a forty-five degree angle. I'm not an expert at anything, but one could say I'm sort of a jackass of all trades. I know enough about painting, engines, music, engineering, business, health, weapons, computers, construction, and many other subjects to do what I need and want.

The most important lessons have come the hard way, which stick the most. Just because I learn a lesson doesn't mean I can apply it either. Be able to have a couple drinks, but don't get wasted. Show her you're interested, but don't smother her. Conserve, but enjoy. All three of these small lessons lead to the big lesson of moderation. The more encompassing the lesson, the more useful it is. A basic observation is that car insurance is increasing. Maybe the insurance salesperson is being greedy. If so, the deeper reason is poor moral character in the salesperson. A more insightful reason for high insurance might be crime, which is again the result of poor moral character. A person could also blame lawsuits, which are again linked to poor moral quality in both the people looking for an unjustified payday, and the ambulance-chasing lawyers. Taking it a step further identifies the problem causing poor morality as a general lack of positive and negative reinforcement in today's society. Objective reason identifies that what Bubba calls the pussification, or softening, of our society directly contributes to high auto insurance. We're making our own problems, and only we as a society can fix things.

If I had to reduce life's guide down to as few words as I could, I would say, "Appreciate, think, and act." People who don't stop to appreciate what they have are never happy and will eventually suffer regret when they realize it later. It floors me how many people believe a scary portion of what they see and hear, especially from the media. Boiling out the bullshit and objective analysis of the facts from both perspectives are critical for proper decision-making and learning. Once a person thinks about something enough to understand it objectively, then proper action may be required. It's too easy to sit back and think someone else will take care of an issue, but that mentality is for the trusting and the lazy.

That sums the rules to succeeding in life, but life's success is truly measured by happiness. I try to find what makes me happy, and do those things as much as I can, short of interference with other needs or wants. I accept the things that make me unhappy, until I've been able to think and act to change them. Bitching accomplishes absolutely nothing. People want solutions not problems.

When Newton asked me what I'd learned though, I had to think about it. In the last two months I've reflected on the main points of thirty-five years of life, now looking at my past through a set of new eyes. The vision may not be 20/20, but what I now see is much clearer.

The biggest lesson driven into me in the last two months is that taking care of your own health should be the highest priority in anyone's life. Some may argue that their spouse or children's lives are most important. Crowley pointed out that if he isn't healthy, he can't take care of his family, so even if a means to an end, his health is paramount. Without your health you don't have shit, so you do what you can to maximize it. Health, like money, is simply a vehicle of freedom. Nobody likes to be broke or sick, but what health and money really do is enable us to do the things we enjoy.

I learned how I personally found it easiest to deal with a potential life-ending experience. Not everybody thinks about it like this, but I learned to accept the known and not to worry about the unknown. I wasn't pessimistic to think I could die; I was realistic and accepted the possibility expecting nothing past the point of flat-lining. Every minute since then has been a pleasant surprise above and beyond what I expected.

Nikki was on to something when he said, "You can't live until you die." I'm not sure why people, for all our alleged intelligence, are too stupid to enjoy something until we lose it. When I woke up from those surgeries alive, I hadn't appreciated what I had so much since the Illinois courts allowed me to leave the state and return to Florida.

I used to think I needed to live every day like it was my last with no regard for tomorrow, and scoffed at people so worried about tomorrow, that they never lived for the moment. Now I realize it's not a matter of living today like it's my last, but enjoying it to the fullest knowing that it could be my last, and simultaneously being ready to enjoy tomorrow as well. Call it balance or call it moderation, but it's the key to everything. Maybe an alcoholic can have just a couple drinks, a hooker can have a heart of gold, and now and then even an extremist can be tempered.

Part II
Die Neuen

Chapter 5

Reinvention

Sun 19 Jan 09

I really didn't plan on writing any more entries, except maybe one final conclusion in a year, but I never really did know when to stop, and I need to document how fucked up my head is right now in case this ever happens again. I know I just bought tickets to see "Gran Torino" and then sat down here on this bench in the mall. I'm not sure how to explain it, but I feel like I just dreamed it versus actually remembering it happen. I ask Sunshine questions about my conversation with the cashier, and I don't remember some of the things she points out, but I do remember things that didn't happen. Something's very wrong with my brain right now. Why the hell is this happening? The only thing I can think of that would cause this is the beer cheese soup I had at A1A Aleworks right before this. I'm still on some medication, but could that tiny amount of alcohol react with the medication to cause this?

I still feel weird, but we go into the theatre and sit in the back row, so I can leave if I need to. This is the phone commercial where they're tearing around in the Nissan. There's the outside of the Nissan zipping around the curve. Wait a minute. How the fuck did I know it was a Nissan? I've never seen this commercial before, have I? Like most people, I've experienced Déjà vu, but this is different. I always know what's going to happen right as or after it happens. I've realized there's no way I could ever know what will happen before it does, or that would be evidence that it's possible to foresee the future, and that's impossible. Nonetheless, I really knew what was going to happen next in that commercial. I had to have seen it somewhere else, but I haven't been to a movie for months, and barely watch TV. It feels recent. I ask Sunshine if we saw that commercial earlier that day at her place or anything, but she says she's never seen it. No fucking way could I know what was going to happen. I'm not buying it. I really want to enjoy this movie, but this dream feeling is really fucking with my head.

That was an awesome movie. Old or not, Clint is still one bad mother fucker. The way he talked to his buddies reminds me of our group in college. Our group had a German, Italian, Czeck, Irish, etc. and we all pretty much made fun of each other with no holds barred. It was never hateful, just all in good fun. If we wanted to get mean with each other, it was usually about something a whole lot more personal than our backgrounds. It thickened our skin too. As much abuse as we took from our friends, nobody would ever hurt our feelings. That night Fatman spit on Stu's slut for making out with some other dude and called her a fucking whore, her friend told him he was fat. We'd called him much worse, and he told her, "Sweet, bitch. I've been called that since second grade. You're going to have to come up with a lot better than that."

We're walking out of the theatre and I'm trying to remember parts of the night, but half of them feel like a dream. It's almost like I dreamed a similar experience to the one I actually had, and now have two parallel memories of the same event. Wow, this is fucked up. Even with all the drugs they put in me in the hospital, this is a completely different phenomenon. Sunshine can see that my eyes are very confused right now, and she asks if I want her to drive. I just laugh. It's nice of her, but I don't need to add fear to my confusion. I just want to get back to her place, lay down on the air mattress on the main floor so I don't have to walk all the way up the stairs to the bedroom, and rest my bewildered mind.

Fri 13 Feb 09

It's Friday the 13th and I'd really like to see Disturbed in concert tonight. I saw them with Jagette a couple years ago, and they were intense to say the least. I don't really remember the first time I saw them at that Ozzfest back in San Antonio. I drank a bottle of Jager for breakfast that morning and washed it down with some Natural Light, so it's not surprising I don't even remember lunch at Hooters that day. After pissing on myself that day at the concert and riding home in the back of Chip's truck while puking on myself, I was in serious need of a shower. Chip, Kramer, and I still made it out that night to the Riverwalk. Chip happened to snap a picture of me talking to the hot senorita architect I used to date. She had an awesome rack and ran four miles a day, but it was pretty difficult to date anyone while only spending two weekends at home per month. At least Chip was nice enough to leave a picture for the ex to see later and give her something else to use against me.

I really don't need to spend the money on the tickets, but fuck it'd be cool to see them again. My chest still hurts like hell to even sneeze. If someone rams into me, which is all too likely at a general admission Disturbed concert, I wonder if my sternum could actually break again. That would suck ass. Fuck it, you only live twice, Mister Bond, although I guess I'm at least on life three already. Good thing I live in a twisted cartoon and not a video game with only three lives, or it would be game over by now.

Tickets have gone up a lot since the twenty bucks I paid to see Kiss's *Hot in the Shade* tour when I was sixteen, but it'll be a sweet show. Sunshine will get off work as soon she can and meet me out here in the parking lot at the Auditorium. The Train, the Snake, Large, and his girl are going to meet us inside. I can hear the opening band inside. It would be cool to see them too, but I need to wait out here for Sunshine so I can give her the ticket. The last time I remember being here was when the radio station hotties sold me a spot at the beer fest to promote YCC. I really enjoyed running a custom bike shop and doing things like that, but it's too bad I couldn't make any money doing what I loved. At least I can still do it as a hobby now. Here comes the Curve with all its war wounds from her driving skills. Show Time!

Fortunately Snake and the rest are hanging at the back of the Auditorium. I'm not as crowded around my chest back here, and we can still see fine. Holy shit, Snake got fat. He has a full beard and I've got a clipped head and face now. That's a switch. I guess he kicked back on the workouts. Fuck, this music is badass! Sure beats some razor boycotter whining about how drunk he is, the job and wife he lost, the dog that died, and the sheep he finds sexually-appealing or a beat void of instruments combined with rhymes about smoking weed, shooting at cops, and slapping ho's.

Every song by these guys kicks me in the senses. Alice Cooper's "Poison" was the first song I ever heard that just grabbed me by the soul and shook it. Bands like this are why I really love hard rock. I've told people it relaxes me, which is subject to interpretation. It fires me up, which is the opposite of relaxing. However, I enjoy listening to it, and dislike listening to pretty much anything else, so I'm happy listening to it, and at some level relaxed as a result.

Look at those crazy fuckers in the mosh pit up by the stage. It looks like a blast, and I'm getting the itch to join them, but I know I don't dare with this fragile sternum. Large is getting the itch to go out there as well, and his girl is successful in keeping him at the back so far. He already had to have his tricep reattached from the mosh pit at a Godsmack concert years ago. I feel bad for the people on the receiving end of any impact from Large. I used to really enjoy the pits, but by the end of college, my endurance was so shitty I'd be out of breath within one song. Being drunk didn't help I'm sure. Right now it's tough watching them and not being able to dive into the frenzy. My strong preference has always been to be a participant in life versus a spectator. I'd rather screech tires around a clover than watch NASCAR, I'd rather fuck than watch porn, and I'd rather be jumping into that mosh pit than standing here.

Alright, they're doing the encore. I know I can't go into the pit, but Large is heading that way, and it looks like he got Train to join. It wouldn't hurt to just go watch. Sunshine and I make our way through the crowd and perch at the edge of the pit with a safety layer of bodies to minimize potential sternum damage. I'm so fucking glad I came! I'm fucking jacked from the energy of those crunching guitars, pounding drums, and that evil voice screaming! After spending the last several months hiding from everything that might hurt, I want to destroy something or red-line something. I feel alive. I feel wicked. I feel intense. I'm starting to feel like me again.

Thu 26 Feb 09

Unlike Humpty Dumpty, the Anarchist engine is back together again, complete with the higher performance Lightning heads, jugs, and pistons. This is the first Evo I've rebuilt, so hopefully I didn't fuck up anything. Before I bolt all the sheet metal back to the frame, I better make sure the thing starts. I pour a little gas into the carb, put the battery back in, and hit the start button. What the fuck? Sparks are flying by the body of the starter. Did I see that right? Yep, it did it again. Fuck. I'll go ask the Swede if he's got any great ideas. We try checking grounds, which seem to be floating. This thing worked fine before I took it apart. How would the ground be floating from rebuilding the engine? I did weld the frame when I modified the seat tab, but the battery was completely out of the bike. Did I fry the starter somehow? Fuck it. I'm tired and pissed. I'll think it over and make it work tomorrow, one way or another.

Fri 27 Feb 09

It has to be the starter. There's no other explanation I can see. Fortunately I have an extra starter on the shelf from when I replaced the starter, alternator, regulator, and battery a year or two ago. I was so fucking pissed when I realized the culprit at that time was a bad starter cable. It had a couple unbroken strands that gave a twelve-volt reading, but the others were broke so it wouldn't get the amperage it needed. To top it off, when I shoved the new cable in place, the bike fell off the jack. The kickstand ended up wedged inside the frame of the jack, so it became like a pair of Chinese finger cuffs. The harder I pulled, the tighter it got, and I finally had to pull the whole fucking jack apart to get the bike out of it.

The new starter works. Sweet, or as Stuey would say, "Victory is mine!" Now all I have to do is bolt everything together and I'm golden. Over fifteen years ago I was a nineteen year-old staring at a '77 FLH basket case in Mom's and Dad's garage like it was the space shuttle. Dad told me to go uptown, buy a manual from Royal, and figure out what was wrong with the clutch. Now I'm staring at not only a fresh engine, but the metal and paint work I'm ready to bolt back in place. I'm pretty stoked with the sheet metal. My gothic-cut fenders and tank are all painted black with red she-devils and covered with candy red. The realistic orange flames are without a doubt the best set I've done to date, now that I've figured out how to fade from orange in the background to the yellow highlights in front to add to the 3D effect. The baseball mitt leather seat is complete with perimeter stitching and the anarchy symbol I burned into the leather matching the ones I painted on the oil tank and primary cover and have tattooed on my arm. The exhaust is cut to a point and balanced, painted black, wrapped, and loud as fuck. No two ways about it, I'm getting major wood looking at this bitch!

Now both bikes are ready to roll. I had my hesitation, but the Ape looks pretty good with the bright red underbelly and white Aprilia stickers as opposed to the flat black I had it before. The updated skull on the tank and skeleton hands on the side fairings look much better than before too. It's got freshly adjusted valves and now sports a lighter 520 chain with a bigger rear sprocket, as if the torque to pull the front end up in third gear before wasn't enough.

I haven't ridden either of these since I got back from surgery, besides the short careful ride to the shop from the shoebox on the Ape. Hell, driving a car is still a challenge, let alone a bike. The biggest concern is of course breaking that sternum. The car and bike are both manageable to drive, but if something would go wrong, I'd be fucked. As I've found in the past, flying over cars, running into them, and bouncing off airbags is all fine and good under normal conditions, but with this chest still fragile, I need to watch my ass. Since I know I'm piss-poor at moderation, as soon as I was able to start turning wrenches in the shop, I tore the bikes apart and slowly got them back the way they needed to be. That way there's no way I could get a wild hair and go drive them when I shouldn't. Mission accomplished. It's been about four months since I got cut, both bikes are 100%, and I can't wait to hit the road.

Sat 28 Feb 09

It's a little chilly out this morning, I don't have any hair yet, and I don't have much for insulation fat, so I better where the skull mask and the YCC beanie. I'm driving to Starbucks on San Jose so I can meet Yoda. There he is on his big old dresser, which looks huge next to the little Sportie basis of my Anarchist. We're driving down 13 to Obi-Wan's place. That bike of his is an '03 and looks brand-new. You can tell he never rides it. He gets on it even less now that he's moved to Oklahoma. He and his wife saddle the attention-starved Hawg and the four of us point our bikes toward the ocean, after Yoda and I remind Obi-Wan both my bike and I have freshly rebuilt pumpers, and we need to take it easy. They agreed to take A1A to Daytona so we could watch the sun coming up over the ocean. How people survive without motorcycles is completely beyond me.

I'm glad it's time for a gas stop, because my ass is killing me. The minimal padding and hard leather on that seat is a far cry from the pillowed seats Obi-Wan and Yoda have, but it looks cool, so I need to deal with it. Those clip-on bars are just a little too much of a stretch, so the back is sore as hell too. Minor details; I'm fucking riding again. I'm still weak, and still get little blurry vision spells on that right side. I'm slowly getting better though, my blood pressure and sleep pattern are drastically improved, and I can't even describe how incredible I feel to be on two wheels again! Doing things like this that make me what I am is the difference from just being alive and really living.

Sat 7 Mar 09

I'm glad Sunshine's such a good sport about my passion for bikes. She probably still hasn't thawed from our ride down to Daytona and back on the Ape Wednesday night. We had on power ranger gear and she was behind me, so I took most of the wind, but it was still cold for her I'm sure. I used to ride the old General when there was snow on the ground in Iowa, and I can remember riding to work on it in Texas when it was 28 degrees. The body gets spoiled though. I rode that Stripper bike to Cousin Reno's for his newest loin trophy's birthday a couple years ago in February. I hadn't even gotten out of town and had to stop to see if I could find some mittens, as the gloves weren't cutting it. Walgreens didn't have any mittens, so I had to make due by buying three pairs of socks and putting three socks on each hand. That way the fingers would all stay together per basic mitten technology. I needed a way to keep the wind from going through them, so I got some packing tape and used it to block the wind on my hands. Of course after getting all bundled up, it was a bitch to try to turn the key, but I made it all the way down to Deltona like that. His warden had to turn the bike off for me when I got there, as I was pretty numb. The ride back that night was even worse. By the time I got to the shop, I'd lost all feeling in the outer two fingers on each hand and one or two toes on each foot. That's the coldest I've ever been, aside from my swim in Illinois and that day I left the hospital. At least J3 and J2 let me thaw in their shop, so I wouldn't have to break any stained glass windows.

It's still dark, but I'm awake and jacked. I feel like Harley in "Harley Davidson and the Marlboro Man" when he gets up in the middle of the night to fire up his custom bike, except he leaves his girl behind. My girl is trying to wake up and get ready so she can follow me down to Daytona for a while before she has to leave for work. I'm putting my Anarchist in the Rat's Hole Show today, and this way she can haul the YCC bike and bikini calendars down for me so I can give them to people at the show. It's nice she lives in Staug, as it shortens the trip. The fact that she has a garage is nice too. I wanted to leave in the dark so I can see the entire sunrise over the ocean. Earlier this week I bought and installed the throttle brake shoe so I can have cruise control. If I can sit upright instead of leaning over for those clip-on handlebars, the back pain should be a little less brutal. As soon as we get outside of Staug and are looking down a dark A1A, I flip on the throttle lock and let her buck.

The sky to the left is starting to turn orange, and here comes the sun peeking over the water. In just a few miles it's gone from pitch black to a gorgeous sunrise. I can hear and feel the rumble of the engine I built. I see the she-devil I painted scowling up from the tank, and feel that hard leather seat I made torturing my ass. No phones are ringing, no one's bothering me, and the only other person close is Sunshine following behind me in the Curve. The sun is shining and is painting the sky that beautiful combination of orange fading to blue. This is as close to heaven as I may ever be. It can't get any better than this, and I didn't even have to take opiates or any shit to fuck up my brain to appreciate it. Maybe those drugs don't fuck your mind up and make you see colors. Maybe they do just dumb down your mind to allow it to appreciate beauty. If that's the case, then right now I've relaxed my mind enough to appreciate all this. I feel absolutely stupid that I used to take things like this for granted, or worry more about answering a phone or sending an email than tasting every single breath of air like it could be the last. The sun is shining, the ocean is beautiful, I'm riding again, and most importantly, I'm alive. I'm so fucking alive, I want to scream. In my head I can hear the Crue singing, "Primal scream, shout, tear that fucker out. You've just gotta say, "Hey!"" I've ridden the whole way so far with the throttle lock on, so I sit up straight in the saddle, take the deepest breath I can, look up, raise my fists in the air, and thrust the air out of my lungs as long and loud as I can. Fuck that feels good! It feels incredible to be me again, but better.

Tue 12 May 09

It's different looking out of a second-story living room at the parking lot now instead of a first floor living room at trees like I did a week ago. After remembering that moving in with the Unicorn ruined that relationship, I debated for months whether or not to try it with Sunshine. She'd brought up the fact that both of our leases were expiring, and the fact that she was paying a fortune to live where she was. I'd told her I was considering cohabitation, but had my hesitations. It's so nice that the two of us can openly discuss such things without someone getting pissy. Eventually I told her if it's going to break, we might as well move in together and break it now so we know without wasting another year of our lives. It's not like marriage, it can be easily undone if things don't work.

We decided since I have the shop and job here and she bets better mileage on an older vehicle, it made more sense to upgrade to a two-bedroom in my same complex, and let her drive back and forth to Staug for work. I didn't have much of an option besides to hire movers this round, so last weekend they brought everything from her place in Staug and moved it along with my stuff into our new pad.

It looks like it's starting to rain, and the Ape is still sitting outside, so I better go move it to the garage. It'll be nice when they move my garage from the one over by the old shoebox to one closer to the new place. I walk outside and see a little cutie jogging by trying to get home in the rain in dark shorts, a sports bra, and a pony tail, and she definitely eats her vitamins. Once I get the Ape started and begin driving toward the garage, I can't help but notice the ass on her ahead of me. If I were still prowling, I'd stop and offer the girl a ride home, but before the thought even gets rejected in my brain, she turns around, waves at me, and asks for a ride to her apartment. She hops on the tail, grabs around my waist, and I take her to her apartment. A single me would be asking if I could come inside and dry off. She's very attractive, seems friendly and not really shy. Nonetheless the good boyfriend in me waves goodbye, parks the bike in the garage, and walks back into the apartment soaked.

I always think that things like that would never happen if I were single, as girls, cars, and jobs are all easier to get when you already have one. There will always be those temptations, but they're good reminders to me to remember why I'm with Sunshine. Yes, I could be a scumbag and screw around, but that's not something I've ever done, and I sure don't plan on starting with the best girl I ever found. If the day ever comes where I just have to have other girls, then I'll be honest with her and tell her versus fucking around behind her back. For now, I'm going to continue being happy with who I have.

Chapter 6

Vacation 101

Sat 08 Aug 09

Damn I'm dragging ass, but considering this week, I'm not surprised. What time did we get to bed? I got in from California around midnight, so it must've been 1 am before we got to sleep. It's too bad I didn't get a chance to go surfing this time like the last few trips, but San Diego is still one of those cities I always enjoy visiting. It was really good to see Sambo and Hollywood this week, but completely different than going out with them in the past. We all have significant others, they have kids, and I don't drink. Ten years ago San Diego would've been a dream playground for three kids like us. I'm not sure if we've really matured, or if we just better control our primal urges for debauchery. I guess one could say they're the same thing on a basic level.

Sunshine and I are up and ready to hit the road to my homeland of Ft. Lauderdale. It's nice to have a dependable car like the Goat that I can drive somewhere and not worry about it like the Serious or Scrotus, rust in pieces. Sunshine's wanted to do an actual vacation for some time now, and this is a nice way to do it. We get away for a few days without being gone too long, and we get out of the area without having to do extensive travel. I'm still not very good at the vacation mindset, but I'm going to try to forget about work and the shop and just relax. So far, so good.

We're at Lion Country Safari. Mom and Dad took me here when we still lived in Florida. Considering we moved when I was only six months old, I don't remember it, but I came here once a few years ago, and thought it'd be something cool we could do on the way today. The ever easily-cheered Sunshine is pretty excited to see real lions out in the controlled wild. They look like husbands on 210, with the freedom to roam the driveway and garage, but barred from true freedom outside of the set boundary. The last time I came here, there was no fence or anything between the lions and the cars, but there is now. I'm sure that fence is the result of some lawyer somewhere continuing to make rules for the litigious and lowest common denominators of society. There's a baby rhino that has been added recently. Damn those things are big. Fortunately the ostriches aren't eating my windshield wipers like they tried to do on my rental car during my last visit.

We're finally at the hotel in Lauderdale. Of all the travel points I accumulated flying around for my last job, Best Western was the only one that honored my points. The hotel is nothing fancy, but it's free and right by the beach. It's time to check in and start relaxing, or continuing to learn how to relax.

Sun 09 Aug 09

Sunshine wanted to either rent wave runners or go parasailing. All the years I went to spring breaks, and I've never done either. All I ever focused on was getting completely wasted and hitting on everything around me, but since I don't drink any more, I'll be able to explore new horizons. Not sure about either of these options, but wave runners keep us at ground level, so we'll try that. She used to ride them when she worked on the yacht, so I'll let her drive first. The numerous dents in her Curve are testimony of her driving skills, but at least out here she'll be hard-pressed to find anything to hit. I still know that falling off this thing and skipping across that water would hurt. The speedometer says 20 mph, but it sure feels faster. This is pretty choppy water, and not like the glass surface of the water further south where she drove on the previous ones.

Okay, it's my turn to drive. We only rented it for a half-hour, so we switch seats quickly and successfully without either of us falling in the ocean. I'm used to twist throttles, so this trigger throttle might take some adjustment. There are no brakes either, which will be different. I'm trying to get comfortable at 15 mph, but the choppy waves are making it a little rough. I put one finger under the trigger so I can't go full throttle. There's 25 mph, and coming down across these waves is pretty abusive on the crotch. I try to sit up on it during the jumps, but that just makes my nuts hang down as the first impact point against the seat on the waves, which is less than pleasant. I wonder if I can lean this thing over like a sport bike. It's similar although coming over a wave in a lean and hitting the next wave about tips us over, but I barely keep it from tipping and am starting to get the hang of this. Fuck it. Let's see how fast this sonofabitch goes. 40 mph is the fastest I've seen, and I'm hooked. Flying over these bumps is going to give me black and blue balls, and my hands are hurting like hell just from trying to keep holding on, but this is a fucking blast! Without having to pay attention to any obstacles besides the buoys identifying the limits of our area, I'm staring at the waves and the slowly changing surface of the water. Noticing the lulls in the water help me anticipate the angle of my sharp turns and leans and the resulting bounces against the next high spot.

It's been great walking around and relaxing on the beach, seeing new things, and forgetting about the rat race, but the most fun part of this vacation has been the exhilaration of tearing across the choppy waters at 40 mph on this thing. It's fitting that my favorite experience of a relaxing event is the most intense part of it. I'm extremely glad we came down here. Vacation, novel concept.

Thu 03 Sep 09

This fucking backpack is already uncomfortable. Eight hours on the Ape with this monkey on my back isn't happening. Hopefully the rain dies down or this will be one long trip. I better go back home and swap out the backpack for the gym bag.

Ah, much better. We're off. I let Tracer lead. I'm sure I can find Franklin, North Carolina, but it'll be easier to follow him since he's been up there a few times already. I'm curious to see how this radar detector works now that I have it mounted on the dash and the LED flicker gadget in my helmet. Tracer sure gave me a lot of shit for modifying my dash and making the mount pieces for the Valentine One instead of just buying one of those awful looking mounts like he has on the triple tree stem. Heaven forbid I do anything the easy way. My detector is better concealed from sticky fingers and Mother Nature than his and looks better, so the time I spent mounting it is worth the effort.

The rain is gone and the sun is out. Excellent. This will be the second vacation I've taken in about a month. I had a great time with Sunshine in Ft. Lauderdale, whenever that was. The weather was great, sun was shining, and even though Lauderdale has often been a threatening environment, I made it the whole weekend without a drop of booze. It's always fun to drive around, look at the Ferraris, Lamborghinis, and

Porsches. I was pretty impressed too with the ten rounds we cranked out on that three-day trip. I'd just thought the diminishing libido was part of aging and damage from the excessive drinking, but obviously it was all related to the heart. My favorite appendage has done nothing but impress me since surgery. I almost feel a little bad for all the girls of the past and the poor show I gave them, but with an equally hungry girlfriend and more lead in the pencil, I enjoy fucking more now than I ever have.

It's been eight hours on the Ape, but we're at the Franklin hotel dropping off anything we won't need on the bike to go hit the mountains. Tracer leads us right to the twisties, mostly with posted limits of 25 or 35 mph. I think back to the first time I saw him dive into a turn when I'd first gotten the Ape and saying to myself, "Fuck it. If he can do it, I can do it." I dove in behind him and kept right on his tail. Since then Tracer's been up here a couple times, taken a couple driving classes, and has added some skills to his aggressive driving. So far I've been sticking right to him, even though it's my first time on roads like this. I feel like I'm being a little too ballsy and a little too sloppy. I need to focus on what I'm doing and remember what I've learned so far about looking through the turn, trail-braking, keeping low, and hanging off the bike. This is a lot different than mastering one cloverleaf I drive every day to work. This takes skills I don't have, and I'm afraid I may realize it the hard way soon.

Another 25 mph curve means I'm slowing down to 50 mph as I brake and start to lean into the curve. Oh shit, the curve is tightening on me more than what I'd planned. I must've panicked and squeezed the front brakes too much, because I feel that front tire washing out on me. I can't look through the curve at this point, so I direct my attention to what I may or may not hit. Uh-oh, all I see is about a three foot-wide shoulder and a drop-off into some trees. This isn't good. I knew I was going to do this too. Fuck! I've never left a bike behind anywhere overnight, but I have to abandon ship if I want to survive this crash. I push away with the handlebars trying to force myself toward the centerline of the road away from the shoulder. I close my eyes, and the next thing I know I'm laying on that three feet of soft grass next to the road with one arm hanging over the drop-off. I don't seem to hurt anywhere besides just a slight soreness on my left shoulder. Everything moves, so that's good. Damn good thing no one was coming from the other direction or I'd be a hood ornament right now.

I remove my helmet and look over the drop-off, and there's the Ape about twenty feet down a basically vertical drop leaning against a tree. I decide I better stay on the road so Tracer can see me, assuming he notices I'm missing. Pretty soon he comes back around, looks down, and asks me why I parked down there. Ironically he'd just been thinking he should slow down, as I was less experienced and keeping right with him. This was just before I disappeared from his mirror.

I scale down the ravine and cuss the fact that the tree made a huge dent in my gas tank. There are scuffs on the right side, a broken blinker and mirror, but that's about it. Apparently the Ape really never fell over, but just dropped down the side and stopped at the tree. I guess I should be happy the tree stopped the bike, or it may have ended up fifty feet down. I'm even happier I wasn't on it when it went down. That tree would have done the next round of damage to my rib cage if I had stayed on the bike for the drop.

A local guy is nice enough to stop by and throws me one end of a twenty or twenty-five foot tow rope, which I tie around the front forks of the Ape. Tracer and another local guy flag traffic on both sides since the curves are so tight and blind in this area, and I guide the Ape straight up the hill. I'll be damned if the thing doesn't start as soon as I hit the button. Amazing. Everything seems fine, so we saddle our bikes and Tracer leads us back to the hotel. I'm shaken to say the least, but I'll look at it as a warning shot or wake-up call. It was made clear to me that I was being too reckless, but nothing was broke that can't be fixed. Besides that slightly sore shoulder, I didn't even get a scratch on my helmet. You could say I was lucky, but if I was lucky, it wouldn't have happened in the first place.

Back at the Franklin hotel, Tracer comes back from the store and has an airplane bottle of Jack Daniels sitting by my stuff when I get out of the shower. He tells me that after the wreck, he needs a drink, and thought maybe I could too. I thankfully decline, and he questions if I'll ever drink again or not. Tracer points out that since jail, I've done much better at going out and having just a couple drinks versus drinking a fifth of whiskey. I admit that my moderation skills have improved, but after surgery, my health was of primary importance. The thing I liked about drinking was getting completely annihilated and the drunken escapades that followed. It's obvious I can't go back to that kind of chaos again, and if I can't do that, then why would I drink at all? A couple drinks aren't enough to get me wasted, but does adversely affect my health, finances, and could possibly flag the breathalyzer if I got pulled over. If the only reason to drink now is to give into peer pressure to the twenty-one year-old behind the bar, that doesn't make much sense either.

Nine months without alcohol is the longest I've gone since I started drinking at eighteen. I never drank in high school because I was afraid of becoming the fourth of four on the oldest son of each family to die in a drunk-driving wreck. The first day I drank was in May of 1992. I'd just finished my first day of construction. I was hot and thirsty, and when the customer brought beer, I just wanted something cold to drink. Three beers later I drove home that night with my first buzz, slowly inching away from that guardrail of untainted sobriety. I basically floored it toward the opposite guardrail from there forward.

College progressed my taste from beer to Night Train, compliments of the song by Guns and Roses. By the time I turned twenty-one, the only thing I'd order in a bar was the cheapest rot-gut whiskey available, generally Hawkeye, with a splash of 7-up. After getting plastered all day every Wednesday through Saturday in college, the new career in Texas forced me to take it easier Wednesday and Thursday nights, but I also got worse on the weekends. Drinking a fifth before we'd even go to the bars eventually evolved to drinking a Texas fifth before going out for 190 Octanes, Bull vodkas, and whatever else I could find, including Everclear on occasion. I was definitely grinding harder and harder until I finally crashed through the guardrail of alcoholism and landed in a river at the bottom in Illinois. Jail set me bouncing back off the sobriety guardrail, I drifted closer to the middle of the road, and surgery eventually sent me back against the sobriety guardrail, where I am today.

Booze has cost me a lot over the years, including three cousins, a grandpa, an uncle, countless dollars and hours, relationships, and who knows how many health issues. My heart problem was genetic, but drinking my way into the ER with that pericarditis didn't help things. I have a sneaking suspicion that time I puked a lot of blood over Ricky's balcony in Atlanta was just a warning of what's to come some day from my boozing. I can't undo the damage I've done to date, but I can be smarter about what I do from here forward.

Fri 04 Sep 09

Today we're going to hit the Tail of the Dragon at Deal's Gap. It's over three-hundred turns in just over eleven miles, and I've been hearing about this road since I started riding the Ape. I'm still a little gun-shy after yesterday's debacle, but I'm doing it right today. I'm being more conservative and thinking about every move I make, practicing the proper techniques, and paying attention to every possible pitfall. The Dragon is an incredible road, and I can see why people love riding it. About the time I get confident, I get cocky and feel myself aiming off the road toward a dirt wall. Dammit, I swore I wasn't going to fuck up again, but I should be able to survive if I hit that dirt wall sideways like I think will happen. Fortunately after the sticky Michelins drop about eighteen inches off the pavement into the gully, I'm able to redirect it back onto the road. Unfortunately my speed is still too high, I'm still not in control, and I'm now aiming toward the other side of the road, which drops off into trees. Finally I regain control, focus, and continue improving and enjoying riding.

These roads are beautiful. A rider has to be so focused here though. One mistake and that's it. I approach some of these curves at 70 mph or more leaning about as far inside as I can, and see a one-foot tall guardrail as the only thing between me and an involuntary sky-dive leading to someone finding my skeleton in a tree in three years. This is just the right blend of fear, excitement, and enjoyment. It's where this Ape can perform like it was designed to perform. Every part of me is sore from constant motion and reaction, but I'm enjoying every minute. This is fucking intense!

Chapter 7

Still Adjusting

Fri 09 Oct 09

I have some time before my flight, so maybe I'll check out a book store. I really don't need to buy any magazines, as Tracer gives me all his old bike and car mags, and I just subscribed to a couple more for Cousin Reno's kid's school offer. I finished Dante's "Inferno" though, and wouldn't mind seeing what else might actually appeal to me. "Inferno" was one tough book to read, but what a great piece of work. Not that I'm a big reader anyway, but that's the first book I couldn't read with so much as a radio playing. It required more focus that the average Mad magazine.

"Arguing with Idiots?" This might be interesting. Sunshine always points out that I don't research subjects like social issues and politics like she does. Maybe it would be good to learn some actual facts on some of the issues, as much as I hate to waste any gray matter activity on such subjects. I know in my head because of common sense that if a criminal knows there's a chance of getting shot by breaking into my apartment, he is less likely to break into it than if he knows that laws forbid me from having a firearm and defending myself. I also know that if some criminal isn't afraid to break the laws regarding breaking an entering, theft, drugs, assault, rape, or murder, that individual isn't going to worry about breaking firearm laws. I shouldn't need facts to know this, as it seems like common sense to me. I was absolutely blown away when Hollywood, who I know is a very intelligent person, said he didn't agree with me. I just couldn't believe that a boy who grew up in the Midwest, hunted for years, and has a couple false teeth thanks to the thugs in Waterloo in his youth, could think like that. Is it because he lives in California now and that's the way everyone thinks out there? Assuming we both started life in the same place, and both are intelligent people, what could possibly have caused him to think like this? Is it the news and TV that he watches that I don't? I'm not sure, but maybe Sunshine's right and I need to educate myself more on such subjects. Before I buy this book, I'll check out the other bookstore first.

Is that a smiley face with a Dirty Sanchez? "Liberal Fascism?" Oh, so that's supposed to be a Hitler mustache. This looks more historical and big picture than modern media arguments between two opposing forces while the masses are manipulated and brainwashed in the middle. It's also smaller so it'll be less weight to carry. Efficiency is key.

We're almost to Denver. This book is pretty interesting, and scarier than any Stephen King book out there. So far the book has addressed Mussolini, Hitler, and Wilson with respect to Fascism, Liberalism, Socialism, Communism, and other "isms." I'm pretty blown away and confused right now. It's been so many years since Government class and History class in high school, but I don't really remember learning this level of information back then anyway. I do remember reading Nietzsche in Philosophy 201 back in Ames and thinking that the Existentialist principles had some great points. The line of his that stuck out the most to me was something about a person not striving for advancement, being content in life, humble, and cowering in a corner as the weakest thing in the world, a Christian. At that point, a lot of things became clear. I remembered being very young and telling Mom it was a shitty thing for her to leave her seat belt unbuckled and say, "If God wants me, he'll take me." I understood that the reason Mom's complacency with everything from her job to her health was a direct effect of her Catholic upbringing. Not that it's a bad thing to be happy with your life, but to take no proactive action in your life and just think that whatever happens is the will of God is foolish. God helps those who help themselves, right? Dad was far from Christian, but was also happy with what he had and never really wanted more either. However, despite the fact that I knew I should be happy with all I had, I still always wanted more. I always wanted everything I could get for myself in life within the limits of integrity and with no one else to thank or blame. Mom raised us Catholic, and Dad set a similar example, but that desire to achieve all I could was burned into me early at a deep level, and I never knew quite why.

Now I'm reading that Nietzsche's writings are a foundation for Socialism. I don't understand how this example of how to advance yourself to the next level and become the absolute best you can in every respect can even be associated with Socialism. My feeble understanding was that Socialism wants everyone to be equal, to take from those that have and give to those that need. That's what always disgusted me about Socialism and the idea that a few work hard to carry the load of all. It just pisses me off thinking about this, but I guess I'm learning something about the world around me. I'm just not happy about what I'm learning.

Welcome to Denver. The last time I was here was almost a year ago. I was in my purple joker costume and went to that bathroom right there to put in my contacts and put on the joker makeup. I'll call Sunshine quickly as I walk toward the door, but about the time I tell her I'm here, I see the Beerbarian parked outside and say, "bye" before I climb in the truck.

28 degrees is too fucking cold, but at least I remembered my coat. He's not wearing his to the bar, so I won't either. No Diamond Dolls tonight. We're going to some new place he wants to try. It's a little different drinking water while this clown slams down one Jack & Coke after another. It would be fun to get hammered with him tonight, but I've made it this far without a drop. It's always a good crowd in Denver. These places don't appear to have the modern hippies of some mountain areas, or the pot/coke heads of Jax Beach. It's just a nice selection of apparently decent, attractive people, all bundled up to keep from freezing their asses.

Now we're in some other bar that is slammed after a cold run here from the last place. Sporty Spice is calling Ronan because of a communication breakdown. "I don't want to go" actually means, "I don't want to go to the airport, but I want you to pick me up when you go to the bars." I was not aware of this translation either. She seemed decent when I met her, but like many girls, thinks our balls are crystal. Here come some rugby player buddies of his, who I'd forgot call him Zilla, an appropriate name. I can't say the young drunken guys full of life don't remind me of us at that age. One of them asks us if we want shots. I tell him I can't as I've had recent heart surgery. I realize recent is a stretch, though it's worked so far, but not tonight. "Shots of Jager!" yells the kid, already too intoxicated to care if I had a hole in my liver or not.

I'm pushed into the corner and have to decide now. I've more than proven I can go without booze, so that's not an issue. I've regained muscle, lost fat, have great blood pressure, and am healthier and stronger than ever before, so my recovery is complete. I'm here with one of my old college buddies, and I'm not going to do anything I shouldn't when it comes to the girls around us. You know what, fuck it. Not just Jager, but Jager Bombs. They're pre-mixed, which aren't as fun, but still a great shot. Booze and Red Bull are two things I haven't touched for almost a year. Oh, that shot is good too. In Frank the Tank fashion, we both yell, "It tastes so good! When it hits your lips, it tastes so good!" If only it tasted bad, it would be easier to resist. Here comes another shot. Okay, just one more. Now we each have a Jack & Coke in our hand, and after what used to be a breakfast portion of booze years ago, I can already tell I've drank. There's that warm burn in my stomach and that ever so slight light-headedness beginning. Moderate, dumbass. In other words don't end up freezing to death, drowning, in a hospital, or in jail, and try to make sure he doesn't either.

Ronan clearly isn't driving anywhere, so it looks like not only have I drunk tonight, but now I have to drive afterward. He's already had two DWI's, and I'm not even close to drunk like he is, so this is the best option for all considered. I could be disappointed in myself for drinking, but I think instead I'll be proud of myself that I was able to have a few drinks and a good time without the wheels falling off the wagon.

Sat 10 Oct 09

I haven't heard from Vermin yet, so I better text her and make sure she's in motion. She was supposed to be on the road by now as it's after 5:30 a.m. She texted back and is en route. I'll take a shower and go look at Porsches, Ferraris, and other stuff I can't afford on Ronan's computer until she gets here. The place looks really nice, since they've completely remodeled it compared to my last visit. I'm glad he finally got a place he can keep for a while. He's learned a lot about houses over the years, although some of the lessons he's learned have been expensive.

The roads are pretty bad with this snow and there are plenty of cars in the ditches. We drive by the Duc dealer again, but I don't think

I'll be doing any test drives today. I'm happy with the Ape I have for now. We do stop and get bagels from Panera and take them over to the hospital where I'd resided a year ago. It feels a little strange walking back through the door that I'd exited in a wheel chair that bitter cold night thirty pounds ago. We ride the elevator to the cardiac floor and walk toward the desk. I don't recognize the people behind the desk, but I explain that I'm dropping off bagels for the people that helped keep me alive the year before. I see one doctor, but he's busy with a patient. We also see John, say, "hi," and explain who I am. He remembers me being Organisis's brother and says a quick hello before getting back to work. It would've been nice to see more of the other nurses, walkers, and others, but I'm still glad we made the stop here.

We pull up to Organisis's house and walk up to the door. Vermin was the only one who knew I was coming. I hadn't planned to make the trip, but Mom and Dad are out here, and I need to make time to do things like this when I can. I got a last minute trip, and here I am surprising them. After shaking Dad's hand and hugging Organisis, Mom comes around the corner, and I tell her, "Happy birthday, Mom!" Not surprisingly she starts crying, as she's happy all of us are able to get together. Some kids send flowers, cards, and presents, and other kids might visit their parents often. I've never been too good about any of that, although I do try to call my parents every weekend. By setting low expectations over the years, even a little trip like this is a big deal to Mom. Under-promise, over-deliver.

This is also the first time I've seen Organisis's second ankle-biter. Hogan definitely looks different than Junior. I'm not sure how he got bright red hair, but he's still got the same recessive gene for blue eyes as his parents and big brother. Walking through this house is somewhat strange too considering my condition when I last stayed here. There's that stuffed St. Bernard still staring at my old resting place on the couch. It's sure nice to be able to walk around here without having an oxygen tube in my nose. It's good to see family and friends, and it's good to be healthy.

Sun 11 Oct 09

This was a fun trip, but now I'm back in Denver getting ready to fly home. The more I read this book, the more appalled I am. I'm not sure what pisses me off more, the people in Government who make decisions without having ever lived in the real world outside of academia and politics, or the masses that buy their bullshit. One of the most surprising things I've learned from this book is the perceived differences between Republicans and Democrats, and between conservatives and liberals. The reason I have such a hard time understanding these classifications is because they don't have consistent thought patterns. Republicans promote individual rights be opposing abortion. Democrats promote equality by supporting race-based scholarships and affirmative action. Are all these contradicting ideals just a way to force people to choose teams over issues, since no common-sense option exists?

The book just makes it more and more painfully obvious that people shouldn't trust the politicians, and the fact that they ignorantly do trust them only furthers the demise of our nation. Maybe there's a reason that Dante's "Inferno" put the corrupt in the lower circles of hell closer to Satan. Five centuries ago Dante knew it was a serious problem, and we're still suffering as a species because of our inability to think and act accordingly. This is exactly why I don't pay attention to politics. It just fucking pisses me off.

Fri 16 Oct 09

It's nice of the Hare to remind me I was going to leave early for Biketoberfest. Now he's suggesting I leave and go study the LEED book for class on Monday. Fuck that. Leaving early on a Friday to go home and study would be like hiring a hooker to play Scrabble. I do need to get out of here though. It's not like I haven't put my share of extra hours in this or any other week. Yep, it's time to pull the rip cord. I better grab these fucking LEED books so I can read how reducing or hiding water fountains makes me have to drink water out of a plastic bottle and it's somehow good for the environment. It looks like rain, so I guess today isn't the best day to be riding anyway. Since I skipped my workout and went to eat with Cartmanini and his boss, I better hit the gym on the way home. I did fifties on chest and back day, so I better do fifties for legs today, then call it good.

Fuck, my legs hurt, but in a good way. Who called from an 812 area code? I think that's Ivy's area code, or was it 219? Shit, her mom was in the hospital a couple weeks ago. Hopefully everything's okay. Oh, it's just a woman from the publisher I checked out online last night. I might as well call her and see what she has to say. I don't plan on becoming a professional writer, but I've always been told I should write a book because of my experiences, unique descriptions, and blunt honesty. These notes were just a way for me to document my thoughts and experiences throughout surgery. I didn't intend to do anything with them besides read them later. All the individual entries over the last year have slowly formed a story describing how I've evolved both physically and intellectually from the surgery, and other people might find it interesting. They'll watch TV shows about people so fat they have to enter contests to lose weight, getting fired, or being stuck on an island. Weren't these all things people used to try to avoid? If the masses seem to enjoy reality and things they are not currently experiencing, why wouldn't a book about someone really going through heart surgery and reflecting on his fucked up life appeal to them?

I'm not a celebrity, I'm not trying to change the world, and I'm not the best at any one thing. There are many people that are smarter than me, play guitar better than me, are better artists or writers, drank more booze, banged more girls, have been through more surgeries, worked more, and have been arrested more. Although this is true, there are probably not many people that have such a diverse combination of the above qualities as I do. Slash can play guitar better than me, but can he calculate the volume of an engine? Einstein was smarter, but did he ever do dumbbell curls with 90 pounders? John Holmes fucked a lot more girls, but he's dead, so he can't do shit better than me right now. I guess the distinctiveness in my story lies not within one particular trait, but a combination of multiple extreme experiences and characteristics. The appeal may really be the fact that it's wild enough to be fiction, but so genuine and honest that it has to be true.

This doesn't sound too bad. I provide the manuscript and they market and print the book for major retail websites and book stores. I'm told I can help promote it by doing book-signings as a local author at stores, which will not only help market the book, but might be fun to do as well. I get royalties on ebooks and paper books and pay them less than what it costs me to print the YCC bike and bikini calendars. Worst case I spend a few hundred tax-deductible dollars, which will motivate me to finish it, and I get to mark off publishing a book as one more of my life's experiences. We strike a negotiation and now I've got one year to do this. I'm only going to get one shot in my life at writing a description of the X-rated cartoon world in which I've lived, so I need to make it count. This has to be my Moaning Lisa.

Fuck that feels better with drag bars back on it. I really liked the look of the clip-on bars, but drag bars feel so much better. Now I'll be able to ride to Daytona tomorrow without having too much back pain. Hopefully my tailbone doesn't hurt again though. The forward position actually seemed to help that. This seat is like riding on a fucking piece of plywood, and I know my ass will be numb by the time I get there. That stitched leather seat sure looks bitchin' though, especially with the big anarchy symbol in the center. Once I get back from Daytona, I'll get that Ape tank fixed and put it back together. I'll focus on my customer's chopper too, get that done, then probably try to hammer out this book before I get too deep into building my next chopper. I think I'll set my final entry date as New Year's Day of 2010, finalize and proof-read everything, and send it off to the publisher.

I'm sweaty, I reek, and I'm sitting in my shop in the hood with my Glock on the desk on a Friday night, while many people are at happy hour, dressing up to go out, having dinner, or just relaxing. Today I committed to publishing a book, got my Anarchist mobile again, and did fifties on legs too, which all make for a pretty fucking good day in my world. I suppose I should get my ass home and clean up before Sunshine gets home from work. Then she can give me a ride back here to pick up the bike, get it back to the apartment, and I can head south in the morning to watch the sunrise from the saddle.

Sat 17 Oct 09

Sweet, it's still dark out, so I'll be able to watch the sun rise on the way down. Holy granite nipples, Batman. Sunshine state my ass, it's cold out there. I can't believe I used to drive that old General home from Ames for the winter when there was snow on the ground. It's probably just over 50 degrees, and I'm whining about the cold. No need to torture myself though. I'll eat some breakfast and hang out here for a while before I take off. I rumble through the streets to JTB and down A1A. I95, which would be "the 95" if I was in California, is quicker, but I've come to enjoy the scenic route south. I'm in no hurry, so I'll enjoy the ride and not just the destination. The seat is still like riding a two-by-six, but these drag bars are a vast improvement over the clip-on bars. I should be able to ride all the way without stopping. Pisser, I forgot to get gas. It looks like I'll be stopping anyway, but not because of the handlebars.

A year ago I was doing this as a possible last hoorah depending on the outcome of my surgery. I'm fucking stoked that I'm here doing it again and feeling better than ever. I take in a deep breath like they taught me in therapy and as described in that relaxation book. Damn it feels great to be alive!

Holy shit, is that an RSV4? I tell the guy standing by it that I didn't realize they had them in the country yet. He works for Aprilia and this is the first one in the US. This thing feels significantly lighter than mine, and is rated at 189 horsepower. I need one of these. It would be a lot more cost effective to just do the engine modifications to mine and get it up to 160 horsepower or so. It'd be even more economic to just leave mine the way it is, once I fix that damn tank dent of course. I really never wanted anything that wasn't a V twin, but there's no denying this RSV4 is a wicked bike. I've just never bought a new vehicle or fucked a virgin. Let someone else deal with the break-in period. Maybe in a couple years I'll be able to get a used one that's already suffered the new vehicle's first year depreciation. It's sort of like not dating anyone younger than sophomores in college as they've already depreciated by gaining their freshman fifteen.

The rest of the group has patiently waited for me to slobber over the bike, so we walk over to Froggy's for a while. Not exactly the same as Senor Frogs from blurry spring breaks in Cancun years ago, but still entertaining. I'm getting more and more okay with ordering water or soda, or pop as they say back in Iowa. These events have changed a lot over the years. I've noticed throughout the day they've played a lot of dance music, or whatever the hell you want to call it. Music to me is pretty much rock or not rock, and when I'm at Daytona, I want to hear rock and American V twin's roaring. This is where I should see tattoos, Florida beach bimbos with their ridiculous cosmetic surgeries, and people drinking Budweiser and Jack Daniels and eating burgers. In general, Daytona bike events should be a celebration of the biker trash lifestyle for lack of a better expression. This should be somewhere Kid Rock would blend well. I don't even like driving the Ape down here for bike events, as it just feels dirty on anything not American when I'm here. Is it really that bad to have a rock-and-roll American motorcycle event? Do we really have to let everyone play in our sandbox all the time, or can we just have our close friends in the sandbox once in a while?

When I was still in Iowa and had the old General, Dad and I would ride our bikes to Humboldt for the drag races on the 4th of July every year. You would only see a few foreign bikes, and they were usually British and parked away from everyone else. They wouldn't even let Buells on the drag strip for a while, as they weren't considered a real bike by the crowd, even though they had a Sportie engine. People were allowed to have their events where they could spend time with other people that had similar interests. As HD's became more popular and the yuppies started buying them, the tail trash got better looking, and the crowd began diversifying. You'd hear white collar bike owners talking about porting their cylinders and boring their heads, because they were completely clueless about the internal combustion engine. This all happened because Harleys started becoming a good product, and you didn't have to be a mechanic to work on them. Goldwings were still threatened at bike events, but pretty soon they became common, followed by crotch rockets, and eventually the metric cruisers. Now I have to listen to Bel Biv Devoe at Biketoberfest? Are you shitting me? AJ gives me shit for even knowing the name Bel Biv Devoe, and accuses me of being a closet hip-hop fan. I assure him not to worry. I was happier at these events when it was everything from AC/DC to ZZ Top, but that's it.

It's time to saddle the Anarchist and get over to Lollipops, and it's colder than a witch's tit in January. I'm glad I bought this hoodie earlier in the night. I thought I might need one later, and when I saw the skeleton riding in flames and the caption that said, "Hell didn't want me, so I came back," I had to buy it. There's the Japanese restaurant where we all ate when we were here for spring break. That's been almost ten years ago. Wow. Poor Inbreeder couldn't even eat with a fork that night, let alone chopsticks. That was the Friday when he and I split a fifth of Everclear at the pool. I think Habhab had some too. Inbreeder even came back from the bathroom halfway through dinner saying he'd shit blood. I told him I did that a few times during heavy benders, and puked blood about a year later. Maybe he'll realize that following my bad example isn't the best approach. There's Molly Browns. Nicole and I poured Gameboy over there and Habhab was already sitting in sniffer's row when we arrived that night. It seems like we got our disposable camera taken away and scolded when I was getting a lap dance from the cheerleader instead of the dancers. What a week of debauchery. We felt bad for the creepy old maid who kept eye-fucking Meat when she'd clean and he was doing his hip stretches. She probably had to clean that place with a flame thrower when we checked out. Broken mirrors, sand in the shower, piss all over the floor, and that little Hawaiian skank that several of them passed around that last night made for a good time had by all. Every morning I'd have my hangover-prevention breakfast beers where I slept, usually on the deck so I could wake up listening to the ocean, and walk across the street for the average eighty-dollar liquor purchase for the pool that day. It was downhill from there, but what a blast.

Lollipops isn't as packed as it has been in the past, but it looks like there are plenty of dollar-snatchers on stage. We assume a position against the wall where we can see the show. I keep Sunshine in front of me to insulate me from the clothing-impaired talent attempting to collect donations for their surgeries and prescriptions. They do have quite a few girls in here tonight, and a lot of them are decent-looking. None of them are tens, but most have some pretty good assets. I'm not a fan of these bottoms they wear half way down the cheeks of their asses though. I suppose some slut on MTV wore them and now everyone's doing it despite how stupid they look. We'll add that to the cocked trucker cap for stupid trends generated by MTV that people blindly follow without stopping to realize how ridiculous they look. I am definitely a fan of the music here though. Disturbed, White Zombie, Godsmack, Metallica, and Crue all grace the speakers. They even play the Sweet Child O' Mine video. I'm not sure if it's the fact that I'm in a place I associated with good times of the past, the people I'm with, the music, the girls, or a combination, but seeing that video and absorbing the environment just makes everything feel right. Yes, I am happy right now, and it feels fucking great. The old guy next to us looks happy too. He must either work here or be a regular, because almost every girl walking by him stops to hug him. Maybe he works independently in pharmaceuticals and provides goodies for the girls, or maybe he just sits over there licking his eyebrows.

I'm glad Sunshine's not pissy about these places. I rarely go to ballets any more, and probably haven't gotten an actual lap dance since Spearmint Rhino in Vegas several years ago for Fatman's bachelor party. I like to be able to go if I want though, and don't do well at all with significant other-imposed restrictions. Fortunately she understands, and isn't demanding about anything, which is a nice change for me. She offers to buy me a lap dance, which is all fine and good, but it just wouldn't feel respectful to do that right in front of her I guess. She points at one of the dancers that had fallen against the wall by us earlier from being so fucked up. Now the girl is in the middle of three guys, wearing one of their caps, being held up by them, and mouthing, "I'm going to suck your cock" to one of them. Sunshine comments how sad that is. I wonder if the girl will wake up tomorrow with her new pearl necklace and call her friends laughing about how fucked up she was, or come through the fog and feel like shit about herself. If it doesn't happen tomorrow, there's a better than average chance that some day she will. It might be tomorrow, it might be in five years when she's still doing it, out of shape from the bastard child she had, and has to jerk a guy off to get a ten dollar-dance from anyone. Then again, she might be making money for college and end up way more successful than I ever will. You just never know, and life has a twisted sense of humor.

Tue 27 Oct 09

I hate the news, and about the only place I'm forced to endure it is in the airport. The big news today is that a business owner in Texas asked his employees to speak English around him and the customers. Another story is about a woman wearing a veil who was asked to leave a store as masks are against store policy. I got kicked out of that liquor store last Halloween for having makeup on because it violated store policy, but nobody interviewed me on CNN. This woman was from the Mideast I think, so my story wouldn't be as desirable for modern news. The racist guy that wants the people he pays to be able to communicate with him and his customers and the racist guy that informed a woman of his store policy are much better news and better help portray hardworking businessmen as bad. They're just more fine examples of the liberal media in action.

The last story I had to listen to was by far the most disturbing. Some fifteen year-old girl was beaten and raped outside of a school dance. I didn't catch where this happened, but it doesn't really matter what location, income level, or anything. This is fucked up, not just that it happened, but that twelve other sorry mother fuckers stood there and watched it all happen. The girl's in the hospital now. I really don't even know what to think besides that this is a truly sad testament to the continuing plunge of any level of integrity in the youth of this society. Fucking appalling.

Thu 29 Oct 09

It's 6:53 am Florida time and my Crackberry alarm is blasting Kid Rock's, "drinking whiskey out the bottle, not thinking 'bout tomorrow..." I'm looking back and it's been one year today since I started this documentation of deranged thoughts. One year ago I woke up to Death knocking at my door. What a hell of a year.

That's enough snoozes, I better get my lazy ass out of bed. My sleep schedule will already by fucked up getting in at midnight tonight and getting up at 6 am in Florida tomorrow. I better write back to that gal at the Company that Cat contacted for me. She emailed last night stating that the open position they have is for a senior mechanical engineer, and asked if I'd be interested in a design position since my resume focuses on project management. This needs to be handled delicately, as I need to make sure I don't take a position unless it's at least a lateral career move with potential for more growth, but I don't want to come off as arrogant or insulting either. This would be a shit-load easier if I was at the shop on the

PC, but the Crackberry will have to do for now. Even though it's far from ideal, I have to admit it's pretty convenient to be able to pull up the information on the engineer and PM position for which I applied, have the career summary saved on it, and email it to her, all from a device smaller than my wallet. After dicking around with the whiz-bang, it's probably a little late to go down to the treadmill, plus the belt slips anyway. I'll just do some shadow boxing and sit-ups here in the hotel room. That should leave me enough time to eat breakfast, clean up, pack, and make it to the Reno airport before my flight.

It's 18 fucking degrees and snowing. Awesome. It'll be nice to get back to decent weather. There's something weird about the mountains to me now. Whenever I see the silhouette of pine trees on a mountain against the backdrop of a rising or setting sun, it just reminds me of laying in that hospital bed watching the sun come up every morning. This is a difficult feeling to describe. I can't say the hospital was like a bad dream, because it was a great experience besides the whole almost dying part. It feels like a combination of humility, forced relaxation, and resulting clarity. Perhaps it's because at that time in my life, nothing mattered except just that, my life. I appreciated the fact I still had it, I had no idea how long it would last, and I guess neither of those things have really changed.

I'm still wearing my contacts and it's a short flight to Phoenix, so I'll just read more of this book and further reduce my already minimal trust of any politician. One lie after another all spun as being for our own good. What a bunch of shit.

Welcome to Phoenix. I get to watch the sweet ass on the snobby blonde that was sitting in front of me as she walks off the plane. The airline attendant tried to ask her nicely to turn off her phone before takeoff, and she continued to text while he continued to badger her until she finally sent her text, which was clearly necessary for national security. I realize the plane would still take off with her phone on for thirty more seconds, but the obvious lack of respect for any authority on her part is all too common. I guess whether it's justified or not, I already have a low opinion of her character, so I won't feel guilty about paying attention to the one good asset of hers I can identify. Her and her boyfriend/brother both have their sunglasses on in the airport, so they're obviously celebrities, or just two more idiot victims of MTV-parenting.

I better get something to eat. Route 66 Grill sounds good. The external seating area is surrounded by a guardrail, so I'll sit out here and watch the people while I wait for my dang quesadilla. It's marginal food at best, but this is an airport and it still beats most of the fast food around here. My brain is definitely in neutral, as I'm easily entertained by wondering if the girl's healthy rack next to me is real or not. Well, they're not real when compared to fake, but they are real versus imaginary. Whatever they are, they're more fun to watch than the people walking by wearing dust masks. I would assume they're either cautious or paranoid of the swine flue, which is probably offensive to pigs. I really don't know much about it, and I probably won't as long as I don't catch it.

Did the newscaster really just say, "What you sow is what you reap?" Idiot. The saying is, "You reap what you sow." Has Grammar been tossed aside in the education system for Recycling Studies or something? That song that says, "My heart keeps beating like a hammer" is another literary butchering. Hammers don't beat, but hammers and hearts both pound. For fuck's sake. I'm not all good, I don't get 'er done, I'm not down with anything or in any house, and I haven't been there and done that. I do say, "like" too much, and it pisses me off every time I catch myself using it improperly. I probably shouldn't be so judgmental of people, but I consider myself to be fair because I judge myself too. I could say I have esteem issues developed as a child by an overactive, insecure mind, sickly build, and general lack of confidence. I then withdrew socially, focused on work, lifting weights, and entered college at a solid 175 lbs. During that time I blew up my own self-opinion, degraded my opinion of humanity in general, and still pacified my insecurities by justifying my narcissistic behavior as I plowed through life at 100 mph leaving a trail of empty bottles and empty girls. I could say that I've bounced off the guardrail of arrogance now, and look down at everyone that I believe to be inferior or even different than myself. I'm sure a therapist would have a blast using me as an experimental subject. I'd probably fuck with him or her just as much or more than they'd fuck with me though. When Dr. Touchy-Feely told me the ex was only expressing herself when she cussed and yelled at me, which was healthy, I asked him if should also express myself by saying, "You're being a fucking bitch! Shut the fuck up!" He denied his own double-standard by suggesting I think about different words to use. Loser.

Sat 31 Oct 09

I lived to see Halloween 2009, so I've got that going for me, which is nice. J3 called last night wanting to go out for Halloween, and I instantly forgot how tired I was and started itching to go out. Once Sunshine got home from work though, we decided since we were both dragging ass, we'd stay in last night and save it for tonight. She just left for work, so before I go to the shop, I think I'll check out another episode of this "Dexter" show. It reminds me a lot of "American Psycho," but as if it was done by the makers of "Nip/Tuck." I end up watching the whole dvd. I never was very good about saving anything for later. Even as a kid I could barely let the glue dry on one piece of the Testors model before I was trying to assemble the next piece. If I ever had a virtue, patience wasn't it.

Sunshine rented the "Dexter" dvd because her sister said I'd enjoy it. I will admit she's correct, as the show is addicting. The appeal is probably because I see many similarities with the main character. I'm obviously not a serial killer, but I'm entranced by the character's intelligence, objective and analytical mind, and his constant internal monologue evaluating himself and the world around him. I consider most TV, especially reality TV, to be completely mind-numbing, but this show, twisted as it may be, is at least mentally stimulating. Normally a serial killer would be the villain, but the premise that this individual helps catch bad guys as his day job and kills bad guys in his spare time makes him an admirable character. The show even shows him interacting with his girlfriend's bastards to make him an even more likeable and respectable character. If a person can be truly objective, move past that whole "all life is precious" idealistic notion, "Dexter" can be appreciated for his selfless acts to improve the big picture. That's enough time lying on my ass. It's time to get to the shop and get some work done.

Tracer and Ms. Texas are going to be watching the Florida-Georgia game at bars and J3 and Cartmanini are going to the game, so I've still got time to kill before Sunshine gets home. I already went to the gym, so I'll go put some gas in the Anarchist in case we take it tonight. It's getting later in the afternoon, but it's beautiful out. I should take it for a ride and enjoy the sunshine and blue skies. It will be getting cooler soon, so I should enjoy this while I can. Maybe I'll watch an episode of this call girl show Sunshine rented while I have a protein shake.

"Dexter" was good, but this show blows more than the main character. She's hot, but it just doesn't have much appeal to me personally. I feel embarrassed that I'm even watching to see how this hooker tries to go on a real date with a normal guy. I could date a stripper, but not a hooker. I've never even banged a hooker. I know a lot of people that have, but it's just something I never had the desire to do. For the same reason the Predator didn't kill the unarmed girl, there's no sport to it. As Foxy pointed out, the girl I take home from the bar could be dirtier than a hooker, but for some reason it just seems more acceptable in my mind. Like William Munny said, "Paying for flesh ain't right."

I feel guilty. It was a beautiful day, now it's already dark, and I'm just waking up after falling asleep watching that stupid hooker show.

Even though I'm sure I did more today than most people would on a Saturday, I still feel like I pissed away the afternoon. I better start getting ready for tonight. I don't want the red food coloring to bleed through the front of the shirt to the back, so I'll use Sunshine's cutting boards as a barrier. It shouldn't be too hard to make a bloody crotch print, but every time I paint the food coloring on the shirt, it bleeds out and loses its definition. I've now ruined five shirts and have a red stained counter top. This is the last one, as I already will have to go buy more T-shirts this week. Close enough. Now I better get this counter top clean, but I don't see any real cleaning agents under the sink. All I see are these worthless fucking green cleaners that have no real useful chemicals in them. Here's some soft scrub. This should actually work.

J3 and Cartmanini are stuck downtown and have been walking around for forty-five minutes looking for a cab. I'll go pick them up on JTB and 1 where some bus is dropping them off and give them a ride to their cars at Chili's. The sooner I get them back, the sooner they'll be ready to hit the bars.

Sunshine's home and scrambling around trying to get ready in her German beer wench costume, and I'm trying one more shirt attempt. I use a sponge this time to apply the food coloring, and it's a little better. A few sprinkles of blood splatter should finish it off. The fun part is next. I put the food coloring in my mouth, swish it around, and let it drip out the corners of my mouth and off the end of my tongue. Ever since I saw Gene Simmons's bass solo in "Kiss Exposed" as blood dripped out of his mouth and his abnormally long tongue lashed out, I've always loved mimicking that act. That same routine at the beginning of "God of Thunder" live at their reunion tour was the highlight of the show. His fireball blowing was pretty cool too, which I've performed a couple times with the aid of Everclear. No fire tonight, but my face definitely looks like Hannibal the Cannibal after he ate the victim's tongue in the hospital. I grab my white cigar and am ready to go.

Sunshine's cousin is coming out with us tonight, and is already waiting at the beach for us. I think this is only the second time she's come up from Staug since we moved. Sunshine has tried to hint at setting her up with Cartmanini, but I've made it clear to her that a) Cupid is represented as a baby because of the maturity level required to think matchmaking is a good idea, and b) Cartmanini and her cousin are both very nice, but very different, and would never make it as a couple. The end of the story would be awkwardness for Sunshine around either of them after the inevitable split, if they even got that far.

It's a full moon on Halloween on a Saturday night, so we're taking the Anarchist and meeting everyone at the beach. I don't feel like dealing with trying to park a car, plus I enjoy riding the bike. My only concern is the safety aspect, not for myself, but for her on the back. The beer wench costume doesn't give a lot of protection, and there'll be a lot of idiots out tonight. I'll be sober and careful as always, but I'd just feel like shit if something ever happened to her on this thing. We're hauling ass down JTB as fast as this thing will go, with the slutty devil on the tank glaring up at me through the candy red paint. Every bump reminds me to hang on to the bike and her to hang on to me. Fortunately it's warm out, so we don't need to fuck around with coats or anything. It starts to sprinkle for a few minutes and makes my face feel like a pin cushion, but overall it's perfect weather for a bike ride.

We drive through Jax Beach and find a small spot to park the bike. Sunshine's trying to get the knots out of her hair and rubbing her sore ass from the uncomfortable ride out here. We all meet at Rush Street and get a place on the deck. Her cousin is dressed like a witch, and probably the most conservative costume here tonight. Cartmanini is dressed like some kind of a Miami pimp in his white suit, Cousin Eddy white shoes, shades, and big gold cross. It's one of those risky costumes that people may look at and wonder if it's a costume or if he thinks he's really that cool. J3 and his date show up. He's supposed to be a private detective with Ron Burgundy hair and a mustache, but everyone keeps guessing him to be from the Beastie Boys' "Sabotage" video. His date is a female detective with a short skirt like all the other girl costumes, including Sunshine's. You could put the word "slutty" in front of any girl's costume tonight like slutty police officer, slutty beer wench, slutty devil, or slutty coke whore. The Eve costumes are new, or at least I don't remember them from last year. Sunshine points out that I'm drooling, even though I didn't think I was being that obvious. I usually try very hard not to eye-fuck girls right in front of her, but it's hard not to notice the scenery. No two ways about it, there are a lot of gorgeous clothing-deficient girls out tonight. There are quite a few of the German girl costumes, but I know the best of them will be blowing in the wind on the way home behind me in a couple hours.

The crowd on the deck is getting a little too busy for me in my sobriety, as well as the rest of the group, and the cigarette smoke isn't doing much for us either. We move inside where it's completely packed. I'd forgot they play '80's rock in here, and it's fun people-watching, but the crowd's wearing on us. We go across the street to MacCool's. Joe and I used to hang out here a lot when I was banging one of the barmaids. Unfortunately I've never met anyone more dedicated to partying than her, had to part ways, and really didn't come here much after that. She tried to understand why I rarely slept and accused me of doing coke. Of course after we split, I talked to two people that told me they'd given her nose candy while we were together. It's more evidence of the theory that the guilty are the first to accuse.

Usually MacCool's has a good band playing, but right now it's typical dance club music, which combined with the crowd is starting to get under my skin. The rest of our group is having fun, so I'll stick it out as long as I can, but eventually we all mutually decide it's time to go. Just as we walk down the stairs, the band starts playing "You Shook Me All Night Long." I had to listen to dance music for how long, and now the good stuff starts. Typical, but we're already on the way out the door. We're on the bike and tearing back west across JTB. I take in a deep breath of the night air, appreciating the fact that it's Halloween and still warm enough that I'm on a bike in a T-shirt right now. Overall it was a fun night. I'm still adjusting to going to bars in crowds sober, but it was good to be out with friends, watching the freak show, and now roaring across the concrete. Damn it feels good to be alive.

Mon 02 Nov 09

I'm about as motivated to sit in this LEED class as I would be to fuck a porcupine. I drive bikes, which get better mileage than most cars, and try to minimize energy used at the apartment. Those are more for selfish reasons like my enjoyment of bikes and saving money. I don't litter, Sunshine recycles what she can from the apartment, and I received a letter of appreciation from the environmental group at the city for how I handle paint waste at the shop. I do believe it's important to save energy, and not trash the environment. I prefer wood, stone, and metal over plastic. I am this way because of common sense where logic applies, and old-fashioned construction where preference applies. I'm not this way because I swallow the load the Government and media spray into the closed eyes and open mouth of society about the new religion of environmentalism. I'm not going to give up my 350 horsepower V8 for a fucking flat-assed Prius, which might actually do more damage to the environment with its batteries than the mileage benefits.

What a scam. The Government and media discount religion to make people hungry for something to believe, and then create this new belief system of saving the environment so people have a cause, look to the Government for leadership in their cause, and feel good about themselves. Now a guy can fuck around on his wife without a church making him feel guilty, as long as he recycles the rubber by shaking the fuck out of it when he's done. LEED comes along and creates a metric to measure how much a building or company cares about the environment. They create one of the most cumbersome paperwork processes and make conducting business in America even more expensive than what legal liability has already done. When it comes down to it, I still don't see why anybody would spend the money to do this process, except for the ability to hang a plaque on the wall. All it becomes is a marketing gig with the Government and media as the public relations staff. Brilliant.

Credit scores work the same way as far as a system that makes money by evaluating people with some character attribute. Maybe I could somehow apply the same principles to some other aspect of measuring people or organizations. Perhaps I could evaluate people's moral character and give them a gold halo for every level of goodness they exhibit. The flaw with that is that few people value moral character these days. Clinton's balls on some chubby chic's chin in the White House, OJ's double homicide, and fucking Michael Jackson's molestation of children are all excused by the media and brainwashed masses because they're celebrities. Modern morality would be a worse investment than a Rosie O'Donnell Playboy shoot.

Instead of measuring how green a building or company is, I'll set up a system for measuring how pink a guy is. I never thought I'd see the day where girls feel more comfortable with a guy that's got a stalker site like myspace or facebook, even if he uses it to post his pelvic pelts. I don't know if girls wrongly think that a person has to pass some kind of screening to be on these sites, but a lot seem to act that way. The good intent would be to provide a way for girls to meet good guys measured by how pink they are. In the true spirit of LEED, the well-intended effort would quickly evolve into a completely convoluted paper-pushing exercise with bureaucratic layers, and profit would trump purpose in no time. There could be a looks prerequisite for being below 20% body fat, but credits for every 2% below that. A guy could get personality credits for humor, intelligence, and kindness. The low body fat could also get credits for health.

Like LEED I could incorporate some contradicting credits. Spending money on dinner could earn fun credits and romance credits, but prevent the guy from earning credits for financial stability. I could even incorporate the ebay feedback practice and take the pink certification to the next level in which the guy has to list three ex-girlfriends as references. Most guys would be completely fucked if that were the case, but I'll bet my third nipple they'd be a lot more inclined to part on good terms with girls if they knew it would affect their ability to get laid in the future. Pink certification sounds ridiculous, but how long is it before the next level of some agency is grading people's personal lives? Maybe I should get the jump start on my idea before someone else steals my idea and beats me to it.

Wed 11 Nov 09

Since Sunshine and I are doing those pictures with AJ in a couple weeks, I'm doing something I never I thought I would and going to a tanning bed. I've always thought it was ridiculous, shallow, a potential cancer-causing activity, and just not natural. I live in Florida, so why would I ever even think about going to a tanning bed? However, I have a distinct tan line at the waist, which accents the slightly overhanging blubber at my mid-section, so I want to go enough to make that line go away. Sunshine comes to this place and is showing me how to put the winkeyes on to protect my eyes. Hopefully I don't burn my winkeye. Sunshine and the girl behind the counter recommend twenty minutes, which would barely add any color for that long in the sun, so it should be safe. The car stereo mounted in my bed has 102.9 playing so I get to listen to decent music while I'm lying here roasting.

We were supposed to meet Tracer for Ms. Texas's birthday, but he hasn't called, so Sunshine and I pick up another "Dexter" disc at Blockbuster after the gym. "Dexter" runs through the list of characteristics describing most serial killers including white, male, thirty to forty-five years old, intelligence, and organization. Of course they're intelligent and organized. Some dumbass gets nailed killing someone for the first time and goes to the casa de concrete because he's not smart enough to avoid getting caught. By definition a serial killer is smart enough to kill multiple times without getting busted. We look at each other and laugh at the fact that I perfectly fit the description for a serial killer. My laugh is genuine, her laugh implies, "That's funny as long as it never comes true."

Few people would probably condone, or admit to condoning, Dexter's vigilante style of societal-cleansing. Yes he's a serial killer, which normal would classify him as expendable life. However, he kills for purpose, carefully researching each of his victims to ensure they are, in his perspective, expendable life. The end result is removal of this trash from society, so is there anything really wrong with it? I'd be curious to see what would happen if a real life Dexter were to exist and be caught. Some would say that those criminals he killed had rights, were victims of society forcing them to resort to murder, and Dexter didn't have the right to kill them. Others would say he should get a medal for what he did, and everyone should use him as a good example. I suppose the right answer lies somewhere with common sense in between.

Fri 13 Nov 09

That was a quick site walk. The only thing they could've said that would've really helped is, "You get a couple more weeks." At some level I'm glad they didn't, or it would just give the competition more time to do a better proposal, and me more time to have to scramble on this effort. It will be nice when this and the design submittal for the other job are both done the second week of December. Since the site walk is done early, I can still haul ass back to the hotel, drop off the rep, and do my phone interview in private.

Having passed the initial call with the HR screener last week, I now have my phone interview with the hiring manager. I hesitate to take any kind of engineering position and derail my operations/project management career path, but the screener caught my attention when she told me I'd get instant good health benefits, retirement, stock options, a significant pay increase, and a decent bonus. The more I talk to the hiring manager, the more I like the sound of the position too. I didn't want to end up in a cube crunching numbers or drawing on CAD all day, but the position is far from that. He's describing the role in terms of direct reports, mentoring of the green engineers, and higher level design with respect to R&D and manufacturing. This job sounds great. He tells me about a systems engineering position that coordinates the various aspects of the product, which could put my project management skills to good use too. This will help my chance of getting a job with this Company if there are two positions open. There's also a project or program manager position that's responsible for everything about a product including first year's revenue. I tell him honestly that the PM position sounds like something I'd aspire to eventually secure, but I'd prefer to learn the company before I'd take that kind of role. My honesty and realistic expectations on the border between humility and confidence seem to impress him. He finally just says he needs to get the other engineer on the phone with both of us. The fact that I used to work with her at the Institute should allow me to bring an instant familiarity and comfort level to that call when it happens. So far I feel all the questions have been answered just right on both sides of this process. Now I hopefully get that next call early next week as he states. I'm trying to keep my expectations low to avoid potential disappointment, but I am stoked about the possibility of landing this job. A huge bottom line boost to be back in Texas working for a good stable company would be fucking sweet. With my current resume, and a person high up on the inside, I feel I've got a damn good chance of getting it too. I sure fucking hope so anyway.

That's enough email-checking for now. I call the rep and see if he's ready to work out before we eat. He goes for a run and I go back to the hotel gym, or spa as they call it here, for the second time today. Pictures are coming up quick, so I need to get these abs in somewhat presentable condition. Following a quick shower I trot down to the lobby and meet our rep for a late lunch. I asked Hollywood what he liked about San Francisco, as I just don't think I could live here. Hollywood confirms Sunshine's observation that the restaurants are great. He also says there are lots of hot single women, but I haven't been too impressed so far. This seems like a better place to get slapped than laid.

We're walking everywhere trying to find something to eat. There are plenty of restaurants, but after five-hundred bucks for dinner for three people last night, we're trying to find something reasonably priced and healthy. The rep finally spots a brew pub he remembered from a previous trip. Ironically when I open the menu, it's the same menu as Seven Bridges, Ragtime, and A1A Aleworks back in Florida. I'll be eating something I could've ordered two blocks from the cave, but at least I'll be familiar with it. Even though the menu is basically the same, the tuna appetizer is made a little differently, and comes with much less tuna. The meals here are more expensive with smaller amounts of food. Welcome to California.

As we take the scenic route walking home, it's starting to cool off. Most people are wearing coats, but I'm still in the T-shirt I wore earlier. The more we walk around, the more decent girls I see, but in a city this big, there's bound to be some scenery. They don't seem to be as big on makeup or boob jobs as Florida or southern California. Most of them look not quite gothic, but dark and moody. I could probably handle San Diego, or even LA if I had to, as those places seem more vibrant and happy from my brief exposure to them, but this place is just too gray and way too liberal for me. I'm sure it's a result of my early years raised in the conservative Midwest, but regardless of how the media tells me I should think, I am just not comfortable seeing two guys with their arms around each other in public. It's their choice and their business, but it makes me uncomfortable and I don't like to see it any more than they'd want to watch me eat out that girl over there in the knee high boots and short skirt. It's also disturbing to me that people smoke weed in public here, which is also another likely result of my Midwest upbringing. In San Francisco you can smoke a cock or joint wherever, but don't dare light up a cigarette or drive a car that doesn't get at least 20 mpg. Not right, not wrong, just different, and just not for me. If the people here enjoy the city, that's great for them and more power to them for finding a place and life that makes them happy, as that's all anyone can ask. I just know I won't be showing up here with a moving truck.

Why is it that every time I really need this navigation system, the fucking thing doesn't work? At least the Google map on my Crackberry is working and I can find my way to the main road and eventually the airport. There's the sign for SFO, which means I successfully made this trip without having a cable snap on a bridge and knock my car into the water like some of those poor motorists did not too long ago. I drop the rental wreck off at Avis, and get the frown of disapproval for not finding a gas station before dropping the car off. It seems like few airports have gas stations anywhere close to them, but I didn't feel like driving all over the area and getting lost over ten bucks worth of go-go juice.

After going down to the first floor like that dumbass at Avis told me, I have to ride the elevator back up to the top to get to the train that takes everyone to the terminal. Hearing that monotone voice on the train brings to mind all the future-based movies I've seen over the years with voices from above telling the sheep how to do everything. This train is a perfect example. The robotic voice tells passengers to be careful because the door is closing. Once the door is closed, this train tells passengers to hang on and set the wheels on their luggage to the locked position. I'd ask myself if people were so stupid that they needed to be told these things, but unfortunately I already know the answer to that question, or there wouldn't be a voice telling everyone to do it. I can't help but notice that the sign prohibiting food and drink on the train depicts a fat burger and fast food drink cup. I wonder how long it will be before someone else catches it and changes it to a Starbucks coffee and salad.

I gave Sunshine a bad time about wearing a short skirt and high boots the other day and claiming it was a cold weather outfit, but I notice a whole lot of skirts and boots on girls today between walking around the city and walking around the airport. It looks good on Sunshine and any of the girls I've seen, assuming the girl is built well enough to wear it. People always claim a certain piece of clothing or hat or accessory makes a girl look good. If a girl is hot, she'll look hot in a potato sack. No set of stilettos will hike up a cottage-cheese ass and make it look good either. The wrapping is just that; it's the present under the bow that's either a hottie or a nottie. No complaints here on those short skirts. Legs underneath are either in tights, nylons, or my favorite, raw. Some of these skirts look like just a long shirt with a belt around it, and if they were much shorter I could read lips.

I'm in the last row but in an aisle seat. Red-eye flights blow, but hopefully I'll be able to get a few "z"s on this flight. I look across the aisle and see a young mother with her likely fatherless child that's crying already. We're taking off and that kid is screaming like hell. Even with my MP3 player I can hear that kid. I feel even worse for the poor bastard sitting next to the possible bastard. This is going to be a long night, but at least I'll be home in the morning, can get a good day's work done at the shop, and I really had no reason to spend another night in San Francisco.

Am I asleep? I think I was until that fucking screaming kid woke me. I would've thought between the engine noise and my music I would be able to tune out that kid. I should be able to. Why won't it shut up already? Why am I letting this bother me so much? I've made such strides in stress management, and now I'm sitting here dazed as I fade in and out of a half-assed excuse for sleep because of this little demon. In Colorado I learned how to manage stress from Junior crying all the time. I can do this. Tune out the brat, listen to the tunes, close your eyes, relax, do your breathing exercises, and go back to sleep.

Sat 14 Nov 09

Now that I've snarfed down the same Quizno's steak and egg sandwich I ate Thursday at JAX, I'll walk down to the gate. Since I'm in Charlotte, I should text Captain D, let him know I'm passing through again, and end the text with Napoleon's "Gah!" I haven't talked to Uncle Slim for a while. He's not answering, so he's either busy driving the mail truck or eating something. I still have an hour and a half to kill, so I'll see if Dad's up and about.

He's waiting in the truck for Mom to pick him up since his car got stolen this week. I point out that he just told me last weekend about how he's had very little trouble with crime in his life, but now just had a second car stolen. I have to ask him if it was locked, and he shamefully admits the car wasn't locked, was parked in a dark part of the parking lot in a sketchy area, and there was a key in the ashtray. After thirty-five years of lectures on my stupid behavior, I always savor these moments even more than seeing politicians get busted. I tell him that I'll refrain from saying what I'm thinking, and he responds before I finish with, "I know, I know."

I tell him about the call I had with the Company in San Antonio, and as per all too often Dad manages to burst my bubble of excitement by telling me that there's a lot more to know about manufacturing than I know. The discouraging words stem from good intentions of caution and realistic expectations, but the results are still the same and his doubt in everything is just something I've learned to accept over the years. I'm quickly reminded why I tell myself not to bring up anything possible for the future until it happens to eliminate this type of conversation. I'm not sure if I'd say Dad is negative necessarily, so much as he seldom believes anything or in anything and often looks for the reason why something good won't happen. In his eyes he's protecting us from disappointment I'm sure, and I find that I've adopted his philosophy of hope only leading to disappointment. On the other hand I've learned how I and others perceive this gloom and tried to be better in how I deal with people by trying to point out potential pitfalls while staying positive and wish them the best. The ironic thing is Dad tackles any project like there's no chance he won't eventually complete it successfully. By comparison I try to look at pitfalls in my own projects so I can address them early and hopefully avoid them. Dad has a lot of similar DNA to me, so I try to watch and learn from him in both what to do and what not to do. Sometimes I have to laugh though as I observe. Keys were in the car with the doors unlocked in a poorly lit area. Awesome.

After Sunshine picks me up from the airport before she leaves for work, I shoot to the shop so that customer can drop off his bike. I'm dragging ass, so I'm not sure how long I'll last. I hear a bike, which is no Hawg, so that's probably the guy on his VTX. While I've got it, he wants the seat completely recovered in gray ostrich, but I tell him it'll look better if he lets us put a black border around the edge of the seat. With no border and a gray seat on silver paint, it just tends to all blend together too much. He agrees. I give him a couple calendars and a card, get my five-hundred dollar down payment, and he hops in the car with his wife to enjoy the rest of his weekend. As much as I need to do today, I've got that hollow feeling from lack of sleep and need to go recharge my batteries.

I needed that snooze, and still have time to hit the tanning bed and gym before the party. There's a hot blonde working behind the counter that looks like she's spent too much time in the bed herself. Maybe that's why she's wearing that stupid looking hat and hopes it distracts people from how leathery her skin will be in a few years. Another girl is getting ready to go tan and I ask her why she asks for seventeen minutes instead of twenty. I was hoping she may tell me something useful about the amount of time in the bed correlating to how burned she gets. My ass and upper thighs are so fucking burned already and itching like a sonofabitch. Her response is simply because it gets too hot for her. How helpful. About that time a girl with a ten-point rack walks by on her way out of the bed. The face is rough, but the perky tan rack under the wife beater looks good. My internal monologue catches the words on the way down from the brain before I ask, "So do you both work at the same strip club?" Good thing I don't drink anymore and don't actually say what I just thought, or I could have a red handprint on my face to match my red ass.

The girl behind the counter can't seem to get my bed to operate for startup. As I get dressed again for the third time to walk back out and tell her, I feel like a stripper myself as much as my clothes have come on and off in the last few minutes. Now there's another top-heavy girl in the lobby who's so kind as to offer to come look at the bed to make sure it's not working. Unnecessarily insulted I reply, "I know what a "17" looks like and an "on" button." It sounds snappy as I hear myself say it, but I'm getting a little annoyed with this. Finally it's working and I'm roasting again. I'll be glad when I never have to go to one of these again. There are definitely a lot of girls coming in and out of here concerned with their looks. If I were single I have to admit I'd consider coming here once in a while just to meet girls. Dirty said when he was on work-release from jail working at the tanning salon, he was regularly banging about three girls, and I never saw him with any girl that wasn't top-shelf in the looks department. Some had a body by Fisher and a brain by Fisher-Price, but they were always hot. I couldn't believe a guy on work-release from jail was getting laid more than me, but he had the looks and the charm and I can't fault him for making use of his strengths.

Sunshine's calling for the second time after I didn't answer the first time. I hate talking on the phone in a car, as I already wrecked one car that way, plus I just don't like to do it. I'll answer this time just in case it's important. She was hoping I was still home so I could grab different shoes since she brought heels and just realized it's an outdoor party. I tell her I'm already on the road and assure her she'll be just fine in her heels. It's a damn good thing I was born with the twig and giggle-berries as I'd make a terrible fucking girl.

That must be Kimber's place with all the cars out front. Kimber greets me with a big hug, and it reminds me of how much I really miss her since she got laid off. She always did great work and was just a treat to have around. DB welcomes me to their home as well. EA is here and the Hare brought his new ankle-biter since his wife's out of town. DM seems to be happy with his new job, and is now looking for another Hawg. Nutzack brought his wife and kid. His wife seems very happy at her new job and explains all the things better about her current employer compared to the Office. That's four of four people here that used to work at the Office that all seem happier now. I see a trend. Eventually Smooth shows up with an oversized bottle of white zinfandel. He might as well have worn a skirt and hooker boots to reflect his masculinity as he stands there drinking a glass of the feminine fuel on the rocks. We all point out the need for the ice to dilute it so it's not too strong for him.

I'm informed that KL has not only been removed from his duties over the other division he took on recently, but that he's been knocked down a level. Wow. I can't say I disagree with the decision made by the executives. The division has done terrible lately, largely I feel because of the leadership, or lack thereof. There has to be negative and positive reinforcement for people to stay motivated to do their best. It has to be embarrassing as hell for him, but maybe he'll start running the group more like a business and less like a sandbox. This doesn't do any more for my faith in the success, or even survival of the group. It's a really bad sign when the leader of your division has just been demoted, especially when there's been almost no work brought in since last December. I used to think I was just looking for a new job to see if I could find something better, but now I feel like I have to do so before I come in and find a "closed" sign on our floor one morning.

I've had a long fucking day and it's time to go. Smooth invites Sunshine and me to the Mushroom with him to meet his friends, but I decline. I just want to go home and lay in bed with Sunshine. He follows me since the Mushroom is just up the street from the cave. I can see the xenon lights of his 911 keeping close in my rearview as I shoot down 295. Usually he doesn't break 60 mph, but maybe he's hopped up from that girly wine. I'll see if he wants to keep playing as I downshift to fifth gear and punch it. I miss my 911 Turbo more than anything I've ever had and lost, but fuck I love the sound and feel of this V8 grumbling under the hood. A car gets out of my way and cuts off the car in the right lane as I aim up the 95 North ramp. What matters is that they're both out of my way and I put it to the floor around that big ramp in the sky passing three digits on the speedometer and eventually heading back downhill. I can feel my heart pounding inside my chest with adrenaline as I take a deep breath and relax my white knuckles from the steering wheel. I slow back down and eventually I see the xenon lights behind me again, so he's still moving at a good clip. We exit to JTB and I punch it again until I slow down for the 270 degree exit that provides my rush on the way home every day. I can hear just the start of a howl from the tires as I leave him behind around the exit, so I know I'm pushing the Michelins' limits, but they stick just fine. I'm tired as hell after the last couple days, but I'm wound up and intense from the drive home. This rush from intense driving is better than any drug could ever be for me.

Fri 20 Nov 09

Good deal. The conference calls and meetings at the new building are over at 4 o'clock on the nuts. This group over here seems like they have their shit together. I'm impressed with what they've already done in terms of site layout, the questions that they're asking, and their professionalism in general. I drop my proposal book off at my desk, grab my empty lunch bag, and the weekend begins.

I need to de-hair myself for pictures tomorrow, get the Anarchist operating well enough to make it to the shop, and then of course do all the things at the shop that need to be done. I suppose I'll clip myself first, or I'll put it off and have to do it in the morning. It's a pain in the ass to have to remove all my body hair, but it's either that or look like a fucking Wookie. Since I'm not sure exactly what poses might be used tomorrow, I better get everything, versus just the torso like usual.

Damn that's a big pile of hair. Between the full body tan, the year of disciplined healthy living, and now the man-scaping, this is the best I will ever look again in my life. I'll still keep the hair tamed, and I may even improve my build a little bit, but I'm not getting any younger and I don't plan on ever laying in one of those fucking tanning beds again. My ass still won't quit itching. I'll definitely need a mirror for the pics so I can make sure I'm sucking the abs in correctly. For just a small group of muscles, it sure makes a big difference when you hold the muscle differently. You have to balance the tension of the upper and lower abs, remember to tighten up the camera side of the obliques, and figure out if sucked in abs with an expanded chest looks better in the shot versus a dropped chest and contracted abs.

There'd be a lot more to bodybuilding or modeling than just the exercise. Learning to pose, control each muscle, flex it without shaking or losing focus on the other muscles, and keep a smile the whole time would be tough. Girls like the ones that model for my website or calendars have to look their best knowing that they're constantly being evaluated or picked apart every minute. I've seen potential models before, appreciated the beautiful face and incredible rack, but wondered if the ass was going to look good in a bikini. I can remember telling a girl at Bourbon Street Station one night that she looked great in jeans, but I'd need to make sure her ass wasn't going to show hail damage in a bikini before I could use her. I still laugh thinking about when I tried to get that Barbie doll from the radio station to model, and she told me she didn't think she would right then, but maybe later. I told her to be realistic and do it now or never, as she looked the best she ever would right then, and it was downhill from that point forward. I think she took it as a mean comment at first, but then realized I was exactly right. Some people might feel a little shallow for assessing someone like that, but it's no different for me to evaluate a girl's looks for a modeling gig than it is for some company to evaluate my resume for a job.

I spent years evaluating girls' looks, so at least I'm applying my skills for something both useful and entertaining. I wish I would've thought of this gimmick years ago. "Hey, ever done any modeling?" It's great to watch a beautiful girl's eyes light up when I ask that. A girl that knows the modeling game will look at me as a potential customer, proceeding with hopeful caution while looking for signs to help them decide if I'm being genuine or just a scum bag trying to get some filthy pictures of them or trying to bang them. An inexperienced girl will instantly put on her best smile and look at me like I'm her ticket out of whatever bar currently employs her. I can see through the sparkle in this kind of girl's eyes and see the fabricated images she creates of herself walking down red carpet somewhere while she rambles on about the teen pageant she won in high school. As Cat pointed out when I got sucked into that sketchy modeling agency scam in San Antonio, it's genius to prey on people's vanity.

I may not have the washboard stomach or be able to see every vein trying to burst through my skin like in college, but I have the first six-pack I've had in years, and can see pretty decent muscle separation. 208 solid pounds is a vast improvement from a year ago when I was a scrawny and fat 185 pounds and couldn't even walk around without an oxygen line in my nose. For being almost thirty-six years old, I have to admit I am very happy with how I look right now. Does that mean I'm narcissistic or just proud of my accomplishments? I don't think there's much of a difference in the trait, only the description.

Now that I'm hairless except for the half-inch left on my head, time to get this Anarchist running again. I haven't had a running bike since the ignition ate her pigs over two weeks ago. That's way too long for me not to be on two wheels. Unlike that fucking Twin Cam at the shop that became more complicated in efforts to make it simpler, this ignition is very easy to install. Three wires run up to the coil, I make the plug wires, and now I just have to get the timing close enough to get to the shop. It starts and sounds close enough for now, so I'll be able to take it over to the shop to fast-time it tomorrow. I'm off to the shop in the Goat now to work more on that Ape tank.

While that putty dries, I'll call the folks. Dad's not answering, but Mom's home. Mom's grim reaper report is absent this week, which is a nice surprise. The last few weeks have seen the death of one of Dad's good friends and the kid of another friend of his. Mom asks me what I want for Christmas, and I tell her, "nothing" as usual. I always feel guilty when she sends me stuff, since I rarely send anything. I got spoiled being a broke sick-dick in the ghetto without money for food for years, so people understood why I didn't buy gifts. I suppose I should make more of an effort to find stuff for them. I tell her I want that job in Texas, and just at that minute the Crackberry alerts me of a new email. Sure enough it's from the Company in San Antonio. The woman I knew from the Institute is apologizing for the delay and wants to do the next phone interview next week. Sweet! I let Mom go so I can reply to the email while ensuring my response is quick and error-free. All I need to do is lose a job because I misuse a word trying to multi-task.

As long as I'm sitting on my ass, I call Aunt Kat. I haven't talked to her for ages, but she was nice enough to buy one of my calendars, so I talk to her for a while. It sounds like she's been drinking, which doesn't surprise me. Dad and his siblings definitely like their booze. It may have killed Grandpa, an uncle, and three from my generation, but it still holds a place in the family lineup. She genuinely appreciates the fact that I called and wishes her kid would call more. I see her point when she says that Uncle Slim found out that her kid lost his job and just plays in the band now through myspace or facebook or some stalker site, and she didn't know it. I think it's a shitty way to communicate with people, and self-indulgent to think that people even care enough about day-to-day bullshit to look at other people's pages to see what they did that day. On the other hand I guess it's efficient. Instead of calling or emailing people about what you're doing in life, you just post the information and let them look if they want. There's no wasted time for unsolicited social updates. Sites like them could have their merit, and I probably resist more on principles like reduced perceived importance of personal communication with family and friends and the fact that it's trendy. The sites are probably a fine social outlet for people who are married and have hours to kill at home waiting for their kid to take a nap or need to eat or get a diaper changed, but I really don't have the time or desire to dick around updating some site like that. I spend way more time than I want in front of a computer already.

Sat 21 Nov 09

My stomach feels like it completely deflated and wrapped itself around my spine. I barely ate yesterday, but I'll be able to eat in a few hours. There's not enough time to go to the gym, but I can squeeze in a quick workout at the apartment's fitness center before AJ gets here. You've got to be shitting me. They changed the code for the fitness center and I have to go to the leasing office to get the new code. I'm glad they do security procedures like this and bracelets for the pool, but it sucks when it's an inconvenience to me. This is just one more example of low-life people causing me inconvenience. If no one tried to sneak in here that didn't belong here, I wouldn't need a code in the first place. Chances are there's no one working at the leasing office at 6 am, so it looks like I'll just do a quick run down to Gate and back to burn off whatever fat I can before the pictures. I just have to shave the chest now, take a quick shower, and I'll be as ready as I'll ever be.

AJ's calling to confirm the apartment number. There are never any parking spaces in the lot, so I tell him to park in front of my garage. We set up the lighting umbrella, move the dining table, and tape the brown comforter to the wall since AJ forgot the black sheet. Before we start the pictures, I tell AJ and Sunshine I'm fine with anything, but each of them needs to say what they're comfortable showing or photographing, since clothing will be minimal. AJ takes a few test shots of me to get the lighting right before we start taking the actual pictures. We'll crop out the head and everything low enough to be obscene for the final product, but right now we just want to get the right shots. I set up Sunshine's mirror so I can see that I'm sucking my abs in properly and looking my best. I try a few poses on my guitar amp in the position of Rodin's *The Thinker*. I remember seeing a shot of Stallone doing that pose years ago, and thought it was rather appropriate considering my excessive mental commotion.

Next we do shots of me standing behind Sunshine with my hands covering the lights and lips. I'm a little surprised I convinced her to do these shots considering her perception of her looks. I knew as soon as she told me she estimated herself a five on a ten scale, that she had a warped self-image. It would seem that because her older sister was very attractive growing up, Sunshine always felt like second place. She's a beautiful girl and has improved her physique even more since she started working out seriously. Unlike most girls whose breasts shrink when they work out, hers actually got bigger. It's genetic as her sister and cousin said the same thing. I try to instill positive self-image into her, and I'm glad to see she's at least comfortable enough with how she looks to agree to these photos.

These should come out looking good. We're facing each other and I'm holding her forward leg up. They're not pictures we'll put in Christmas cards, as if I'd send out Christmas cards anyway. They'll be some nice pictures for the bedroom only, and let me take down that awful water color painting she has over the bed right now. It's time for the pictures of just her. We move the dining room table back in front of the dark background, put in the extra leaves, and have her arch over some black sweatshirts on the surface. Seeing her balance on one ass check and her head with her back arched as far as she can and her elbows acting like training wheels looks horribly uncomfortable, but very sexy. I'll look forward to seeing how these come out once AJ gets them on his website so we can take a look.

AJ needs to run errands, Sunshine had to get to work, and I have to meet Obi-Wan at the shop so he can drop off his bike. I'm pulling in a few minutes late, he's waiting by his bike, and his wife is in the Jeep. I'm famished so I invite them to breakfast. The food tastes good, but I eat way too much after a week of fasting and feel like shit now. As usual I go from one extreme to the other and hopefully eventually find some balance in the middle. Between the fact that I'm dragging ass and feel awful now, I suppose I'll take a quick snooze.

Damn, that was over a one-hour nap. I need to get my lazy ass to the shop. The Anarchist makes it to the shop, so now I can fast-time it properly. I finally find the clear timing hole plug so I can check timing without spraying oil everywhere. Even after using a paint marker on the TDC mark, I still can't find that fucking timing mark through the clear plug. Fuck it, I'll take it out and see if that helps. Sure as shit, there's the mark and my timing by ear was right on the gnat's ass. I button up everything and decide I might as well switch out the handlebar risers while I've got time. Now I should be able to ride a little more comfortably. The bars are now exactly where they were when I bought the damn thing. I changed bars three times only to end up where I started. That's efficiency at its finest. Should I even try the mid-controls or just leave the damn thing alone now? I wonder if Steven ever started on my new front wheel. He hasn't returned my calls recently, but hopefully everything's okay and my wheel is in progress. I can't help but notice I'm in a pretty damn good mood right now. A big part of that is because I have my bike running again, and I've noticed in the past the strong correlation between the operational condition of my vehicles and my mood. The pictures went well too, I got to see Obi-Wan, and overall life is good.

I'd like to take the bike out tonight, but I'll be nice and give AJ a ride out to the beach. We get to Sundog and meet Tracer and Ms. Texas. I've been disciplined for a while and think I'll take this week to slack off before I get back to the routine. After plowing through a burger and fries, I add apple crisp and ice cream to the pile in my stomach. I order some crab-stuffed shrimp so it's here when Sunshine gets here, and end up eating half of that too. I don't feel so sweet. Yuck. I could vomit right now. I've only thrown up from eating too much once before. Jagette and I went to Golden Coral and I had five full plates of food including one salad plate, one plate full of desserts, and three heaping plates of everything between. I had to go home and gag myself that night, and I feel like I might do that tonight. Let's get the hell out of here.

Before I get in the car, I better launch this gut bomb. Years of inducing vomit by finger-banging my tonsils after too much booze comes in handy at times like this. Seafood tastes pretty nasty coming back up. I'm through Sunshine's leftovers now and I can taste the returning dessert. Five full loads up the throat later I have puke all over my boots, and just threw up forty wasted dollars worth of dinner, but at least I feel better. Sometimes I wish I would've learned a little moderation at some point in life.

We all meet at the Twisted Rock or whatever the hell they call this place now. It used to be a great time on Thursdays when it was the Twisted Sister. They had dollar Yuengling drafts and a lot of hot young girls who seemed a lot more personable than the coke whores at the Ritz. We always had a good time there; even the night that asshole in suspenders puked on the floor and it splattered my foot. He apologized and there was really no point in getting pissy with someone that drunk, plus it's not like I didn't use to behave as bad or worse. Later that night some girl walked by with toilet paper stuck to her shoe, which was great for an opener. I acted helpful by pointing it out, made a joke about it to show humor, and reassured her I didn't think she was an idiot after she embarrassed herself. J3 was a little embarrassed but appreciated the entertainment. After she turned away from the bar with her hands full of drinks and a purse, she thanked me again. Not only did she seem like a nice girl with a good sense of humor, but she also didn't have a free hand to slap me. I said, "Wait, you have some on your ass too," and blatantly grabbed a full palm of her ass while smiling at her. She looked back, looked up at me, smiled, and said, "Very nice." J3 laughed again as if he felt guilty about it, as he's usually not quite so forward. I assured him I wouldn't have done it if I didn't know she'd think it was funny. Later that night at the Atlantic club she came up to me drunk and smiling and babbled, "Hey, you! You're the guy that grabbed my ass! I told all my friends about you!" Bond, James Bond.

There was a bike and car show here earlier today, and there's still quite a few wheeled creations out in the parking lot. Several chopped, black Sporties are out here, some ape hanger bars on a couple big twins, and even an old BSA. Tracer is fascinated by the old Honda sitting there. I tell him I can understand why he's intrigued by the technology of the modern ones, but old Honda's like that were disposable pieces of shit that people drove around the farm until they died and got thrown into a grove. They weren't even worth fixing. To each their own, but I did point out that the one chopper with a Japanese engine wouldn't start and the owner was pushing it up and down the parking lot trying to get it to fire. I ask Tracer if he thinks the guy is appreciating that Japanese reliability right now.

The lead singer of the Kings of Hell stops by to talk to Tracer, since they've grown to know each other pretty well over time. He seems like a decent guy and shares the same interests as I do in terms of bikes, music, and tattoos. This is a crowd to which I feel a little more connection because of those interests. About that time the two guys with him start attempting English slurred by an afternoon of drinking and start to annoy me a little. I'm glad they like my shirt with the big middle finger on it, but I'd prefer they not stand this close laughing about it.

The girls went inside earlier since both of them had to piss. Sunshine comes running out because some dirt bag sat next to them, and Ms. Texas had to grab him by the shirt and push him out of the booth. As we all walk inside, it's obvious they really did change this place's layout. The bar is still on the right and the booths are still on the left, but that's about it. Ms. Texas is already a little tipsy and continues to point at the guy that sat with them, as Tracer and I tell her to quit pointing already. I like bikes and people who are into bikes, but the Kings run tight with the local biker gang, so it's best to mind your own business at their shows.

With the drunks invading my personal space outside and now Ms. Texas chirping and pointing at the guy who was harassing them, I'm already annoyed by the crowd. My seat is facing away from the stage, and even when I turn around, I can't see because everyone's standing right there. Sunshine asks if I'll dance with her, and I tell her, "no." I'm trying to absorb and deal with the crowd as it is, and unfortunately right now she's another variable I'm not able to process amidst the others. I'm getting more annoyed. Sunshine puts a hand on my arm, and I find myself even annoyed by her simple gesture of affection. She pinches me and I reactively ram my knuckles into the edge of the table. Now I'm pissed, and it's showing more by what I'm not saying than what I am saying. I look at her and she knows I'm pissed and is just looking down and upset. I feel like complete shit now. She's such a sweet girl and wants nothing more than to enjoy life with me. Here I am acting like an asshole because I spent my whole life drunk and can't adjust to sober social interaction, and now I've made her upset. I apologize and explain that I'm not upset at her, but an apology is like an abortion; they're just desperate attempts at a clear conscience after you've fucked someone. How do I explain the fucked up mess that goes on in my head sometimes when I don't even understand it?

I try to relax and enjoy the show and eventually we get up and walk closer to the crowd so we can see. Cartmanini shows up and tells me he had to call to find me because there was too much white trash in here to pick me out of the crowd. He does come up with some good one-liners, but we'll see how far that gets him in this crowd with his fancy collared shirt and dress pants. It's no worse than Tracer in the middle of the bikers with his sport coat and T-shirt carried over from Miami Vice popularity. Between the tattoos, unshaven face, and black T-shirt, I can definitely blend into this crowd easier than the others in our party.

The moshers in the pit knock a monitor off the stage, and the singer even tells the crowd to cool it. Is that asshole in suspenders and a Mohawk the same one that puked on me when this was still Twisted Sister? He's swinging his slutty girlfriend around and she bumps into a few guys knocking a bottle of Budweiser on the ground, which shatters at our feet. As I look up from the broken bottle I see some jackass on the bar taking pictures while the bouncer tries talking him down. Instead of climbing down, the guy jumps and lands on some guy just standing there watching the show. The guy buckles, and I think it might be AJ, but fortunately it's not. I'm just standing behind Sunshine trying to make a barrier with my arms between her and whatever obstacles are coming near us. Ms. Texas already tried dancing in the mosh pit with a glass of wine, which she's now wearing. We step back to a table and hang out there for a few minutes before just leaving. I usually enjoy this band, but the crowd tonight that's been drinking since noon is more than I can handle in my new sober state.

I drop off AJ at his place and aim home where Sunshine is already waiting. Both of us are tired, and after a somewhat unpleasant evening, we crash. A few hours ago I was appreciating how good of a mood I was enjoying. I need to learn how to identify problem areas, and the obvious problem is that crowd at the bar and how I deal with it. The crowd never used to bother me when I drank, but it sure as hell does now. It's a problem I'm going to have to overcome. Nights like this make me feel bad for Sunshine. She spent six years with a guy that didn't make her happy. Now she has a guy that can't just go have a few drinks, have fun, and dance with her. She's such a good person and times like this make me feel like I just don't deserve her. If she found a guy that could be everything she wants and told me she had to leave me for that imaginary Prince Charming, I'd be perfectly okay with it. Of course it would sting at first, but I'd find comfort if I knew she was truly happy and had found something better. Maybe some day I'll be able to enjoy a few drinks with her and even dance with her and be more of what she deserves, but maybe she will end up finding someone else that can first. I'm not sure I'll ever be able to go relax and have a few drinks occasionally. I'm not sure I really want to ever do it again. I am sure that I can't afford to slip back down that slope and get anywhere close to that guardrail that's brought me so much angst over the years, or neither of us are going to be happy.

Chapter 8

Holidays My Way

Thu 26 Nov 09

It's cold out, but driving the Anarchist out to the beach will allow for significantly reduced parking-related stress. I wish I would've worn the skull mask. Every so often I'll where less because of how it will look or the convenience, and I usually end up regretting it. My ears feel like they're frostbitten since the beanie won't stay down over them at these speeds. Cold or not it sure feels good to have this bike running again. As we park it, a few people come over to check out my handiwork.

I build the stuff I want how I want it to look, but it's always a nice compliment when someone comes up to admire my craft.

It still surprises me a little bit to see all these people out here on Thanksgiving morning drinking Bloody Mary's in front of Pete's. I don't think I've actually ever been in the bar itself except for a couple years ago when I came to this with Tracer. It's a smoke-filled pool hall without much eye candy, so I never had much reason to go into the place. Has it actually been three years ago that I was out here with Tracer that time when we first ran into Ms. Texas at Sundog? Last year I was in Colorado with everyone. Four years ago is when I went down to Cousin Reno's for Thanksgiving, and finally had to leave after listening to his warden nag at him past my limit. Three years ago would've been the year I boycotted holidays. I thankfully declined Cousin Reno's offer for Thanksgiving dinner that year and just went to the shop. I always enjoy seeing Reno, and used to enjoy going down to visit, but that nagging from the year before was too much. At that point holidays went from a fun time to get together with family and friends to obligation. It was a few days away from work to do what I wanted, and I just liked the idea of going to the shop and working. It doesn't mean I don't like holidays, it doesn't mean that I don't like Reno and his warden, it just means that year I wanted to take a step back from holidays and enjoy my time off at the shop.

There aren't near as many hotties out today as there should be, but I suppose most of the Ritz and Brix patrons are still doing the walk of shame, finding a ride home, or sleeping off a hangover. People of all ages from rug rats to the retired wealthy of Ponte Vedra are all here. Many people brought their dogs since it's primarily an outdoor event, even though some of the bars are getting pissy about people walking outside with drinks. I'm not sure what the official policy is, but nobody seems to care that I'm drinking water outside, so I don't concern myself with the issue. Ms. Texas is using intoxicated sign language again, and as her hands wave everywhere, one of them spills my water. Minutes later her flailing hand is holding a Bloody Mary, which ends up mostly on Tracer's motorcycle jacket and partially on Sunshine's white coat and white cashmere scarf. I can see Tracer's annoyed, and he comments that it'll be a few minutes before he's not annoyed, which is another characteristic we share. That makes it even more funny only minutes later when he's turning his wrist to check his watch and pours his Bloody Mary on the ground, though far enough from the coats to avoid further damage. Speaking of annoyed, I've had about enough of this crowd. Sunshine can read my mind and asks if I'm ready to go. We walk through the crowd, watch a few people point and laugh at my crude "choking hazard" shirt, fire up the bike, and ride back to the cave.

The turkey is done way earlier than Sunshine expected, but since she has to get everything else ready, I've got a little time to shoot over to the shop and finish the primer on the Ape tank. A little putty, a little primer, a little sanding, and I'm still done in plenty of time to get home and help get dinner ready. This is a lot of food for two people, but she enjoys cooking and I don't mind leftovers, so it works out well for both of us. The turkey isn't even close to dry, and it's been sitting here for a long time. The chef tells me it's because she soaked it in the brine, which also explains why it's a little salty. This is a damn good turkey. I can't help but pick at it while I carve it on the board and end up with a huge platter of segregated meat. I guess we really don't have to separate the light from the dark meat, but it's a force of habit from the days in the restaurant.

We watch some Vince and Reese Christmas movie about a couple that ignores the holidays so they can avoid family and spend the time vacationing together. Eventually in true holiday movie form the couple realizes that they do enjoy family, Reese decides she wants a brat, and Vince chooses to give on having a kid so as not to lose Reese. I'm glad Sunshine and I are able to speak honestly about trying to figure out what lies ahead for what we want out of life in terms of each other, but it's still sometimes a little awkward watching movies where the same discussions occur that mimic our thoughts. As I lay on her lap, I can feel a few tears dripping down on my head. I taste for the salt check and confirm they're tears. I ask if the conversations of this movie couple are generating thoughts in her head about our own screenplay. She explains that she wishes her family would've come to visit. When she found out her dad changed plans and wasn't going to come here for Thanksgiving, I told her I'd completely understand if she wanted to go home for Thanksgiving instead of spending it here with me. Family is family and it's poor practice to put yourself between a significant other and anything that was there before you. She'd chosen to stay, but that doesn't mean she doesn't miss her family on a holiday.

I'm not going to puke like the other night at Sundog, but I'm on the brink. She's putting everything in Fatman-sized Tupperware containers and I'm cleaning dishes before I cram them into the dishwasher. These fancy pans of hers are heavy and expensive, but they cook well and are easily cleaned. They're even higher quality than my kitchen in a box I bought a couple years ago at Target, though one of her pans probably cost five times what my whole kitchen in a box cost. As I start to wash the gravy pot, it reminds me of the last time I probably washed gravy out of a pot back at the We-3 when I was in high school. Every Sunday and holiday we had gravy, it always stuck to the pot, and I usually had to scrub like hell to get it out. By that point in the day the hot water was warm at best, which made the task even tougher. $2.85 per hour and all the food I could eat was worth it at the time though. As kids our family would spend holidays at an aunt's and uncle's house, Grandpa's and Grandma's house, or at Mom's and Dad's house with company. The beginning of my job at We-3 also began the end of my childhood appreciation for holidays. Most of my high school Thanksgivings were spent working at the store. In college I always came home for the holidays or went back home with Sambo and his posse to go hunting with them. Once I left home though, I left holidays behind. I always figured holidays were time to spend with my family, and since I wasn't around them, I didn't have much use for holidays. They became another day off from work I could drink away. I can remember Flanman insisting that Fatman and I go with him to get the stuff to make Thanksgiving dinner one year after a particularly drunk night, and I'm glad we did. I can also remember the ex being at her parents for holidays while Fatman and I drove around looking for strip bars that were open. Like many things, holidays are different things to different people. They're a day for people to do what they want, whether it's stuffing dollars in a g-string, putting a wrecked bike back together, or reaching up a cold turkey's ass to replace its guts with bread and vegetables for a feast.

Now that the domestic chores are done and I've tagged to the dishwasher, it's time to let the digestive juices do their work in front of another movie. It's called "Funny People," but it's far from funny. A comedian is going to die of leukemia, so it's technically about funny people although the title is arguably misleading. It's not going to make me laugh, but I do find it interesting how the main character deals with knowing he's going to die, considering I had to come to grips with similar thoughts not long ago. Sunshine's already out cold or I'd give her shit about picking yet another depressing movie like that Ben Button movie. Besides the turkey dinner for three I ate, I almost forgot it was Thanksgiving. This year I'm thankful for everything good in this little fucked up cartoon world in which I live. Maybe thankful isn't the best word, because I'm not really thanking anyone for anything. I'm not thanking Mom and Dad for having me, I'm not thanking my boss for my job, and I'm not thanking the doctors for saving my ass. I'm just appreciating everything I enjoy in life. It's not just the things I enjoy, but I also appreciate how happy my sisters and parents are right now, and the cute girl passed out on the couch next to me. Had I gone any further down the gutter a few years ago, I'd probably be lying next to some crack whore passed out right now, but I'm thankful the only chemical in excess in this girl's system is tryptophan.

Fri 27 Nov 09

The Ape tank is painted and the carbon fiber fenders have a fresh coat of matte clear on them. Tracer and Ms. Texas are already at Land Shark and J3 and his girl are on their way. Dammit, my neoprene skull mask is still in Sunshine's Curve from yesterday. It's too damn cold not to wear something on my face and ears. Here's my old Jagermeister bandana I got at one of the Daytona bike events from Timia, one of the Jager girls. It's too bad it rained the day she invited AJ and me do go down and meet the models for her calendar she produced as a scholarship gig for local talent. I recognized her at the Ritz a year later, and then never heard from her again. I never touched her, but she's still another pretty ghost from the past.

Dammit, I need gas too. I'm bundled up in the leather coat, YCC beanie, Jager bandana over the face, and sport bike gloves on the way down JTB to the beach. Fuck it's cold out, but it always feels good to be on two wheels. I should've worn my sweatshirt under the leather coat too. Obviously I didn't learn yesterday why I should dress with more clothes rather than less when out in the elements. Idiot, gah!

I'm surprised my bike is the first in the parking lot tonight. There were quite a few old bobbers last week at the Twisted Rock or whatever it's called. Tracer, J3, and their girls are here already, but the Kings haven't started playing yet. Even Scot from the Office is here hanging out with some beach girls. He can't contemplate why I would ride the bike in cold weather or why I'd have my Spyderco in my pocket. I carry it in the Office; I'm definitely carrying it in a biker bar. The band is firing up and I'm enjoying tonight a lot more than last week. Sunshine shows up in her preppy white sweater and jeans. She forgot to take a black shirt with her when she left for work, but it's cold in the bar so she's covering up with my leather coat soon anyway.

Tracer explains the whole retro '50's culture of this little group from the hair to the music to the cars, and states that the '50's are a dead era. I point out to him that his standard Miami Vice garb is from the '80's, which are also passed. Tracer's a sharp guy, and I think he gets both irritated and somewhat impressed when I can turn something back on him. He does it to me too. I notice he's not wearing his sport jacket tonight, possibly a result of the text I sent him this afternoon. I'd asked him to wear a black T-shirt and jeans and get some tattoos so he blends in versus wearing a suit to a biker bar like he always does. I pointed out that it was just like the dirt bag coming into Bonefish dressed like a slob among well-dressed people trying to be different and hungry for attention. He fucks with me plenty, so I always enjoy a chance to return the favor.

Tracer and Ms. Texas are out bouncing around on the dance floor. It's funny to watch him out there partying with tattooed bikers. Sunshine asks me to go out and dance with her when the Kings start playing Social Distortion. I decline and feel a little bad thinking back to last week. However, I am having a good time enjoying the company and the music, and I'm not going to get greedy. This is good. I'm able to be here at a bar, not drinking, having a good time with friends. I'm not sure if I'll ever be able to or have the desire to dance sober, but one step at a time.

Sat 28 Nov 09

Today's been a great day at YCC. The Ape is all back together except for this stubborn rear fender. Carbon fiber is like anything else with aging characteristics in that it looks great when it's new, and ragged out shortly after. The matte clear took to the front fender fine, but this rear piece keeps getting fish eyes on me. I've sanded it down for the third time now and one more coat will do it. All I'll have to do is bolt that on next time I'm here and I'll have two complete bikes again. I do need to remember to order that new gas line though. It's looking a little worn and I have to order the decals for the red underbelly anyway. The Goat has a new alternator and lower radiator hose, so that should be good to go for our trip south tomorrow.

What the hell is that noise outside? Fuck, I forgot my Glock at home today. It sounds like just thunder. I hate it when I end up here late at night and forget a gun. I hope I never have to use it, but I'd rather have it and not need it than vice versa. If it weren't for having a gun, I would've been terrified living over here for those years. There's a comfort that comes with knowing you have a fighting chance, just in case. I guess for now I'll hang onto the framing hammer, get one more coat of clear on that rear fender, and then get out of the ghetto for tonight.

Sun 29 Nov 09

I usually get up at 5:30 am anyway, so this is no big deal for me. It looks like Sunshine doesn't feel like getting up at this time on the first Sunday she's had free in weeks though. Let me flip on the light to help ease her waking. I'm not being a dick. I'm just being helpful. Alright, maybe there's just a little schadenfreude at work. Even though it's early for her, she bounces out of bed smiling as usual.

It's a little past 6 am, but we should still be in Deltona by 8 o'clock as planned. Early Sunday morning is a nice time for a drive. There's minimal traffic, and it's light enough to see the FHP hiding up the road in the median in time to slow down to the generally safe 10 mph over the speed limit. The bad thing about early Sunday mornings is the fucking rock stations are doing community service programs. It has to be some kind of do-gooder requirement for the stations. Sunshine points out that most people listening to rock will be asleep at this time on a Sunday, which is a valid point, but it still pisses me off. After hearing "Ball and Chain" at the Kings show Friday, I've got an itch for some Social Distortion. *Live at the Roxy* will be providing some soothing Sunday tunes for the drive down.

I guess we are about twenty minutes early, as everyone's just getting ready at Cousin Reno's place. We're packing up his Pilot and on our way to Sea World. I ask him what's wrong with the Uncle Rico van sitting in his driveway, as I can see wires hanging out of the ceiling right next to his double secret compartment stapled shut for his Glock, which is the identical .40 cal to mine. He'd removed the antenna off the top of the van, and the wires were the result of that unfinished task. He'd also taken the stereo and the blue LED speakers out of it and given them to his oldest boy for his car.

Eighty bucks for each of us even with Reno's AAA insurance card? Are they going to kiss me first or just fuck me? Oh well, we came this far and it should be a good time. It's also a good idea to charge more and keep the trash out. Sadly these days, economic restrictions are about the only way to do that. Money doesn't beget class or vice versa, but it's the only metric short of subjective judgment available. It's been too long since I had breakfast though, and I see a bakery. I could eat enough to get sick here, but I'll just have one cherry Danish and get Sunshine a blueberry muffin. I'm sure she'll only eat about half of it and I'll end up eating the rest of it anyway. Reno and Sunshine both look up at the Manta as we walk by it. Not only is it a rollercoaster, but you hang down from it instead of sitting in it. Fuck that. I didn't deal well with that little Space Mountain ride at Disney, and that wasn't anything like this.

Reno's kid wants to see the cat and dog show, since he missed it last time they came here. The young girls doing the show may not be Oscar nominees with their acting, but their training is impressive. The vicious ditch tigers and ball-lickers are doing some pretty cool tricks. It's one thing to teach a dog how to sit or lay down, but how the hell do they even communicate to the dogs to go knock a phone off the hook, bark, pick up flowers, and bring them back down? The animals may not cooperate 100%, but pretty damn well overall. I notice the trainers feeding a lot of treats to them, which I'm sure is an integral part to the training. I could compare it to the training of a younger me when people would buy me a drink to act like a circus monkey, but that would be degrading to the monkey. Unfortunately I bought most of my own drinks, and those of many people around me, so I was sort of a not-for-profit train wreck.

You can't have an animal park in Florida without having flamingos. I send a picture of them to Organisis, as it seems she'd accidentally called them penguins when Mom and Dad took us to the Minneapolis zoo years ago. I think that was the summer before I left for college as kind of a last family vacation with all of us kids at home before we started going our separate ways. We went to that Renaissance festival after the zoo. I still wish I would've bought the executioner's axe they had for sale at the blacksmith shop. It's not like I needed it, but it would've been cool to have. I figured it was one of those things I could make myself some day and passed on it. Organisis is texting back denying my accusation of bird confusion, but I still think it was her.

Stingrays, an octopus, and seahorses are all residents here. Jellyfish look so bizarre like an empty sac with tentacles floating in the water. How the hell do they even function? I don't see a brain or anything. It's like seeing a clear Plexiglas computer tower with nothing inside and wondering how the hell it's producing activities on the monitor. There are a couple manatees in desperate need of a personal trainer. They look even bigger than the ones we saw at DeLeon Springs.

A mime greets patrons at the entrance to the next show. We watch and laugh as he mimics people entering. He struts behind the girl walking with her chest out to show off the all-too-obvious aftermarket rack and leads people all the way to the exit just to fuck with them. Most of the people never realize they're being mocked. Now that I think about it, he could've been walking behind our little group making fun of one of us, and I'd never have known it. That prick. I guess as many times as I've made a joke out of myself, I shouldn't be mad if someone else does it. Several trainers/actors dressed like pirates run around the large ship set interacting with an otter, two sea lions, and a walrus. Damn that walrus is fat. The people working here sure seem to enjoy their jobs. Novel concept.

We've been watching animals eat fish all day, and when in Rome… This is a unique restaurant. All the tables are surrounding a giant shark tank. I wonder how mini-Jaws feels about me eating his cousin. The food is okay, but it's a place where you pay for the ambiance, not the food. I tell Reno and the warden I'll pick up their lunch and to consider it their Christmas present. A hundred and twenty bucks for lunch? Holy shit. They split an entrée, and so did Sunshine and me. That was some expensive ambiance, but it's not like I didn't used to blow that on any given night at the bars. Of course mistakes of the past don't justify mistakes in the present either.

The next show is the dolphins. This is more serious ballet than the light-hearted skits in the last couple shows. Fancy costumes, trapeze and bungee cord acts, and the music in the background are interlaced with dolphin tricks. The part that amazes me is how the performers ride on the dolphins noses. I can see the dolphins swimming side by side under water through the glass, and the performer has a foot on each dolphin's nose. All you see on the top of the water is this torso being pushed quickly through the water with arms spread wide. Besides the training of the dolphin necessary for that, the training and balance required by the performer has to be extensive too. The performers seem incredibly happy doing their job, though a couple of them should have shed a little weight before cramming into the wet suits. There's an apparent passion for what they do. I wonder if it's all an act, and they get up in the morning saying, "It's off to another fucking day of playing with dolphins."

I'm trying to take pictures of the dolphins as they do their tricks, but why am I doing this? Instead of watching it really happen in front of me, I'm watching it through the screen on my Crackberry. I might email the pictures to Mom and the girls, but otherwise I may never look at them again. If I were going to watch it through a screen, I might as well be sitting on my ass in front of a TV at home. I'm putting the Crackberry away and enjoying this show the way it's supposed to be enjoyed. Between the sheer enjoyment of the performers and the talent of both them and the animals, this is a hell of a show. I find myself envious of not only the performers who truly enjoy their job with a passion I've only enjoyed with bikes, but of the dolphins. I can't even fathom the simplicity of their life. Everything is easier for them as they swim effortlessly through the water waiting for the next handful of fish. There are no worries of material possessions, careers, food, care, or social dynamics. On the other hand, they'll probably never know the thrill of accomplishment or the agony of defeat. They lead a very monotone life, but again as Mr. Crowley pointed out years ago, you can't enjoy the real high highs without enduring the real low lows.

Sunshine and Reno look up at the Kraken, another roller coaster, and decide they want to ride it. Like a sober Cliff Clavin, I remind them that the Kraken was the mythological sea monster that Perseus killed with the head of Medusa in "Clash of the Titans." The fact that I always enjoyed mythology has zero bearing as to weather or not I'd enjoy this ride. In fact it seems like I got scared watching the movie in theaters years ago when the goons captured Pegasus. However, parks like this are going to make sure they're safe, and no one's ever been hurt on this ride. Fuck it, I'm going to ride it too. I can survive heart surgery and whipping through the mountains hanging sideways off of the Ape, and I should have no problem doing this ride. As I get ready to board, I look at Reno and Sunshine and repeat John Candy from "Vacation" by saying in a full-cheeked voice, "I have to warn you, Rusty. I had a bad experience on a ride like this once."

I have the edge seat with Sunshine next to me and Reno behind me. The harness feels a little tight if I try to take a deep breath, but as long as it holds me in place, I'm content. I can do this. Nothing is going to go wrong. All I have to do is stay calm, sit back, and watch the ride. Who knows? It might be fun. We're getting higher, and it looks like we should be dropping pretty soon to the section right over the water. Don't grip the harness handles so hard. Relax. Here comes the drop and holy shit this is steep. Oh fuck this doesn't feel right. It looks like we're going to drive right into the fucking ground. Oh, shit! I have to close my eyes. Mother fuck, here we go. I don't see it, but I sure fucking feel that we just took a sharp turn from straight down to straight ahead, and I open my eyes again. Shit, we're going straight back up and going to go upside down. My eyes close again. Every time I even try to open my eyes, there's another corkscrew or 90 degree turn coming up and I can't help but close them again. I'm not nauseous and I don't feel like I'm going to get sick or anything. I don't know if it's because I'm an engineer familiar with how physics work or what, but mentally I just can't handle seeing those hard turns coming up. Everything I've read and learned is that motion is fine until a sudden force is applied before all hell breaks loose, and that's what each turn feels like. Why the fuck do people do this for fun?

Finally I open my eyes and see the landing pad instead of another turn that's going to jar my brain loose again. Mother fuck I didn't like that. As I try to climb out of the thing, my legs aren't yet willing to cooperate and feel like complete Jell-O. My forearms are killing from the kung-fu grip I had on the handles the whole ride. Sunshine looks at me and tells me I look even paler than when I was in the hospital. I feel mentally thrashed, rode hard, and put up wet. The ride, much like the movie that featured its namesake years ago, has psychologically beaten me. Sunshine expresses her utter confusion with how I think nothing of driving a bike or car at well over three digits, but am so bothered by a roller coaster. I explain to her the main difference is that I'm driving the bike or car. It's not logical to feel safer in self-controlled risk versus uncontrolled safety, but it's a quirk of mine I've relearned and have to accept. I don't like things out of my control. Period.

Once I get some color back in my skin, we go see more sea lions and birds. Sunshine buys some fish to feed to the animals. It's interesting to watch their little community. There's one sea lion up front that gets the most fish because he's large, up front, barking the most, and displays his tricks like holding up a flipper. I can relate that one to a very successful person that worked hard to get to a high position. Some could say that lion is closer to the whore on the street who sacrifices pride for reward. That raises the question as to whether there's really a difference between the whore and the successful hard worker. Both do what's necessary within their abilities to get what they need and want. There is another sea lion laying back in the water that doesn't look capable of crawling up the rock. It's barking just as loud as the one in front, but I don't think it can do tricks. Because he is making efforts within his ability and still barking, people throw him quite a few fish. It reminds me of the blue collar working person who didn't have the means to pursue further education, but works hard with what he or she has to earn a respectable living. Next to that sea lion is another who's just laying there. No one knows if it's lazy, already full, or can't do more than it is.

Sunshine feels sorry for the inactive one and throws a fish to it. This particular sea lion could be equivalent to someone disabled, homeless, or even just happy with what they have and letting the others who need fish more sit up front. Unfortunately this one misses the fish, and one of the scrawny white birds on the rocks next to the sea lions eats it first. Most of the birds are standing right up front by the sea lions, but aren't doing any tricks, making any noise, or doing anything but trying to get free fish for no effort. They steal from both the sea lion working for his fish, and from the helpless one in the back who probably needs it more. These birds to me represent the expendable members of society. They purposely contribute nothing to this portion of the park because they know they can get enough to survive by leeching off the sea lions. They steal from both those who have and those who need with no guilt or remorse. How could this be corrected? What if no one threw fish near the birds? Would they eventually learn to earn fish, or just steal more from the sea lions? At what point would the fish become limited enough before the hard working sea lions grew tired of supporting the expendables, and start acting to prevent what's happening? I wonder the same for our own society. I look up as we're walking away and see the Kraken peeking out over the trees and taunting me over my mental defeat.

We're sitting in our seats ready to see Shamu the Killer Whale. I'm sure there have been multiple creatures by the same name over the years. Every famous animal is replaced as the old ones die from the Georgia bulldog to the Ultimate Warrior, and I'm sure Shamu is no different. Reno's youngest loin trophy and his momma are sitting down in the splash section per the youngster's request. The first performer comes out, and she is built much better for a wet suit than the main character in the dolphin show. The black and white wet suit is a creative match to a killer whale's natural pattern. Huge screens behind her show her magnified so the crowd can see her. Here comes the killer whale. Damn that thing's big. It's amazing to see that huge animal jumping out of the water. Other performers in black and white wet suits appear. There are more videos of inspiration urging the crowd to follow dreams and save the earth. Normally I don't like to be told how to think when I just want to be entertained, but this is tolerable. Soon there are two whales, which are then replaced by the actual Shamu. That thing makes the others look like minnows. The most incredible part is watching the guy stand on Shamu's nose as the whale comes straight and completely out of the water. That guy must be thirty feet in the air! I'm impressed. These people are even more passionate about their job than anyone else I've seen today. I notice none of them look more than thirty, so it must be a short career for them. They find their passion and enjoy it every day they can until it's over. At their young age they've figured out what most people never do in a whole lifetime.

Thu 03 Dec 09

I needed that nap considering I'd been up since 2:30 am and have been scrambling all day. Soon after I started dating Sunshine, she asked if I'd go to "Nutcracker" with her. Mabel had asked me the same thing my second year at college, and my response had been, "Isn't that a fucking opera or some shit?" She told me it was a ballet, as if that was supposed to make it more appealing. I told her, "No fucking way." However, when Sunshine asked me if I'd go with her, I told her I would go someday with her. Last year I got a pass on that commitment by having heart surgery. It was a lot of pain to get out of a ballet, but well worth it. This year when she brought it up, I told her I'd seen an ad for the Trans-Siberian Orchestra and suggested that as a compromise. I'd heard commercials for them in San Antonio every year, but was always too busy drinking to check it out. Tonight I'll get to see them, she'll get to enjoy a holiday cultural event with me, and I don't have to go to a dance event that doesn't involve dollars and chrome poles.

These seats are straight up the left of the stage and close, though they won't provide a direct view of the performers. We should still be able to see fine. When I came here to see Tool and Disturbed, I wore jeans, biker boots, and a black T-shirt. Tonight I'm seeing an orchestra and wearing dress slacks, a white collared shirt, a black sport coat, and similar black boots. Dammit. I notice I didn't have time to polish the boots and there's still residue from my recycled apple crisp dessert and stuffed shrimp from when I vomited outside Sundog a while back. I'd like to think I'll find time to polish these things soon, but realistically I'll be lucky if I can remember to get them polished in the airport on my next trip.

The band is starting to enter the stage as the lights dim. The guys are all dressed like orchestra conductors without ties, and the girls are all wearing flattering black dresses. The male singers have shaved heads, and the other guys have long hair straight off of a heavy metal stage from the '80's. All the girls have long hair ranging in shades from jet black to beach blonde. I see a bassist and two Les Paul guitars, likely running through Marshall stacks in the back. There's a drum set, two keyboards, a string section, and a girl with a wild-looking violin. Seeing that reminds me of Mark Wood, the voodoo violinist, from years ago. It's been a long day, and I'm having a hard time forgetting about it. The new Rammstein cd blasting in my office was about the only thing keeping me sane today at the Office. Even sitting here I feel a little on edge about this huge proposal, and little things like Sunshine resting her warm hand on my knee bothers me a little bit when it shouldn't. I tell her it's warm, pick it up and put both her hand and my hand on her leg instead. There's no point in being uncomfortable when there's a good compromise. Alright, take a deep breath, relax, forget about the stress, and just sit back and enjoy the show.

It's bizarre to see these guys in coats and tails head-banging with their Dave Mustaine hair and Les Pauls cranking. Even more wild is watching the brunette's dark hair flop back and forth as she thrashes that violin. Traditional Christmas songs start with soft tones from the keyboards, and are quickly joined by pounding drums and screaming guitars while sparks and flames occasionally burst in the background. It's great to here a song paying tribute to the U.S. soldiers that begins with Metallica's "Don't Tread on Me." Now that I think about it, these guys were possibly inspiration for Metallica's *S&M (Symphony and Metallica)* cd. They tell a Christmas story in between songs. In the first year I've felt like the politically correct world has killed Christmas with its great trees and holiday parties, it's refreshing to hear someone putting on a Christmas show and telling a Christmas story. The Trans-Siberian Orchestra isn't worried about offending any non-Christians in the crowd or afraid of a lawsuit by its employees. This group is simply exercising their American right to celebrate their traditions and share that with other people like Sunshine and me who, religious or not, still consider December 25th to be Christmas.

I think I'll take a picture of the head-banging violinist on her platform. I see a missed call from the 800 number that looks like the number from the Company in San Antonio. Last night I finally got a chance to talk to the engineer who'd worked at the Institute with me. The call went well, but she was honest in that she had no openings right now. Another call this soon is either really good or really bad. As I put the phone back in my pocket, Sunshine asks why I'm not going to check the voicemail. I tell her I'm here enjoying the show, and I'm not going to distract myself with career right now. The Trans-Siberian

Orchestra isn't going to stop while I make a phone call. If the message is a flat "no," then I'll continue to be happy to have the life I have like it is. If it's a step toward a better life, then that's great too. Either way, the voicemail doesn't have an expiration date on it and will sound the same now or after the concert.

One of the singers appears at the rear of the arena. At first I think she's playing a piccolo, but it's actually her voice. How the hell does she make her voice sound like that? All of the singers have incredible voices, and every performer gets a few minutes in the limelight. They're all incredibly talented at their chosen method of musical generation, and they show off just enough to remind you how good they are without going too far. I thought the animal trainers at Sea World looked like they enjoyed their jobs. These people are having a blast as they put an obvious amount of passion into every note, lick, strum, and strike. How great must it be to do exactly what you love and make a living doing it? I used to love pouring a whiskey on the rocks and breaking out the guitar. I loved playing guitar in general, and at the time I enjoyed whiskey with almost everything. I feel pretty shitty that I haven't even pulled the guitars out of the cases in a long time. It's sad that something I loved so much has had to take such a backseat to other things in life. With Vermin's wedding coming up in May, I'll have to get back into playing, figure out what songs to play for the event, and make sure I know how to play them. Seeing this show makes me wish I could put on a great show for Vermin's wedding. It'd be great to come out and play the beginning of "November Rain" on a keyboard. Then I could pick up the twelve-string and play the verses until I pull out the electric and rip through the solos and eventually the outro. With enough time I'm sure I could relearn all those portions, as I used to be able to do that. On the other hand, Vermin probably isn't looking for some extravagant concert. I'm sure she just wants a little background music and the basics, which I can surely do as well. Maybe I'll pick one Elvis song for Mom's enjoyment and one Dylan or Cash song for Dad.

Now that we're home, I'll check my message. She left her cell phone number asking me to call back, so I'd say that's a good sign. I always relate business to dating since it's something easily related. A potential date with a blocked number would never leave her cell number if she didn't want you to call back. Excellent. I leave a message, but it's pretty late, so hopefully I'll hear back from her tomorrow. I'd told Sunshine if I can get a job making a hundred and fifty K a year, I'd buy her a Jetta so she can let that Curve rust in pieces. A long time ago she also put the restriction on me that if we move to Dallas, I have to buy her an aftermarket rack. Tonight I make a deal with her that if I get a job with the Company, we'll talk about the car and we'll also seriously consider planning a trip to Germany. We both know that she likes to travel, but I hate sitting still in a plane and traveling. I tell her that since Rammstein won't be touring in the States, Germany might be the only place I can see them in concert. If I can see them live, I'll consider going to Germany with her. If I get that job and it pays what I think, it's a fair deal to make this arrangement. The way I look at it, this is like paying commission to get a sale. Who knows? It could be fun. I'll hate the flight over and back, but a Rammstein show would be bitchin', and I may have to find that section of the Autobahn where you can still drive like hell. I wonder how much it'd cost to rent a car that'll do 200 mph.

Wed 09 Dec 09

Kid Rock on the Crackberry is telling me to get my ass out of bed. I can't be wasting time when I have this proposal due in two days. I better get up or I'll dose off for nine more minutes and then start my day off in a shitty mood because I slept late. Two years ago I was averaging two hours of sleep a night between bars and early work mornings, but since surgery I've spoiled myself with at least six hours of sleep a night. How the fuck did I used to live like that? The stupid amounts of Red Bull probably had a lot to do with it.

The Anarchist will be the choice of vehicle this morning. It hasn't been ridden for a while and some fresh air will do me good. There are still a few cars at the House of Ale as a drive past my old stomping grounds shortly after 1 am. It's hard to believe I used to still be there at this time a couple years ago, as Tuesday was ladies' night, and the best night to be there. Mitchell, J3, and I used to go there on Tuesdays, and on Thursdays we'd go to Atlantic for its ladies' night. It was fun then, but I wonder if I'd really be able to enjoy doing that again. Between my newly acquired sleep constraints and sobriety, I just don't see it. If I were single, I'm sure I'd try to step back into that lifestyle at some level, but I've got Sunshine, so no need for that tomfoolery.

I'm pulling into the parking lot and it's no surprise that my vehicle is the only one in the lot, except for Tricky's car left in VP row while he's on travel. I still can't believe all three of our VP's went to Vegas this week while the worker bees are all back here working our asses off on this proposal with no divisional adult supervision. What the fuck were they thinking? Maybe they're networking at the convention for their next career.

My water glass is full, the Netbook is fired up, Rammstein is blasting, and I've got three work days to finish this thing. Getting up this early blows, but it's a great chance for the division and a couple other internal groups to get some desperately needed work. Whether the division stays open or not and whether I stay or not, I have a job to do and I'm going to do it balls-deep like anything else I'd attack. Another hundred emails arrived yesterday that I never opened. I look through them for the ones relevant to the proposal and blow off the rest, as it's the only way I'll get this done. Here's that email from Tricky. Even though he's supposedly responsible for commercial contract aspects, he has the balls to email me from Vegas telling me that since I'm the developer, it's my responsibility to determine what we're excluding contractually. What the fuck? He's never impressed me, but this email was the icing on the cake of a lot of shit with him pushing that other

RFQ to Nutzack and a half-assed job at the items he was supposed to contribute to this proposal. He and KL both tell me to have him help, and then when I assign him tasks, instead of just doing them like anyone else here would do, he tells me how to do them. I had to tell KL last night about the contractual buck-passing and embarrassment of having to ask another division to clean up Tricky's messes, but I doubt it made a difference.

Here's an email from KL that came in overnight informing us that there will be no raises. All he did was forward the email from MS with an "fyi" at the top. That's sure a sackless approach, but I'm not surprised. Reality is we're all lucky to have jobs, and if no raises means no unemployment line, then I tend to agree. My aggravation lies more and more in the way that our management is in my opinion completely failing our division. Three VP's and a developer that just started are in Vegas with wives blowing division money in a market in which we're getting beat, while I'm back here running a forty million-dollar cross-divisional proposal with no help from them. Good thinking, guys. My lack of sleep and aggravation has me tempted to write back to this email and tell them it's a hard bullet to swallow at 2 am while they're in Vegas, but I better not. I'd really like to write back to Tricky and copy KL and tell him what a boar-tit worthless job he's done, but I need to find a better way to approach it than what I'm considering now. I better just get to work.

Today is Dad's birthday. I better call him, even if it's 3:30 am his time. Usually I wait until 4:30 his time to call, but it's a special day. How old is he? 2009 minus 1945 is sixty-four years old. I bet he never pictured living that long. Of course I never pictured living this long either. As of late I won't make any bets on who dances on whose grave. He's not answering, and I don't blame him, so I'll just leave a message for him.

Stabby comes into my office behind Smooth and the Hare and announces that he just resigned. I'm the first one to respond with a sincere "congratulations" to him. That's great. He hasn't been happy here forever, and I don't think he ever would be. He's one of the best workers I've ever known, but that perceived negativity of his has screwed his career here and he needs a fresh start. I'm really happy for him, but we'll have to discuss it later. I've got two weeks worth of work to do in the next couple days.

I have a missed call from someone from the Company in San Antonio. They have an interview arranged for next Tuesday. It's too bad I couldn't get a trip over a weekend, as it'd sure be nice to spend some time back in the great state of Texas. That will work well though, as I can come in Monday morning for half a day, fly out, and be back for work Wednesday. After the last two weeks, I don't think anyone will question me taking a couple days off. Part of me feels a little slimy about sneaking off to an interview, but I just don't have confidence in my management's ability to save the group, let alone help it succeed. Even if we get the order on this big proposal, it could lead to success for the group, but at the group's efforts, not the management's Vegas trip. If that Company is going to give me a big pay increase to go there, I'd be a fool to stay here anyway. I get the impression that it doesn't matter how many of these proposals come out successful, the Office would pay me just enough to keep me for as long as I stayed anyway.

I know these group meetings are necessary, but they're taking up my valuable time. KL is on the phone dropping calls again from Vegas, and you can tell it's irritating MS. Someone even makes a joke about KL having hookers around him that cause him to drop calls. This is embarrassing. When the contractual E&C's subject arises, I state that Tricky is doing them and I confirm it with KL. He says that Tricky sent them to TD to review. What a dick move. TD is busting his ass and doesn't deserve to get thrown under the bus, especially as a sacrifice to save face for that worthless Tricky. I wish I could find a way to point out that fact without making myself and our division look bad too, but I can't, so I sit there more pissed than before. There is some schadenfreude I enjoy as MS looks at me and asks why Tricky is in charge of contractual items and hasn't been in any of the meetings or calls so far. I'm ashamed of my leaders, but at the same time I'm glad to see others notice the clusterfuck that's unfolding like I do.

What a doll. Sunshine has ribeyes and sweet potatoes with a salad for dinner when I get home. She's even bought some toy cars of a GTO, Ferrari, and Lamborghini. It's frivolous, but she enjoys doing things like that. I'm not used to girls doing nice things like that, but she's gotten me more accustomed to such behavior. She also picked up the next dvd of "Dexter." Unfortunately I fall asleep half way through the show after dinner. I'm so tired I can't even enjoy a one-hour show with my girlfriend. 1 am is going to come early tomorrow.

Fri 11 Dec 09

Fuck, I overslept by an hour and a half! I should be sitting pretty well on this proposal and hopefully just have the loose ends to button up today. I was hoping to be done a couple hours early and take a few of the primary contributors out for a drink. I wouldn't drink of course, but it would be nice to at least get them a couple beers for their work. It's drizzling out, so I'll be a pussy and take the Goat today. That exhaust wrap on the Anarchist is torn anyway from where I turned too sharp going over that manhole in the parking lot and drug the bottom. That's one more thing I get to fix, but will enjoy doing.

All the written documents are finally done and I've got a half hour for SH to finish pdf-ing the last document while I start uploading the rest of the files. The directions say to hit the "firm" button, but I select it, and the whole fucking thing locks up. Shit, is that what you do after you've attached everything? You have to be shitting me. I didn't bust my ass for over a month to get fucked by technology. I'll email it until they respond to my emails and unlock my account. I really doubt they'll disqualify me for it, but it still pisses me off because I feel like a fucking idiot. I'm not sure why KL is standing over me thinking I want to discuss our rep's commission on the job right now, so I'll need to make it more obvious with more cussing at a higher volume to less subtly invite him to leave so I can do my fucking job. He hasn't been here all week, so I sure don't need him hanging over me now. I just have a hard time looking him in the eye today with all that's gone on this week. How can he be so clueless as to take three VP's and another guy to that show when this proposal is hot and heavy? How the fuck can he either be clueless or just look the other way while Tricky fucks off, slides by responsibility, and passes the buck?

Now that everything's submitted, I type an email of thanks to everyone in the Office that touched this proposal. I feel like just moving the VP's names to the "cc" line instead of the "to" line, but resist my urge for stabs right now. If we get this job, I owe a lot to everyone that busted their ass on this effort, but I feel like about zero gratitude is owed to the VP's. I also send one to the other division's VP and thank him specifically for his group's hard work and copy all of them on the email. It's not political, and it's not ulterior motives. I just sincerely appreciate the work all these people contributed, except my own management. Speaking of the VP's, CL is calling. He wasn't involved on this at all, but he is involved in the show in Vegas, so I can't fault him for anything. I'm just burned out right now and want to get the fuck out of here, so I'll talk to him later.

TD and SB are over at Monkey's Uncle, and I told them I'd stop by. I don't need it, or even necessarily want it, but I'm in a bar with these guys and I order a Jack & Coke. Mmmm. Damn that tastes good. They comment that they thought I'd go easy with a beer since I hadn't drunk for so long. I tell them if I only had a chance to fuck someone once every six months, I'd rather fuck a model than a nasty old boiler. I'll allow myself just one though. The more I talk to these guys, the more I like them. They both suggest that they should find a way to get me over to their division. I would probably be a good fit over there between the construction experience and Government work I've done. That's an interesting notion. Maybe if the Texas deal doesn't come through, this group would be a way to stay where I am with a better outlook. I like these guys, but I like the people I work with too. The leadership seems like it would be a vast improvement, but the grass is always greener on the other side. I finish my drink, plant that thought in the back of my melon, and walk outside.

I haven't been to the gym in several days, so I walk to my car, grab my gym bag, and walk to the gym. After about a half hour of cardio and abs, I drive home feeling a lot more unwound and relaxed. I'm also completely thrashed, and badly in need of sleep. There's that leftover ribeye and potato in the fridge, which will make a perfect minimum-effort dinner. Since I keep falling asleep during the last two "Dexter" episodes, I'll try again.

Sat 12 Dec 09

5:30 am is still early, but it's a more civilized time to be waking up when compared to the last two weeks. I don't even remember Sunshine coming home after the art show last night. I just remember waking up on the couch freezing in front of the "Dexter" home screen and going to bed. That's the first eight-hour night of sleep I've had in weeks, and I have to admit it felt good. I don't want to be lazy though, so I'll get up and watch the last two "Dexter" episodes. That sounds stupid as I say it in my head. I'll prevent laziness by lying on my ass in front of the TV. I can't seem to stay awake watching them at night, but I should be able to finally get through them this morning.

Where do I even begin? The VTX is waiting for the wheels from the chromer, but I should get his seat over to T-Roy. Obi-Wan's bike needs to be put back together, and I need to figure out the air cleaner. I still have to figure out the fucking wiring on that Twin Cam too. That thing would be together by now if it were an Evo. I'm so glad the factory changed from the simple three-wire ignition connection to two twelve-pin connectors in the name of progress.

I'll work on Obi-Wan's first, since I'll have to order parts to finish it. The carb support I've got laying here should work. I'm surprised I have to drill these threads out, but at least I don't have to buy another one. What the fuck? I could swear these holes lined up a minute ago. That's fucking sweet. I just butchered a good part I could've used on my next chopper and have to order a new one for Obi-Wan's anyway. Sonofabitch. I figure out what pieces I need and send an email to the supplier to get the carb support and the new air filter. I think I'll go on a parts run before I fuck up anything else. I need some fuel line for the Ape, so I'll get that on the way.

I put the oil and filter down by Obi-Wan's bike for when I get back to that project, and start replacing the fuel hoses on the Ape. Gas is leaking all over the place as I try to hold my tongue right to get the banjo bolts where they need to be before the whole floor is covered in fuel. I put the white stickers back on the bright red underbelly and the Ape is officially back in one piece. I give it a quick bath and have it all ready to swap with the Anarchist tomorrow.

T-Roy is over here picking up the seats for the VTX so he can add the ostrich inserts to match the bike. He tells me I need to do a little more metal work on the chopper's seat pan before he can foam and cover it, so there's a little more work to be done on that. As with most of our less frequent conversations these days, we both update the other on common acquaintances. I tell T-Roy about Captain D in Charlotte and he tells me about the Frenchman's debacles. Not so many years ago we were both here on Bert Road working our asses off every day trying to survive. We'd spend our days in our shops and our nights at Bourbon Street, beach bars, or the House of Ale with other cohorts. Those were tough times because of our financial situations, but great times in that we were just tattooed derelicts enjoying life and the fact that we did what we loved for a living. We've both quit drinking and hanging out in bars since then, and we both have serious girlfriends. He works for an investor doing the same thing but for a paycheck, and I went back to the white-collar world and kept the shop as a hobby. Maturity is such a strange thing to watch sometimes, especially in a mirror.

Sun 13 Dec 09

The fact that I'm waking up at 4 am with no alarm is evidence that last week is still affecting my sleep schedule. It's for the best as I have to get something done on the chopper today. I still haven't figured out this fucking ignition, but at least I think I have the charging system under control. Naturally the spacers the shop recommended aren't quite right, but I've got a spare that will work. Both primary drive pulleys are in place, everything's bolted down, and I forgot the fucking polished plate behind the drive pulley. Sonofabitch. I take everything off again, install the plate, and finally the driveline is together.

I'll send the belt drive cover and axle covers to Mr. Crowley so he can machine the YCC logo into them. I still have to get that license plate holder design done so he can get started making a few of those too. There's never a dull moment, but it's only 9 am and I've gotten quite a bit done already this morning. I take a quick break and see Sunshine before she treks down to Staug for work. Now that I have the Ape roadworthy again, I ride the Anarchist back to the shop for its repair and I'll take the Ape home tonight.

Mon 14 Dec 09

Last week really fucked up my ability to sleep late, but I'm only working half a day today so it doesn't hurt to be here at 6 am already. After neglecting a lot of items while I worked on that proposal last week, I need to catch up. I crank up Rammstein's "Liebe Ist Für Alle Da" since I'm the only one on the floor again, and start wading through incomplete tasks and unread emails.

If the 1 pm flight to ATL is delayed, I wonder if my 2:15 flight will be late as well. I ask the lady at the desk and she puts me on the

1 pm that's now leaving at 1:30 so I make my connection in ATL. It's a damn good thing I got here early or I would've been screwed. I've got no books, no laptop, and a couple Muscle & Fitness magazines. It's ridiculous how much this magazine has become just a paper commercial. I count eight two-page advertisements before I even get to the table of contents. There are thirteen ads before the editorial, fifteen ads before the letters from the readers, and eighteen fucking ads before the first article containing actual training methods. This is sad at best. If it wasn't for Cousin Reno's loin trophy selling magazines for his school, I never would have subscribed. Unfortunately they didn't have Maxim, and Tracer gives me all of his old sport bike magazines, so I got this and something else. Was it Hot Bike, Road & Track, Car & Driver, or even Rolling Stone?

I take a deep breath of Texas air as I get off the plane, and soon re-familiarize myself with the SAT airport. Years ago I was in this airport once or twice a week, but I haven't been here since last October when I had a work trip out here right before surgery. The airport's changed a little, but the restrooms are still hidden down this hallway behind baggage claim. After putting in my contacts, I walk to the rental car counter. I'm impressed that the guys recognize my name and identify me as an applicant for the Company when I check in. I mention the Institute and the guy talks about all the secret projects going on out there. You have to love this Texan hospitality.

PT's has changed its sign to say "Perfect Ten." That was the first strip club Sambo showed me in San Antonio. Big Earl's in Ames had a falling ceiling, full nude cases of Gardnerella adorning the stage, and some crack whore smoking a cigarette in her pussy. PT's completely blew my mind as a new standard in strip clubs, soon joined by the Palace, Sugar's, All-Stars, and XTC. I couldn't believe so many hot girls were willing to lose their clothes for my entertainment in those adult candy stores.

It's foggy here today, but I see Sugar's is still in business too. It was Club Hollywood when I first moved to San Antonio. I remember

Flanman sitting on the curb shaking his head worrying about who was going to drive home since we were all fucked up. Sambo and I convinced him that if we all went inside, they could drink more, I'd slow down, and I'd be able to drive us home. Somehow Flanman bought our jiz logic, and an hour later I had a date with the waitress while Sambo puked under the table. Hopefully she didn't have to clean it up.

It was Sharky's for a while too, but when it became Sugar's, we were there for lunch almost every Saturday. They had three-dollar steak and fries and jumbo shrimp for two more bucks. If you could go in, have lunch, and leave, you made out like a bandit. It was the nights we didn't leave until 6 pm after drinking and feeding dollars to the entertainment that got expensive. There were a lot of good times there. I wonder if V or Misty or Jessica Rabbit work there yet, or if they look even as close to how hot they did back then. Much like how my friends and I have been replaced with the newer generation of alcohol-enhanced patrons, I'm sure the girls have been replaced by a newer generation of saline-enhanced ballerinas.

It was very nice of the Company to put me at the Omni. There are Christmas decorations, Christmas music is playing, and people are just as happy and friendly as I remember. Even though I lost my taste for holidays when I left my family in Iowa, I have to admit I almost feel a little of the Christmas spirit right now. I know exactly what I want for Christmas too. If I don't get this job for Christmas, it'll be another year of my current management stuffing my stocking with their seagull management tactics by swooping in when unwanted, shitting, and flying away again. Like I promised myself after surgery, I will continue to appreciate what I have though. They did give me a decent raise and promotion at the beginning of the year and were accommodating of my recovery, for which I'm very grateful. No matter how annoying the job may get, it still beats being unemployed, and it is a great bunch of people.

It's Chip, Vice, and me for dinner. Cat chose an approach from the J3 handbook in choosing to not communicate at all versus communicating a decline for the evening. Pappasitos sounds good and is jut a couple blocks away. I don't think I ever ate here when I lived here, but it's a good meal. I'm glad I can still sit socially with Vice. The prick Nowork below him was the problem, not Vice. It's just that I lost some respect for Vice when he took that asshole's side at my termination, even after the interviews with everyone in the department backed up my accusations of Nowork's bungee cord ethics. Once he fucked Vice out of his position, I guess it put Vice and me on the same level again, and we've remained friends. Vice has an early flight to Hill tomorrow, so he leaves as Chip and I aim toward the Flying Saucer. Huebner Oaks is still a nice area. Gladys's has changed names, but overall this area looks basically the same as when I left.

The Flying Saucer is pretty busy, but after taking a seat, Chip decides we should go to the La Cantera Yardhouse instead. I don't remember this area, but the only time I remember being close to here was when Sambo and I picked up Sleaze from the hotel to go to All-Stars when he was in town. A couple young cuties leave the patio and walk across the street to contaminate their breath and their lungs with a couple cancer sticks. I find that since I'm retired from hitting on girls, I notice a stronger urge to ask those girls if they realize how stupid they are for smoking. Maybe by telling them they are beautiful and it's such a waste of that beauty to smoke, it might make a difference. Who am I kidding? I've tried telling past girlfriends I'm ditching them if they don't quit smoking, and nothing changed. Those two girls would likely say the same thing to me that little Marie said to Rocky. "Screw you, creep".

Tue 15 Dec 09

Why do I even bother setting my alarm? It's only 4 am here in the great state of Texas, but I'm awake so I do some shadowboxing, sit-ups, push-ups, and anything else I can do in a hotel room. I walk down to the business center and spend a little time catching up on any hot emails before going to breakfast. I've gotten spoiled by hotels with full breakfast buffets that cost more than most of my dinners over the years. The omelet chef asks about my shirt, which I bought at the Dragon store in North Carolina. He's an older guy and like many others, he dreams of the day he can afford a Hawg. People like this make me appreciate the fact that I have the ability to hop on a bike and just go when and where I want. He's fascinated by the fact that I not only ride, but build bikes, and checks on me every few minutes to ensure I'm finding everything easily and enjoying my breakfast. I really miss how nice everyone is in Texas.

I'm waiting in the lobby for someone to get me in the door, but it is a little before 8 am. It's hard to imagine anyone not starting work before this time, but I'm the minority for preferring early mornings to late nights in the Office. There are real wood panels on the walls and stone tiles on the floor, which I'm now educated enough to recognize as possible signs of a LEED-certified building. After looking over the artistic display in the lobby and noticing the various ways the pieces are fastened to the stand, I look up at the Company logo. It appears to be laser cut from stainless steel. It could be mild steel that's been coated to prevent rusting I suppose. The middle leg of the top and bottom swoops is ever so slightly off-centered. That could be deformation from the cutting process. That's going to bother me. I wonder if they'd let me come in and reshape those middle pieces to make them centered. OCD is a bitch, and I probably should refrain from pointing out that their logo is off-centered during the interview, or they'll think I'm off-centered. Here comes my potential future manager, and she looks just like I remember her from the Institute. Not only did the Institute provide me with a good job for six years after college, it may help me get a good job now. It's a good thing I started getting fucked up with Sambo and the rest of those guys in college since he helped me get the job at the Institute. Finally, only in sobriety, my drinking is beginning to pay for itself.

I'm back on the plane ready to head back to JAX, and my head is spinning. Eight interviewers make it difficult to remember if I'd already told someone something, or if I was confusing the current conversation with a previous one. The questions they asked were regarding real challenges they face at their job, and the answers required weren't from any textbook or training course. Five years ago I couldn't have come up with the answers as well or quickly as I did today. Fortunately I deal with many of the headaches they endure, and that experience combined with quick social analysis of the situations allowed me to give what I considered good answers. The interviewers seemed to agree, and at the risk of stepping from confidence to arrogance, I feel like I really nailed the interviews.

The last thing I heard on the way out was, "You'll hear from us one way or the other soon," which is neither encouraging nor discouraging. The HR gal asked how soon I could start if I got an offer next week, but that could be hypothetical. The facts are that they just opened a position for January, they couldn't have interviewed anyone else yet, the interviews went well, I had the Institute commonality with several of them, and their option is to hire me or go through a lengthy resume filtration and interview process between now and January. I need to keep plowing forward down my current path, as that may be the future I have, but I am so fucking jacked over the idea of getting this job. I'm going to be doing cartwheels out of the Office if I get this. I'll also be more disappointed than Fatman at an empty buffet if I don't.

Fri 19 Dec 09

Sunshine texted me to call asap to answer a question. I'm not sure why, but I always get uneasy when I see or hear messages out of the ordinary that sound like emergencies. If Mom or Dad call at a time they wouldn't normally call, it always makes me think it's bad news. I call Sunshine and bad news was an understatement. Tracer and Ms. Texas had gone to "Nutcracker" recently, but were disappointed because it was a kid's version. Tracer griped to someone, and he was given four free tickets to the adult version tomorrow night. Fortunately for Sunshine and unfortunately for me, the extra two tickets were offered to us. Sunshine is extremely excited about getting to see it and views the gesture as one of kindness by Tracer and Ms. Texas. Tracer was aware of Sunshine's and my agreement to skip "Nutcracker" and attend the Trans-Siberian Orchestra instead, so I'm sure he's enjoying a lot of schadenfreude at my expense, regardless of the bow of kindness he's wrapped around the tickets in his presentation of the event to Sunshine. Despite how much I dread the event, I'll obviously attend as she'd do the same for me, and it's not too much to ask considering how much she does for me.

Sat 20 Dec 09

The Florida Theatre is a very interesting old building, and this is the first time I've been inside of it. I can't help but notice how much it reminds me of the Majestic Theatre in downtown San Antonio, where I saw "Defending the Caveman" years ago. Supposedly it was a one-man Broadway show, but to me it was more of a comedic, intelligent look at the primal differences between men and women and reasons each acts differently than the other. The example that stuck with me most was how women have a party, run out of dip, all do a conga line to the kitchen, and get more dip as a group. In the same scenario, the men will identify the empty dip bowl, and the first response is, "Fuck you. I brought the dip." The next is, "Fuck you, I brought the chips." The performer pointed out that both of these situations are fine by themselves, but problematic when combined. A woman points out an empty dip bowl, and a guy says, "Fuck you. I brought the dip." The responder isn't being an asshole as the woman will assume, he's just being a guy. The comedy of the show was very entertaining, and the insight it provided to both men and women about each other was very thought-provoking. That show should be a prerequisite for any new couple before seriously dating. I have a feeling that "Nutcracker" will not be nearly as entertaining or insightful as "Defending the Caveman," but Sunshine is excited, so I remind myself what a great girlfriend she is and put on a smile as fake as a wedding cake for the show.

Finally the pain is over and we're across the street at a new place called Dos Gatos. Behind the bar is an eye-catching painting of a senorita and a cat at her feet. Sunshine points out the two cats or pussies in the picture per the bar's name, which I'd just noticed as well. It's a dark little bar and both barmaids are covered in tattoos, which normally makes for a more comfortable environment. It just makes me feel out of place because we're here in collared shirts, sport coats, and dresses. In discussing the play, I point out that despite the three major errors I saw, I'm sure the dancing took hours of practice and the guys had to be strong to hold the girls in the air. Whether it's a dancer executing an impressive move, a guitarist cranking out a fast solo, or a fabricator forming a piece of metal into a work of art, I always try to appreciate someone taking pride in creating something worthy of admiration. I did express my surprise and display my ignorance in ballet by noting that I've seen better plots in porn flicks. I thought it had a pretty weak story line that barely held together a lot of separate dance acts. The part of the event most unbearable is having to watch guys bouncing around the stage with their packages wrapped in spandex almost as to call attention to their crotches. It would've at least been fair if the girls had similar spandex displaying their crotches, as they were all very fit, but all the girls had skirts or dresses. However, it appeared that some of the cast was pretty young, which makes the whole thing even more disturbing. Any dancers I see from now on better have names like Destiny and Bambi.

I chose not to bring up the part of the play I found most interesting, so as not to turn the conversation into some kind of social debate. Most interesting to me had been the parts of the play that illustrated its age when compared to modern society. Each family of children arrived with two parents. The sets of parents danced with each other as a group while the kids played around a Christmas tree. The little boys played in one group with swords, while the little girls played in their group with dolls. An older uncle picked up the young girl and danced with her. The different groups of dancers represented their countries of origin in dance style and costume. I was almost surprised the politically correct dingbats haven't gotten on this play's ass and demanded an updated script. I can just imagine them insisting that instead of each family having two natural parents, there needs to be a pair of remarried parents with step-children, a single-parent father and a single-parent mother to create sexual tension, and a same-sex couple raising a future confused child to help ram acceptance of everything but the nuclear family down our throats and encourage the demise of the family structure. The next thing they would bitch about would be the clearly sexist display of girls playing with dolls and boys with swords. PC Nazis would demand that girls play with dump trucks and boys play with dolls to promote gender confusion and androgynous behavior. They could never allow an uncle to pick up his niece and dance with her either, or this would make him an obvious incestuous pedophile. The fact that the dancers from other countries dressed and danced according to stereotypes would be considered completely racist. The PC Nazis would have an absolute fit that someone dare make a play about Christmas in the first place. The play would have to be celebrating the holidays with a great tree and eliminate any traditions so as not to offend any religion or belief system and further break down American traditions, including Christianity. Thinking about how societal fascists are fucking up everything I was raised believing really pisses me off, so I'll enjoy the conversation's other aspects like cars and the new bar we've found and are enjoying tonight instead.

Wed 23 Dec 09

Sunshine's smiling, the sweet sounds of the Bloodhound Gang are playing on the Blaupunkt, and the V8 under the hood of the Goat is growling down the interstate toward Miami. Hearing *Hooray for Boobies* as we drive through Daytona Beach brings back memories of Chip, Gameboy, Inbreeder, Meat, and I raising hell down here for the fifth and final full week-long spring break I did. That trip was filled with eighty-dollar liquor store bills every morning, pitchers of Lynchburg Lemonade, sunshine, and clubs. It was a lot of fun for me at that point in life. All of it just leads to the fact that I'm extremely happy with my life now as I drive my Goat down to Miami with Sunshine, so at some level I have to be happy with all the events that lead to this point. There may have been an easier path to get here, but the easiest way isn't always the best either.

I'm glad I took the Valentine One off the Ape and put it in the Goat this morning. I'm not driving crazy fast in my opinion, but it's nice to avoid tickets. It's going off and I see signs reducing the speed to 55 mph. Some Buick SUV tears by me in the HOV lane as I'm slowing down and as expected, it gets nailed by the cop on a bike that flagged my detector. There's a patrol car in the HOV lane ahead too, and the officer just climbed back in the car. No alerts on the Valentine, so they must be going somewhere. Why is he behind me with his cherries lit? I move over and he stays behind me. What the fuck? I wasn't going any faster than anyone else in traffic, and there were no alerts. I pull over, and I'm not happy, but I'm not going to let this ruin the trip. I'll take the class as opposed to driving all the way back down here for court. I give the officer my license, registration, and insurance card. There's no need to bring up the Glock under the seat. I have my concealed weapon permit, so I'm legal, but there's no need to bring it up if he doesn't ask. I wish I'd put that sticker on my license plate from the sheriff's office or wherever I sent money that time, although that sticker's no get-out-of-jail-free card.

He writes me up for the full 75 mph in a 55 mph. I'll say, "thanks" to an officer that lets me off the hook, but I refuse to say, "thank you" to this guy for giving me the full penalty on the $281 fine. I know he's just doing his job and I can't fault the guy for doing as he's told. I also admit that it's my fault for speeding in the first place, but that doesn't mean I'm any less pissed about it. Isn't West Palm on the high crime city list for Florida? Aren't there bigger threats to society here to worry about than a guy taking his girlfriend to Miami for Christmas? This Simon Says law enforcement is ridiculous. Simon says, "Don't speed." Simon could say, "Don't wear a popped collar or sideways cap in public," and fine you if you do it. In either case, you're doing something that doesn't hurt anyone else, so what's the fucking problem? Of course it's possible they can lead to wrecks, but I've effectively committed a victimless crime and am being punished for doing something that could possibly lead to hurting someone. What happened to being innocent until proven guilty? If a person thinks about killing someone else, it doesn't mean he or she gets the chair. This isn't the fucking "Minority Report," is it? It's still better than the ticket Sunshine got from one of the communist traffic light speed detectors at Baymeadows. That's even worse because it's a Simon Says law that isn't even critical enough to warrant an officer spending his time monitoring it. Some company makes up a rule, sends you a ticket, and splits the proceeds with the municipality. It's not a big enough deal to affect your driving record, but the company can pursue collections if you don't pay. It's beyond fucked up and one more move in the wrong direction for free Americans.

I'm pissed, but in the big picture of things, this just boils down to a fine, a few hours to take a class, and keeping my nose clean for another year. When I was in court for that speeding ticket I got on the Ape following Tracer's bonehead driving, the judge said one ticket per year is basically excusable with court or class so no points go on my license. Even if I do get another ticket this year, I can try court, or just pay the fine and take the points. If I have to get a ticket, I'd rather it be for twenty over and not more. The last time I got pulled over I was leaving Doc's at 5 am going twice the speed limit in a construction zone, and I talked my way out of that. When that officer asked how fast I was going, I told him I'd just changed the battery and hadn't reset the dash from km/hr to mph. It was true, and he made me sit there and figure out how to change it back to mph, but didn't give me a ticket. As a result of his humanity, I was sincerely apologetic, respectful, and grateful. I didn't get caught going 144 mph on the Ape on the way to Jennings with Bikey or driving 160 mph north of San Antonio in the Grauer Geist years ago. I didn't get nailed to a judicial cross when I got pulled over after Sambo got us all turned around at 4 am going back toward Austin after just coming from there either. I was pretty damn glad to hear the cop say, "I'm trying to ask which of you two is less fucked up. You get some coffee and you get your asses back to San Antonio. I've got better things to do than chase you two idiots around all night." All that considered, this ticket is pretty minor compared to what the law could've nailed to me in the past.

We find the hotel at noon, but they won't let us check in until 3 pm, so we've got time to kill. Part of the reason we chose Miami was seeing the Cuban club in "Dexter" and deciding we could enjoy the Miami sites and a little Cuban culture at the same time. I'm driving back across the water while Sunshine's trying to Google "Little Havana" so we can have an authentic Cuban lunch. We find a place called Versailles with a safe parking lot, friendly service, a good crowd, good food, and lots of it. Next we Google the Lamborghini dealer and shoot over to Biscayne to check out their stock. Ronan and I checked out this place on our trip here years ago, and I called the boss the next week to arrange an interview. The hiring manager told me despite the fact that I'd never sold cars, he'd hire me on the spot because I knew cars, and I was a go-getter. His estimate was around $100K the first year, but I'd have to start selling Audis before I could sell the Lambos. I may have really enjoyed it, or I might have hated it, but the ex wasn't too thrilled about it, so I'll chalk it up next to V and Rachel as one more opportunity I was never able to explore due to my bad decision-making in spouse-selection. There's a badass flat black Murciélago sitting here, but someone ruined it with a big yellow "SV" on the side. None of them even have manual transmissions. They all have the paddle shifters. The paddle shifter on the Camaro I rented in LA was unique for me, but it's just not the same as a manual, and it seems sacrilegious to even make a car like a Lamborghini that's not a stick.

As we leave the dealership, Sunshine says that she likes the look of the Ferraris better than the Lamborghinis. I explain to her that the Lambos are truly the strippers of the car world. They're high-maintenance, undependable, and can break down on you at any time. Their sole purpose is for exotic looks and bragging rights about how hard you drove them. Next I describe the Ferrari as the car equivalent to a model. The looks are still exotic, the performance is still incredible, but they're much more refined and better built. Although they're more dependable, they still require a whole lot of maintenance, but if maintained properly they can be worth the investment in the long run if you don't abuse them too badly. She asks where Porsches fit into the analogy. I tell her that I've always viewed Porsches as the hottie next door. The beauty and body are still off the charts, but with more elegance than the pasta rockets. In addition to the great appearance, the hottie next door demands only the respect and attention she deserves, but returns that attention and pleasure in the sheer enjoyment of the ride. Because of the upbringing or engineering of the design, you have more dependability and they don't require near the maintenance of the Italian counterparts. These qualities are what make both Porsches and Sunshine so appealing to me. She also asks about the Goat, a Corvette, and other cars, as she gets a kick out of my use of experience with automobiles to explain my classification of girls and vice versa.

The hotel is a pretty nice little place for eighty bucks per night. The building is far from modern, but shares the intriguing design of the Art Deco district in which it's located. The room has a low bed that reminds me of the years of sleeping on a mattress thrown on the floor. Over the bed is a hanging light, which I hope is secured safely. The bathroom has one of the same half glass shields for the shower like La Mansion where Ronan and I stayed years ago, except this shower is mounted to the ceiling and rains down. Overall this is a nice little place in South Beach for the price.

It's a little cloudy, but still a beautiful day to walk around and check out the sites. We walk down Collins and look at the various shops, pointing out dresses we like or don't like. Senor Frogs has changed to something else, so I guess we won't be going there. We both laugh at a mannequin in a store that has a giant fake rack like the ones we saw in Lauderdale, and she brings up again how she'd like a set of aftermarkets. As usual I tell her, "It's your money and your body." I did agree to buy her a set and a Jetta if I get a job making a hundred and fifty K, so we'll see what happens. We walk over to the ocean and there are still a few people out in the sand. The water is much bluer down here than Jacksonville, but still pretty choppy today. We walk back up Ocean and I point out the TGI Friday's where Ronan and I slammed several Long Island Ice Teas on our trip here. La Mansion has changed names since then, but it was one of these hotels on this block.

Every sidewalk restaurant through which we walk is equipped with some young cutie trying to tell us quickly about the drink and food specials. We continue saying, "no thanks," and keep going. Apparently everyone is hurting, even the hotels, bars, and restaurants in Miami. I laugh at a couple guys trying to give us a cd for their band that say, "We like Guns N Roses too, bro. Don't shoot us, man." I guess between the militant haircut, Guns N Roses shirt, and stern look ahead so as not to be drug into a sales pitch, they make their assumptions about me in the same way that I assume based on their looks, the cd is probably rap or hip-hop and I won't enjoy the music burned on it. Nonetheless I can't help but turn around and laugh as they laugh back following their comments. They're funny, but I'm still not going to carry one of their cd's around.

Häagen-Dazs sounds tasty, so we spend over six bucks for a single scoop of ice cream. Fuck that's high. Bienvenidos a Miami. We look over at the petite blonde working across the street trying to draw people into her restaurant. Some of these baitresses are pretty hot, but I wonder how many girls get a reality check when they move here. I can imagine some homecoming queen from her little town in the Midwest that moves down here or to LA to make it big, and soon realizes that even though all twenty guys in her high school class would've rolled in razor blades and dove in lemonade to get a taste of her, she's just another face in a crowd here. She soon burns her winterized skin trying to get a tan, but without a fake rack or decent wardrobe, her looks can barely get her a job hustling potential customers on a sidewalk in a city like this. On the other hand, there are probably lots of young people that can get by enough on their looks to survive in the city and enjoy it enough for a few years until they progress in life or realize they need to move to do so. Miami is definitely a city that could be enjoyed if you had money, but would cruelly remind you of what you're missing if you didn't have money.

As Sunshine enjoys a glass of wine and I have an alcohol-free Mojito at the hotel bar, we somehow get on the subject of marriage and why people resist it. I ask her if she'd ever take a job knowing she had to keep that job forever, and she agreed that would be a hard decision to make. I also point out that in business, it would be stupid to sign a contract stating that you'll only get your goods from one source forever, whether the goods change, or even if the source decides to no longer provide those goods. She turns that one back on me stating that it represents a desire to have the freedom to get your goods from anyone you want any time. I refute and state that it's not a matter of insisting on variety as much as fear of unknown changes in the goods and source. We also discuss that when she left her ex, it was probably more headaches than my divorce because of a common house and their longer time together, but she doesn't have to mark the divorced box like I do. It's not that I worry about that, but it's just more significant for someone to have to accept that failure in their life as a failed marriage versus just another failed relationship, let alone multiple failures at it. I'm glad we can always openly discuss such issues to help each other understand the other's perspective, but I do fear the day those differences become an issue for us. Maybe that day will never come, but if it does, I'm going to have to figure out all those answers to the unanswered questions that torment my mind about the future. I'm happy with things just like they are, and the last thing I want to do is anything to change that happiness.

These sidewalk restaurants all look similar as I try to remember which one was the place where Ronan and I sat down with two girls at a table. We each had two drinks and the girls that night each had an appetizer, and the bill was a hundred and eighty bucks. The girl by Ronan straddled him, but when the other one looked at me, I confessed that I was engaged and couldn't do anything fun with her. Ronan was pissed since my moral structure was preventing him from scoring in Miami, but without some kind of code, you have nothing by which to live.

One of the baitresses makes sure to let us know it's 30% off all menu prices, so Sunshine and I decide to have dinner here. We're on the second level, and enjoying her lobster ravioli and my tilapia and shrimp. Unfortunately the assbags right below us on the sidewalk level are smoking, and the smoke is blowing right at us. I've gotten spoiled by most of Jacksonville restaurants' no-smoking policies. My first reaction is to pour my drink on their cigarettes like I used to do when I was younger, but it's difficult to determine whose rights are at risk. Does this situation encroach on my right to enjoy a meal without breathing that cigarette smoke, or their right to enjoy a cigarette with their meal? We chose to eat here, so I suppose one could say it's our fault, but we may have chosen differently if we knew it was a smoke-friendly restaurant. Regardless, the food and company are good, and I'll enjoy it and try to ignore the smoke.

We leave the restaurant and identify Mango's as a place we'll stop by later. Clevelander's is a place we've both been before, so we stop for a drink. I tell her that Ronan and I saw an extremely beautiful girl in a sundress sitting at the bar the night we came here and wondered out loud if she was wearing anything underneath. Two guys standing next to Ronan overheard our comment, and excitedly said that she wasn't wearing anything underneath, and they'd stood there for the last hour waiting for the next crotch shot. Despite the other guys' best sales pitch on why we needed to stay there until the girl got up and flashed snatch again, we moved inside that night. I hesitate to tell Sunshine things like this, as it just reaffirms her image of me as an irresponsible sex-crazed alcoholic in my younger years, but we both have our pasts and try to walk the line between honesty and discretion.

I don't remember a stage from my previous visit, but there's a band tonight and they're just starting to play "Sex Type Thing." I haven't heard that song in a while, but we used to listen to it constantly in college. Sunshine and I sit here in our snazzy attire head-banging with the devil horns in the air singing along and cheering. We can tell the band appreciates that on a slow night. At least someone is showing some enthusiasm and enjoying their music. They play "Plush" next, some Led Zeppelin, and a couple Van Halen songs including "Ice Cream Man."

The band is great, but they take a break, so we decide to visit Mango's. The place is definitely hopping, unlike Fat Tuesday's, which is completely dead. That's too bad, as I used to love Fat Tuesday's. I guess people these days just aren't as excited about getting wasted on 190 Octanes. The guys working at Mango's are either bulky 'roid monkeys or lean and very ripped. Six-packs are definitely a hiring requirement for both sexes, as well as salsa-dancing ability. The employees partner up and dance to the music of the live Cuban band on the dance floor or on the wide portion of the bar. It's great that we're both able to point out impressive physical attributes of people without making the other one insecure. We both know these twenty-something people are built a little better than us, but we both know that we're still built better than most people in the thirty-plus age range.

The girls at Mango's have skimpy, tight, zebra print outfits. Most are pretty decent looking to say the least, but there's one behind the bar that definitely stands out from the rest. When she climbs up on the bar/ stage, everyone watches. Sunshine and I both agree that she is the most beautiful girl in the place. She's graced with a ten-point aftermarket rack that almost looks real, a ripped stomach, bronzed skin, dazzling eyes, a bright smile, and long, dark, curled hair. As she gyrates on the stage, her most prized asset becomes obvious as it moves in perfect rhythm back and forth to the Latino band. Every shake of the maracas is met with a shake of that quarter-bouncing ass. It's so hypnotizing I couldn't look away if I wanted. Sunshine knows I'm admiring the girl's looks and motion, but she knows I don't want the dancer more than her or anything else besides face value of the situation. She understands me in the fact that I genuinely appreciate objects of beauty from cars to art to girls. Like Dom says, "I'm one of those boys who appreciate a fine body, regardless of the make." It's so nice not having to listen to unwarranted jealousy stemming from internal insecurities like some girls of the past.

Thu 24 Dec 09

The room and bed were comfortable, but caveman needs food badly. Sunshine picks up the fifty-dollar breakfast at the hotel restaurant for one last Miami-priced meal. Last night we spent seventy-five dollars for her three alcoholic drinks and my two non-alcoholic drinks. That fucking speeding ticket is still the hardest cost to swallow, but I'll deal with that when I get home. Right now we're enjoying the last few sips of our freshly squeezed orange juice and the warmth of the sun as it peeks out from behind the hotels across the street. Tiny finches or sparrows bounce across the sidewalk searching for crumbs. Sunshine throws a scrap or two toward them. Their heads rotate in jerky motion like tiny robots that go right to the next set point and stop abruptly. Why do people have fluid motion and they do not? Their low resolution head movements are fascinating to watch, and remind me of the rabbit-fucking motion of those drug-induced visions in the hospital over a year ago. I may not see bizarre visions like that any more, but I feel like I've really been able to appreciate more colors and sights and sounds than I ever did before. Surgery was great for me in more ways than cardiovascular improvements.

We have a couple hours before they boot us out of the hotel, so we walk through a little outdoor shop area. There are a couple more dresses we see that we agree would look great on Sunshine, but there are plenty of gaudy cries for attention hanging on the mannequins as well. I explain that my basic preferences for clothes on a girl are solid colors with basic designs and minimal, or at least consistent, texture. Relating it to a bike or a car, you want to appreciate the lines of the vehicle, the metal work of the body, the complementing accessories like the wheels, but maintain its elegance. Excessive body features, accessories, or loud mixed colors in the paint take attention and detract from the real beauty of the vehicle, and in my opinion a girl as well. I don't like ruffles, bows, or fringe when a simple elegant dress will do. We see one particular dress that is an absolutely awful combination of colors that would make a tie-dye shirt look classy. I point out that the basic rule in colors should be that you should be able to puke on a piece of clothing and tell that you puked on it. Vomit camouflage like the dress in the window should be banned right along with plus-size bikinis.

The ocean is still choppy, but the water is gorgeous. It's barely after 10 am, but the sun feels so good out here. I wish the hotel would let us stay for a few hours so we could come out here and enjoy the sun shining in Miami Beach for a while. What better activity for Christmas Eve in Florida?

Casa Marina is closing, but that's fine as it's been a long day. After sitting on my ass for six hours coming back from Miami and sitting here on the deck for the last couple hours, I'm ready to jump on the Ape and shoot home for the night. I'm sure Tracer would stay here for the next few hours if he had his way, but he has a delayed sleep schedule compared to the rest of us right now. I've always liked sitting out here on the deck and being able to look out into the dark ocean, especially under a full moon. Tonight is windy and cold to say the least, so we've been hovering around the one operational heater unit while the girls have been sitting inside. I suggest to Sunshine that she ride home with Cartmanini so she doesn't freeze, as she's already cold. I also take the chance to question why her vest isn't keeping her warm, and point out that the lack of sleeves may have something to do with it. It's as mysterious as the fact why fingerless gloves don't keep fingers warm.

I need to keep this thing under 70 mph, as I can't afford to get another ticket today. I'm getting closer to the Gate exit and don't see many cars around, so I can crank it up a little. Here comes Cartmanini and Sunshine in his Lotus, so I downshift to fifth and jam it. Here he comes again and as much as I want to just blast down this open road, I'd get zero sympathy from the judicial system having just received that ticket yesterday. Fuck I wish I could just pay some blanket fee at the beginning of the year to allow me to speed for the next year. Even if it would cost more, it'd be worth it. Germany gets the Autobahn, which I think has unfortunately lost most of its wide open spots. We'd never get an Autobahn here in America because of all the idiots on the roads who are texting, wasted, eating their fast food, talking on the phone, and just being stupid. All the rules here are based on the lowest common denominator, but that would be so fucking great if they did have a wide open road. It would let me twist this throttle right now, wrap out that V twin between my legs, and pierce the night with this bitch in a blur of high octane and adrenaline. Just thinking about it has already blown me well past three digits, so I better squeeze in the dual front Brembos and get ready for the exit.

Fri 25 Dec 09

Before I go to the shop, I'll open this box from Mom and Dad since it is Christmas. Every year since I've left home, I've asked them not to get me anything, as I'm terrible at buying presents and never know what to get them. I liked buying the Johnny Cash and Elvis gifts I picked up for them in the Memphis airport that I saw randomly and thought they'd enjoy, but having to buy something because of the calendar is always difficult. Despite my request that Mom not ever send junk food, she sent peanut clusters, the peanut butter-cracker-fudge snacks, and hocus-pocus buns. It's nice of her to do, but I'd rather not eat such things. There's a box of chocolate-covered cherries with a note that says, "paper boy" on it, since I complained as a kid about how many I'd get for my paper route Christmas tips. It seems ungrateful I guess, but I just can't handle that much sugar. Dad sent an LED penlight, which will be very useful at the shop. I like seeing the penlight done in the American flag design, and the cherries have a big "Made in USA" stamp on them as well. It's pretty obvious from where my spirit of nationalism comes. Here's one of my 2009 Y Chrome calendars with pictures of Mom and Aunt Dar's faces imposed on the bikini models. I can't help but laugh, despite how wrong it is. Every now and then they'll come up with some good ones, and this is definitely one of those moments.

I leave Sunshine to her cooking and head to the shop, where I call my parents to thank them for the gifts. Dad says there's a gift certificate from Eastwood coming. Maybe I can put that toward an English wheel or something. The Goat is filthy, so I start washing that while I'm talking to the parental units. The cordless speaker phone at the shop was one of the best investments I ever made. I even polish the hood, roof, and trunk, as they get the most direct sun damage. I throw out the trash inside the car, set Sunshine's relics like chapstick, rings, and hair ties in the glove box to give back to her, vacuum everything, wash the dash, and leather condition the seats. Obi-Wan's bike is running, the Anarchist is all polished and running, and I'm still getting out of here in time to be home by noon as promised. It's raining like hell, but the car is still pristine and the water beads perfectly on the silver surfaces. Damn, that looks good. I feel so much better seeing it the cleanest it's been since I got the car.

Cartmanini has left, Sunshine's zonked out, and Cousin Reno is fading fast. "Superbad" is just ending and that's a good place to close the book on Christmas 2009. It wasn't a huge family Christmas with three generations celebrating around a tree filling Grandma's and Grandpa's house, or a Christmas where my ex was at her parents while Fatman and I cruised around San Antonio looking for an open strip club. It was far from Nikki Sixx's "X-Mas in Hell" where someone was curled up under the tree smacked out on heroin. This was just a simple Christmas with my girlfriend, nearest cousin, and good friend in our small two-bedroom apartment in Jacksonville with enough food, drink, decorations, phone calls to distant family, and movies to make it feel like what Christmas is supposed to feel like.

Sat 26 Dec 09

Reno's back in Deltona, Sunshine's back at work, and I'm back at the shop. I already went with Cartmanini to the gym in a feeble attempt to work off the vast amount of food we ate yesterday. As much as I'd like to do something else constructive, I'm sitting here doing the on-line drivers' safety class. It's not that difficult or expensive, it's just the pain in the ass of doing it. It looks like they've put real thought into making sure people actually go through it. You can't click to the next page until the timer goes off, and if you don't pay attention enough to click the icon just as the timer expires, it just takes that much longer to get through it. I literally haven't read one line of text so far on the screen. The window is minimized and I scroll down, play any videos, answer any authentication questions, and then watch the timer in the window while I do something else on the computer. It's not like I'd normally be out getting hammered at the bars, but there's still plenty of other things I'd rather do on a Saturday night. At least it'll be done and over in a few hours and my penance will be paid for the heinous crime of keeping up with holiday traffic. Only now, after taking an on-line class, will I truly lament the wrong I did to all those people I hurt by going 75 mph in a 55 mph zone. Simon says, "This fucking blows."

Sun 27 Dec 09

I can't believe Mom is up at 6:30 am Iowa time texting me a reminder of my womb-exit anniversary. It's nice she remembers, but I would prefer to ignore the fact that I just got a year older. I suppose that more than anyone, I should be tickled I just survived another year of existence. Birthdays are a double-edged sword in that they're a celebration of the fact that a person made it another year, while also being a reminder that a person has aged one more year and has one less year to live. Besides the fact that at thirty-six years old I can legally fuck a girl half my age, there's really nothing significant about this one. I like the number in general as it's easily divisible by three, twelve, nine, four, two, and eighteen, as well as being a nice bra size.

Dad's calling the shop. In the past I'd completely ignored all contact on this day, but Tracer pointed out that acknowledging family birthday wishes is more for them than me, so I answer. He tells me he feels like a jackass for forgetting my birthday yesterday. Score. I point out that he doesn't have to feel bad about missing it, but can feel like a jackass for not realizing it's actually today and not yesterday. Both sisters call shortly after, so I spend a little time catching up with them as well. I hadn't gotten a chance to speak with Organisis much on Christmas day since she was busy with the little guys. Age progression reminders aside, it's always good to hear from family.

AJ shows up to discuss some lighting fixtures he's trying to plan for some bike and car shots. He's great with a camera, but needs a little mechanical help, so I offer to go to Home Depot with him to find something that will work. We discuss our mutual dilemma of having the greatest girls we could ever hope to have, but dreading the idea of marriage or worse yet, kids. Both of us are happy with our current lives, and although marriage or even kids could potentially be better, we're afraid it could be a lot worse too. It appears neither of us has made any progress in this decision-making process since we last discussed the subject. We both agree to let the other know if any kind of light bulb appears over our head any time soon.

It's nearly lunch time, so we grab a Hungry Howie's pizza on the way back to the shop. While we sit in the dirty office of the shop eating our pizza off some dusty paper towels, AJ brings up the subject of church, as he'd just come from there. His church is one of those new contemporary non-denominational, non-judgmental churches where you can dress like a dirt bag, which is great for attendance here. He hadn't realized that I'd gone to church all through college, and that Mom still worked for the Catholic church back home. AJ's not quite as surprised as Batman back at ISU. He came running into Carpenter house in shock yelling to everyone on the floor that he'd just seen me in church earlier that night. AJ's still surprised and asks where I went astray with the crude language and naked chics on bikes. I explain to him that as a child, Fr. Brickley told me in confession that it's wrong to take the name of the Lord in vain by saying things like "God-damn" and "Jesus Christ," but it was no big deal to say "shit" or 'hell." I say, "fuck" constantly, but try to never say a holy entity's name in vain as taught years ago. As far as painting a naked chic on my bike, that falls into the art versus smut interpretation I guess. It's just application of my love for beautiful women and my love for motorcycles, or the simultaneous celebration of both God's and my creations.

When the discussion evolves from church to charity, it's obvious AJ and I have very different thoughts on the subject. My views are much more objective compared to his idealistic views, which are more common in people I'm sure. If a child not connected to me in any way starves to death or dies of some disease, I feel absolutely no remorse. Mother Nature is just doing her job, and the world can't afford to waste resources on lost causes. AJ insists that giving money to some kid will afford him or her chances to make a better life. I point out that if you could take an infant from a neighborhood like Bert Road, raise them in a controlled nurturing environment, you could make a huge difference in what that child becomes. Short of that level of commitment, charity is reduced to a surface action allowing the donor to feel like a difference has been made when it's just a futile effort to delay the inevitable. I remember the rice bowls as a young Catholic in which we had to put money every time we cheated on our self-inflicted restriction for Lent and thinking the same thing even at that age.

My parents didn't have much when we were kids, but Dad was too proud to even accept free cheese or other items from the food bank. In fact a local drunk would go get the free food and sell it to Dad. It was confusing to me as a kid, but now I get it. I've always worked for everything I had, and if anyone gave me anything, it was a family member or friend or at least someone in the community. As a result of those principles instilled in me, I'd gladly do what I could to help family, friends, and people I knew well, but that's where it stopped. I could see supporting something like the Red Cross because they help people here in this country that are working hard and get screwed by natural disaster or something, but that's about it.

My outlook on charity and humanity was solidified during the years on Bert Road. After my boss going back on our agreement and terminating me, and my wife going back on her word and divorcing me two days after the last paycheck was deposited, I was pretty destitute. I lived on a packet of oatmeal, a ninety-nine cent ravioli cup, and cup of soup a day for a couple years, and I didn't see any charities helping me out. I'd even got fucked by the HR guy who claimed I'd quit instead of being terminated and didn't get a dime of unemployment. When I finally crawled out of that gutter, it was by sheer will with no one else to blame but me for being there, and no one else to thank but me for getting out of there.

With philosophical banter out of the way, I turn to Obi-Wan's bike. With the bowl off, the valve and petcock appear to be delivering fuel at the float's request. The bowl has some obvious residue, which is likely the result of the same gas residing there since 2002. A little carb cleaner takes care of the bowl and allows the accelerator pump to function properly. I spray the cleaner in every part of the carb body as well, put it all back together, and bingo-bango it's running. After an oil change, fluid check, and bath, it's shining and ready for a test ride on the expressway. This thing is smooth and has some decent kick, but the rear brakes are Flintstones quality. After bleeding and refilling the rear master cylinder, the back wheel will lock up on command, and this project is ready for pick-up.

Following a good cardio and ab workout at the gym with Sunshine, it's time for a bowl of cereal to appease the stomach before we sit down to watch Blockbuster's latest contribution to the demise of my intellectual progress. What the hell did we get? I was just there, but I guess I just registered it as "not the last "Dexter" dvd." They must only have one copy of that disc and I'm never there at the right time to get it. Overall it was not a very noteworthy womb-exit anniversary. I didn't take thirty-six shots at a bar, no stripper spanked me thirty-six times, and I didn't fuck an eighteen year-old. There were no parties, no balloons, no streamers, no cakes, and not even a special meal. I started the day waking up, still alive, and not in a jail or hospital. I talked to my family, split a pizza with an old friend, and accomplished a few things working at the shop while being serenaded by the sweet sounds of heavy metal. I went to the gym with my girlfriend and am now about to enjoy a quiet evening at home with her to catch up on each other's days. I couldn't ask for a more perfect birthday, because it was a great day without being a birthday at all.

Thu 31 Dec 09

Obi-Wan seems happy with his bike. The new air cleaner looks cool, its fluids are checked and changed, the rear brakes work, and it's capable of idling by itself. I lecture him about the necessity to use a machine so it stays in operating condition, and he heads into the brisk Jacksonville air.

After depositing his check and returning the Goat's core alternator, I swing by the factory parts counter to see if they have the MAP sensor for the chopper. They don't, but Orange Park has three. I've been meaning to get over to Orange Park forever now, and can't believe I never made it over to Buffalo's for their bike night all year. I haven't seen Ruben in ages either, so I pick up Sunshine and we call Ruben on the way over. Fortunately he's able to meet us at the Orange Park House of Ale for some lunch. As usual, he's got various challenges in life, but laughs it off and sees it all as new little projects to address. It's been six years I guess since Ray passed away. Prior to that, the three of us often met at the Road House for Amber Bocks on Fridays after the base let them go for the weekend. Fuck the years go by quickly. I can't help but notice how I identify times in my life with the group of people in that period. Family stays consistent, but for those first years working in Jacksonville, I associate those memories with Ray, Ruben, the other base people, and the subs like Slick. Shortly after that I was running around with T-Roy, the Frenchman, and J3. Captain D was a friend of that time that overlapped from the group in San Antonio because he'd moved from Texas where he, Cat, Kramer, Flanman, and I used to raise hell. Chip, Sambo, and Fatman were in that period too, but had also been part of the college buddies. Sometimes friends pass on to the next stage, sometimes they become long-distance friends, and sometimes they fade away just like I do to them.

After wishing Ruben a happy new year, we shoot back across the Buckman Bridge toward home. As we cross the bridge I suggest that we stop to see Tracer's cousin and her husband on the way. I've only been to their house twice, so it takes a little while to find the right street, but there's no mistaking that bright orange brand-new Camaro sitting in their garage. After introducing Sunshine to the older couple, she and the wife discuss the art in the home that was bought at the gallery where Sunshine works. I'm a little concerned that the older gal's extreme religious conservatism may clash with Sunshine's opposite views, but fortunately no political issues arise as they discuss their common interest in the paintings and artists.

The proud new car owner is excited to show me that his original automatic Camaro has been replaced by an almost identical model, except with a six-speed manual transmission. I congratulate him and Sunshine and I point the Goat back toward Tinseltown before our guests arrive.

It's pretty cold out, but I just got back from swapping the bikes between the shop and garage, as I may actually do a ride on the Anarchist this weekend. As I'm climbing off the bike in the garage, J3 and his girl come up behind me. What the hell was her name? I just say, "hi" and figure he'll remind me eventually. Not long after Cartmanini shows up, we all pile into his Range Rover Sport and meet AJ and Stretch at Carabbas.

Dinner was good, and I had a glass of egg nog left over from Christmas while everyone else had their beer or vodka. We were supposed to meet Tracer and Ms. Texas at Landshark to watch the Kings of Hell tonight, but our group decides that's not very New Year's Eve-like, so we go toward the beach and continue the evening at Lynch's Irish bar.

Sunshine's unfortunately had way too much vodka and is struggling to stand right now. She's not being belligerent or making a spectacle of herself, but is just doing a drunken impression of "Weekend at Bernie's," and I'm really not quite sure how to handle it. I have such a difficult time dealing with drunken people and just bars in general these days, and now I have one more dynamic to consider. I'm not mad at her by any stretch, just a little irritated about how difficult it has become for me to handle these situations. J3 and Cartmanini are noticing the usual array of douchebags, including a moderately well-dressed, yet somehow less hygienic Jesus and some other ass-bag in a purple running suit in case he needs to do any laps before driving home tonight. We all recognize our age-derived intolerance for those younger patrons around us and the need to get Sunshine to a soft place to land. We stop at Gate on the way home for more beer and watch sadly at Cartmanini's as Dick Clarke struggles to say the words, "Happy New Year." I suppose it's nice he can still participate in the event, but I feel sorrier for him than watching the decrepit forefather of modern heavy metal get abused by his brats and wife on "The Osbornes." Sunshine slept right through the ball dropping, so we might as well call it a night and get her home.

Chapter 9

Man and Machine

Fri 01 Jan 10

It's not as early as I'd like to have been moving, but we were up late last night, and I wanted to get a decent night's sleep. It looks gray and gloomy outside, but like Rocky I've got some things in the basement and need to get on that bike and just drive south. I've got three days with no work and no worries, and I need to make use of it. In reality I could be in Texas next year at this time, and I owe myself at least one two-wheeled adventure through the state that spawned my existence many years ago.

231

Sunshine stumbles into the room as I think about what I need to pack. I really don't need or want to take much with me. I hate carrying too much stuff on a bike trip, so the list will be minimal. It's cold and misting, so I do have to prepare for the weather at some level. I've got jeans over long underwear and those insulated green, fuzzy socks I had for doing the paper route in high school. I used to dread getting out of bed on those mornings when it was thirty below zero to go deliver papers, but it taught me how to handle adverse weather conditions in preparation for stunts like this. It's already getting hot in here with the hooded sweatshirt from Daytona covering one of the Y Chrome T-shirts underneath. My face will be sort of protected by the skull neoprene half-mask, sunglasses, and Y Chrome beanie. The leather biker coat, Redwing engineer boots, and gloves complete the attempt at warmth in a 70 mph blast in January. As far as extra clothes, there's only room for a pair of cargo pants, one extra pair of boxer briefs, one extra pair of socks, and my "Fuck the Factory. Build it Yourself" T-shirt. I wrap the extras in the Guns N' Roses *Appetite for Destruction* shirt from Sunshine and tuck the package and a laminated Florida map in the space between the handlebar risers and the clutch and brake lines. Sunshine asks me where I plan to go, and I tell her I'm heading south and I'll see where the road takes me. That's really all I know, so that's all I can tell her. I let her know the phone will be off, but I'll be sure to let her know when I perch for the night somewhere. It's obvious she's concerned about me heading out on my own on a bike in such beautiful weather, but she knows any display of concern or caution would be wasted breath. With a quick goodbye kiss, I pocket the bike lock, wallet, keys, powered-down phone, and Glock and walk out into the mist.

I've been told before that I need to enjoy the journey and not just the destination. I have always been bad about rushing to the next milestone without taking pleasure in how I get there. I had to be an adult right now. I had to be big right now. I had to be drunk right now. It was always an endpoint, not an experience. Looking back over the last year since surgery, I think I've improved significantly and have appreciated a lot of things I wouldn't have enjoyed before. That being said, instead of just barreling down I95, I've always enjoyed watching the sun shine over the ocean driving down A1A. Unfortunately today there's no visible sunshine, but only a gray sky pissing down on me. The pace down A1A will be much slower, but should be more interesting than three lanes of high speed potential clusterfucks in this weather.

I've barely been to Staug since Sunshine moved to Jax, but still recognize the Old Jail, the Fountain of Youth, and the other landmarks as I drive through town. I'm no waterologist, but I have a sneaking suspicion the water I drank from the Fountain of Youth didn't really make any difference. I don't know that I would ever live here, primarily because I don't know what I'd do beside sling drinks in a bar to tourists and locals or dress like a pirate and try to sell trinkets on St. George's Street. Nonetheless it's a quaint little town that definitely has character and some unique appeal that's fun to see every now and then. Look at these idiots on bicycles out in the rain. Of course, I suppose they are probably thinking the same thing about me.

The rain is really picking up now, as the wet marks on my jeans have spread from the shins and knees all the way to my crotch. My face is almost completely covered by beanie, shades, and mask, but the exposed tip of my nose feels like a pin cushion as it leads my face at highway speed into hundreds of tiny droplets of rain. This route on past trips was great for watching the ocean reflecting the rising sun, but today it looks pissed off as the waves crash on the beach. I wonder if it'd be good for surfing or not?

Visibility has reached Mr. Magoo levels, and it's raining like a sonofabitch. I smell flowers as I enter the northern end of Daytona. I don't think it's actually the scent of real flowers though, so much as air freshener from the elderly in the condos that line this stretch of A1A. I've been on the road for a while, so maybe I'll pull over for some breakfast and see if the weather lightens up at all. I pull into an IHOP, climb off the bike completely soaked, and go right to the rest room to get my clothes in a manageable pile so I can sit down to eat. The Glock is floating around in the torn pocket of the jacket too, so I need to adjust that to ensure it doesn't fall out or anything.

I've barely touched caffeine since surgery, but a cup of coffee might help warm me from the inside out. No need for a huge breakfast, but a couple eggs, hash browns, and sausage hit the spot. Without the distraction of conversation, I observe some of the other restaurant patrons. There are a couple couples in biker garb that probably drove to breakfast in their SUV, as I didn't see any other bikes besides mine in the parking lot. I hear one guy tell the waitress he'll come back to see her in a year when he gets out of jail, while another guy is discussing his concern about getting Daytona 500 tickets already. The waitress asks where I'm coming from and I tell her Jax. She tells me that she just moved from Jax. I'm going to guess the move was to escape an ex more than to pursue the IHOP career, but who knows. Another waitress tells her customers how she moved down from Jersey. I won't even guess why she moved from Jersey to Florida just like J3 did, as that seems like a no-brainer to me, but some people from Jersey may disagree. Hey, that rhymes like, "I got to nail her back at her trailer."

After reassembling myself in the bathroom, I walk back into the rain, which appears to have grown heavier and colder. Maybe I would have been better off just pushing through instead of stopping and trying to warm myself, but it's too late to change that now. I straddle and start the bike and head south again on A1A. It really feels colder, and the thought of turning around crosses my mind. What good would that do though? I'd still have to ride in this shit all the way back home. I could get a hotel, but it seems pretty weak to take a three-day trip and only go to Daytona. Tough, stubborn, or just stupid, I'm heading south like I planned. Every time I hear and feel that rumble resonate from the bike through me when I take off from a stop, it strikes that chord that makes the discomfort worth it to keep driving. That growl of the engine is the reason I'm doing this, and even Mother Nature isn't going to prevent me from enjoying a weekend on my bike.

A1A routed me back to Highway 1 south of Daytona, and I'm staying on 1 as it should be easier to find a gas station or hotel when I finally decide to stop. Now that the rain's cleared a little, it's gotten much colder and I'm starting to shiver to the point of my hands causing the handlebars to shake a little. That's not good. I suppose staying soaked emulated the same effect of the wet suits I wore surfing in San Diego. If those suits kept me warm in that cold water, it would make sense that my soaked clothes worked the same way. Am I really wishing it would start raining again? It doesn't matter what I wish for, Mother Nature doesn't take requests. Vero Beach is thirty-three miles away, which sounds like a good place to stop. I can suffer through another half hour or so. I started the day wishing it would get better, when I would've just been happy if it hadn't gotten any worse. When it got worse, I kept hoping for a clearing in the rain, and when it finally happened, things only got worse. The grumble of the engine made it worth it though and kept me going. This trip has been a fairly appropriate experience for my life. Sometimes I just have to accept the fact that when things are bad, they may still get worse before they get better, and I just have to find the enjoyment in it where I can until things do get better.

It's sprinkling again, which confirms my decision to stop in Vero Beach. I don't see any chain hotels I recognize, so I aim back toward A1A. I'd think there would be some place at the beach to stay, but I'm not seeing anything. It looks like there's another street closer to the ocean, so I'll shoot over there. Finally I find the Aquarius, and it should do just fine or at least beat driving any further today. I tell the desk lady I'll stay if she gives me some time alone with her dryer. Fortunately she's extremely accommodating and lets me park under the overhang to keep the bike from getting any wetter. The first thing I do in the room is crank the heat full-blast and jump in a scalding hot shower. My feet are so cold that the hot water stings them as they begin to regain feeling. Once housekeeping is done with their rounds, the desk lady takes all my clothes and puts them in the dryer. I can't put leather in the dryer, but I lucked out and the room has an oven. I open the oven door, prop my boots, gloves, and coat on the door, and set the oven to warm. It'll probably take all night, but the stuff should be dry by morning. Since I can't really leave, I call the local pizza joint and have a stromboli and salad delivered that will serve as dinner tonight and breakfast tomorrow. I really can't do much while I wait for dinner to arrive, so I text Sunshine the hotel number so she can call if she wants, and I don't have to wear out the battery on my cell.

I've got my stromboli and salad, a warm room, clean dry clothes ready for tomorrow, and cable TV to pollute my mind. I'd be lucky to understand even a fourth of the words from "Gangs of New York" in Spanish, but the Miss World Fitness contest is showing. Damn those girls are in good shape. One is forty years old and still has better abs than I'll ever have. For being that age, she's very rhythmic and fluid in her motion, unlike some cougar her age awkwardly dancing at a bar to modern songs while trying to pick up some younger guy. These girls are hot, athletic, graceful, and would all make great strippers. Even that loses my attention shortly, but "Lethal Weapon 3" is on another channel, and that will do for now as I drift off for a snooze. Hopefully that oven doesn't set my coat on fire and secure my place on a future Darwin award email.

Sat 02 Jan 10

It's a new day. The sun is shining, the sky is beautiful, and the air is just right for riding as I lick my finger and point it in the wind like those clowns in "Men at Work." The Glock will ride in the thigh pocket of the cargo pants today instead of the coat pocket to see if that makes things any easier. I've been meaning to find some place to redo the liner of this coat, and it would be great if someone could make some kind of an integrated holster in that pocket. I'm sure I could go buy a new coat, but I've had this one since my last one got stolen out of Juano's car on New Year's Eve of '95 or so. It's been through concerts, rides, rain, and a lot of experiences with me. As opposed to buying a new leather coat that was cheaply made in China, I'd much prefer to pay someone to handcraft something out of this coat to make it what I want. Leather's supposed to look used. New leather is for doctors and lawyers on bikes, not bikers who need doctors and lawyers.

I'm sticking to A1A, but I can't believe how many times it's jogging me back and forth to 1. By the time I get to Stuart, I've already crossed the intercoastal five times since leaving Vero Beach. Every glimpse I've caught of the water today has been better than the last. As I drive through Juno, I'm extremely impressed with how well-groomed the city keeps their beach area. There are no pot heads on ten dollar bikes driving with beer cans on the handlebars who pack six into a dumpy house like in Jax Beach and many other areas. This beach area is lined with incredible homes on the land side and perfectly manicured hedges on the ocean side. Everyone I see is in shape and dressed in nice clothes, bikinis, or wet suits. I'd think the ocean would be bitter cold today, but I can't blame them for wanting to get in that water. The ocean is that gorgeous Caribbean blue with a hint of emerald and is absolutely beautiful. Ferrari after Audi after Porsche after Mercedes adorns A1A in this area. I need to quit cranking my head to try to identify the car models, so I can pay attention to what's in front of me.

West Palm Beach is more of the same beautiful water, people, cars, and homes. There's the Palm Beach County something-or-other building with a few cop cars outside. I could stop by to see if they got my check and driving safety class certificate, but I'm sure they'll let me know if they didn't. I see about five cop cars as I drive through the Palm Beach area before the road steers me back through a little downtown area. I'm sure the police presence has a strong impact on keeping these beach areas so nice. As soon as I get close to 1 again, the demographics have gone from well-dressed people and nice homes to low-income people and dilapidated buildings. It's such a pronounced variation that it's hard not to notice the abrupt changes in the type of people I see as I drive through the streets.

Soon I'm back on A1A and driving through Pompano, which means I'm pretty close to Lauderdale. The beach layout has changed from the beautiful homes and trimmed hedges of West Palm to hotels and older well-kept buildings. I finally see a gas station and stop so I can fill up the thirsty bike before I get into the main beach area. Before I even get my mask and beanie removed, some guy in a yellow Sexterra is asking me how much I want for the Anarchist. I tell him I honestly don't plan to sell it, as I've really grown fond of the bike over the years. He asks a few questions, I tell him more about it, and he continues asking what I want for it. I finally tell him I paid six grand for it, have put at least a couple more in it, and wouldn't take anything less than seventy-five hundred. I give him my card and tell him if he's still interested next week, he can give me a call. I don't want to sell the bike, but that money would go a long way toward the driveline for my chopper. Is my plan to end up with a blown Goat, another 911 Turbo, my Ape, an RSV4, the Anarchist, and the chopper? Eventually I'm going to run out of room and have to trim my collection I imagine. I'd hate to be without an American V twin for very long, and that chopper won't be done for close to a year I'm guessing. If I had to sell this Anarchist, I'd probably be lucky to get what I paid, so it's tempting to take advantage of finding that right buyer now. I'm not going to worry about it. Right now I'm just enjoying the bike. If he calls next week, I'll weigh the options then. I know it's ridiculous, but I find myself worrying more about the fact that my bike just witnessed a conversation about selling it. My tendency to personify my vehicles is not logical, but uncontrollable. About the time I got ready to sell Candy to buy a 911 turbo, the door lock started showing its ass. When I took the Grauer Geist north of San Antonio for pictures to sell it, the clutch went out on the way home. I had to drive it straight to the Porsche dealer for over three grand worth of repair work. I really don't want to sell the Anarchist. Hopefully it knows that and doesn't develop any issues resulting from it feeling unwanted now.

That tattoo shop I visited years ago should be in this little corner between Sunrise and A1A. I remember stopping because there was an old Sportie parked outside that caught my attention. Was it Bulldog Tattoos? I park next to a few other bikes close to where I remember the place to be. At the same time I'm parking, another guy pulls up with a brand-new bagger, freshly cut white hair, smooth shaven, fancy sunglasses, and a leather vest that looks unused. I can tell he's a hard core biker and probably just rode in from somewhere far away like Oakland Park. As I walk up to where I'd seen that old bike parked years ago, the tattooed guy smoking outside hollers at his dad to help me, which makes me feel better in supporting a father-and-son operation. I explain to the dad that I want a red skeleton hand tattooed on my right trap above the other work and below the collar line. He cocks his head when I tell him it will represent where the grim reaper got his hand on me, burned his print on me, and let me get away. Since I haven't eaten lunch yet, he tells me to go grab a bite while he draws the design. I always go to tattoo shops with a drawn design of exactly what I want, but I didn't have time this round and a skeleton hand is pretty straight-forward.

The bar across the street serves food, but I've got this .40 cal on me. It's not like I can go put it on the bike, so I guess I'll take my chances. Iowa's gun permits were no good in any place that served booze. Texas establishments had to post a sign that said "51%" at the entrance if they made over 51% of their income from alcohol sales signifying that gun permits were not valid. If I remember right, Florida allows you to carry a gun with the permit in the dining area, but not the bar area. The chance of someone actually finding out about it and anything happening from it are slim to none, but I'll sit in the outer dining area just to be safe, as I think that falls within legal adherence.

As I wait for my burger and fries, I ask Chuck if I'm parked safe. He said they still monitor the meters and there are rules about multiple bikes in one spot, so he is helpful enough to go feed the meter for enough time to finish my meal and recommends the free lot behind the tattoo shop for when I'm getting inked. Karnival's across the street is a place I remember having a beer or two years ago, but it's boarded up.

Chuck tells me it's supposed to be reopening under new management soon. There are two other tattoo shops on just this block, but I've already got someone working on it, so no need to bother the other two or piss off the first guy. It's still chilly sitting out here, but overall a nice day, and I can see the gorgeous blue ocean out past A1A from my table.

Even if not for the guy's age, I can tell this guy came from a past generation when compared to most. He carefully inspects every needle, every aspect of the gun, looks at pieces with a magnifier under the light, and even adjusts the rubber band so it's just the way he wants it. That kind of pride in work is something often lost lately, but something I always appreciate seeing, especially for something that's going to be permanent on me. I feel that first buzz of the needle sticking in and out of my flesh. It stings at first, but I've learned to focus on something other than the needle and the pain isn't bad at all. Fortunately this pricking won't be on any bone, nipple, or armpit. The old guy apologizes if it hurts, and I tell him it can't hurt as bad as getting my chest sawed open a year ago. He asks me what I do in Jax. I could tell him I'm a white collar project manager and push papers all day, but instead I tell him that I work for a construction company and build choppers on the side. I'm still telling the truth, but the part that's more appropriate to the situation. The guy getting inked in the other chair is apparently here on his lunch break from a construction site, as I can see the dried concrete on his lace-up work boots. The old guy tells his son he's inking a real biker, and the other patron begins to tell me about his bike. It's a warming feeling to have some commonality with simple people like this who are real artists making a living doing what they love and appreciating the art I do as well. They're simple people not trying to fuck each other to climb some corporate ladder, and they'll get their heart attacks and ulcers from drinking, smoking, and eating instead of office politics and job stress.

Some young girl, who must be kept around for eye candy or because she's getting banged by one of the tattoo artists, comes in with an obvious hangover and sweeps the floors in a mentally-neutral condition.

She's pale as a ghost, has some random ink on her upper arms, pins and needles in her face, bright red-dyed hair, and a phenomenal rack for such a tiny frame. Good thing she's too hungover to notice the fact that I can't help but stare at them, and they even look real too. I give two thumbs up to her parents and the hormones in animals these days. The old man asks one of the other artists for the camera so he can take a picture of his latest work. I think to myself that he probably says this for every customer to make them feel special about their ink. As if he could read my thoughts, he tells me he doesn't get the camera out for many tattoos, but he's proud of this one. I check it out in the mirror, and have to agree it's a good one.

I make fun of people who get a Chinese symbol for spirit or something after they break up with someone or find themselves or whatever. One could say a grim reaper hand print on my trap after a couple temporary deaths is the same documentation of a life milestone, and I can see that point. I like it though, and that's what counts. I ask the guy if he'll throw in an XL shirt from his window that says, "Tattoos are like pussy. If you don't get it all over, you're not doing it right." Unfortunately he doesn't have any stock of them, so he's got his hundred bucks for services rendered, and I'm out the door into the Lauderdale sunshine with some fresh ink.

As I cruise south on A1A, I try to enjoy watching the ocean to my left while trying to find that dumpy hotel I've used on the right. There's one called the Waterfront that looks fairly cheap. I need to remember the Waterfront and that it's right north of the Hilton. I'd love to stay at the Hilton, as that place was badass, but it's a little luxurious for this hooligan's holiday.

Before I go into the Best Western where Sunshine and I stayed a few months ago, I'll call that Waterfront and see what rooms are costing as it's closer to the main drag. The Waterfront is under a hundred bucks, so I'll just aim back that way. The Elbo Room is overflowing with people as usual. I'm amazed that the same place Dad and Uncle Slim used to support is still in business and still always busy. It looks like a lot of locals and some tourists, but it's definitely not the beauties in bikinis that were there when Mom, Dad, and I drove by the bar a couple years ago. I've been through this area enough that I've learned the landmarks like the Elbo Room, the Rock Bar, Sangria, and the Beach Walk complex. Lots of memories, cloudy or otherwise, come back as I drive past them, but this is the first time I've been able to see all of this from the saddle of one of my bikes, and I have to say I'm really enjoying it. It's sort of my home city, as I was born here, but I still feel like a cross between a tourist and a local as I rumble past the people and places of Lauderdale Beach.

This room isn't the fanciest in the world, but all I need is a place to crash. There's a good chance I may go to a bar, so I need to leave the gun in the room. I don't see a safe in here, but I wonder if I can hide it in the air conditioning unit like Dexter hides his blood slides. That's a no-go, so I'll just slide it all the way under the dresser. I'd feel like an idiot if I forgot it there, and I doubt I will, but I'll slide my bike keys under there too so I can't leave one without the other. A nap would be nice, but there's still sunshine outside and that means I should be out there enjoying it.

With the weather this cold and the sun being lower in the sky, there are almost no people on the beach. Several health-conscious people are out jogging on the adjacent sidewalk. I get busted by one pair of girls admiring how ineffective their sports bras are at preventing the bouncing, and I can tell they're not impressed. With a week's worth of beard growth, a biker trash hooded sweatshirt, cargo pants, and engineer boots, I doubt I look like the kind of guy these young girls are trying to attract by keeping their bodies toned. Other people are out for walks, some are taking pictures by the water, and some are enjoying cocktails at the sidewalk bars. The sun has crept below the buildings to the west, but I finally find a nice spot where the sun is shining between two buildings and warming a narrow section of the beach. This looks like a nice spot to perch, so I throw my legs over the wall and stare out into the ocean.

I just can't get over how stunning that blue water looks out past the sand. I usually go into the water at least once when I'm this close, but I don't need to do that today. I can see how beautiful it is without freezing any more than I have this weekend already. That sidewalk is where I followed my crying bipolar ex back to the hotel for one of the most miserable walks of my life. Out there I was on a boat with Becca when she threw her grandma's ashes overboard. Down there is where Cartmanini and I had dinner at Lulu's. Unicorn and I were out in the water and then ran across that overhead walkway to a hotel for another drink. This sidewalk is where I went for a jog the day after Captain D and I got blitzkrieged the night before we cruised down to Coconut Grove to drink more. Down there's the Hilton where I sat naked on the deck after a good drilling session. This street is where Mom, Dad, and I drove in his Jag years after he used to raise hell on these same streets with his brother and partners in crime. Not fifteen feet away are the wave runners Sunshine and I rode just a few months ago.

I've been down here with friends, family, girls, and now by myself. All the trips were enjoyable at the time, except for the one with the ex. The trips I enjoyed the most were the ones with my parents, with Sunshine, and this one, all for different reasons. They definitely have the priorities in my memory bank though. It seems strange to have been here with different girls, almost like the Ghostbusters crossing the streams. At this age it's unrealistic to think that many things you do with a girl are going to be the first time you do those things. Even if I got married, it wouldn't be the first time for me doing that with a girl, as I wasted that cherry on the ex. My trip with Sunshine wasn't the first time to Lauderdale with a girl, but it was the first time on a wave runner, the first time I didn't drink, the first time at a fancy restaurant on Las Olas, the first time able to fuck that much with a new heart, and the first time experiencing all the other things with Sunshine in Lauderdale. It doesn't make it any less special, and it doesn't mean that I completely forgot the other enjoyable trips. It doesn't mean I miss those other girls or wish I was still with them, it just means that I tuck those fond memories away on a mental shelf and enjoy what I have today with Sunshine.

My thoughts for this trip were to spend a few days with just me and my bike in my home state. Maybe at some level I did make it a milestone trip with the grim reaper tattoo, the trip to my home city, my recent birthday, and the new year. Maybe I did come down here looking for answers. I can hear Axle singing in my head, "..searching for answers that never appear. Maybe if I looked real hard I'd see you're trying too, to understand this life that we're all going through." Lupo had told me that after the misfired shot with the gun pointed at his head, he'd scrapped everything, and ended up living in a rental car for a while. Then one day he sat on the beach, staring out at that vast ocean, and realized that his problems were so insignificant in the big scheme of things, that they weren't even worth considering. That was his turning point when he put the self-pity and regret away and just took life with what he had at that minute moving forward. I haven't had any wisdom bestowed on me sitting here on this wall. Maybe I haven't found any answers. Maybe I have found answers like "the trip with Sunshine, the trip with my parents, and the trip by myself," and I just need to find the right questions. One thing I do know is that before surgery I don't think I could've just sat here on this wall with the sun's warmth being absorbed by the black sweatshirt on my back like a solar panel, staring out at the sand and the big blue ocean, and appreciating the beauty of the moment without being distracted by the cars, people and places all around and behind me. I have learned something, I'm just not sure exactly what that is or how to capture it, but it's been a great lesson.

I take a few pics with the phone of a perfect shot of a couple palm trees in the setting sun with the ocean behind it and text it to Fatman and Sunshine. As I walk back to the hotel, I can tell it's cooled off as the sun falls down the horizon, like curtains closing for the set change before the final act of a play. This was the point of the day during spring break where actors on the sandy stage exited slowly to their hotels to change from bikinis and board shorts into club shirts and dresses for the final act. We'd stumble back to the hotel room, pass out for an hour, wake up, clean up, and have a few drinks to rejuvenate our buzz. Dressed, drunk, and sunburned, we'd leave the hotel for the last stage, which was a darkness lit up by the lights of the clubs and restaurants and buzzing with music and drunken youth without a care in the world. I'm not sunburned or drunk, but a nap and hot shower does sound good.

Per the hot spots in "Girls, Girls, Girls," they closed the Dollhouse in Ft. Lauderdale, but Ricky and I have rocked in Atlanta at the Tattletale. I'm going to call that kid and see if I can get a response out of him, since he hasn't answered an email from me for nearly a year now. I always worried a little about him going down to Columbia or Peru or wherever he was last living. He's such a good kid, and I felt bad for him when he just couldn't seem to find happiness in the States, and took off for South America to sort of find himself. I tried to help, told him no place is perfect, pointed out that hiding somewhere from life isn't getting him anywhere, and maybe he just needs to find a place and make it happy by surrounding himself with the right people where he lives. His phone number has changed, which isn't a good sign. I send him an email from the Crackberry as a last desperate attempt to confirm his survival. I sure hope that kid's okay.

Where should I go tonight? I wouldn't mind enjoying some food and entertainment right down A1A at the Rock Bar or thereabouts, but I'll just shoot across Las Olas, and maybe I'll find somewhere to get a bite. Downtown is kind of fucked up with construction. I get distracted by a Ferrari 360 in charcoal pearl paint in a parking lot and almost rear-end the BMW in front of me. That wouldn't have been good. The clutch cable feels like it's getting a little loose, so I need to remember to tighten that when I get back to Jax. There's not a whole lot of activity downtown just yet, and the only bikes I see are crotch rockets. I don't feel like listening to some eighteen year-olds tell me how fast their rice rockets are, so I'll just keep going. Pure Platinum, which I think might be the old Dollhouse, is on Federal, but I don't remember passing Federal and I'm already at Andrews. I guess I'll keep going west, but here's 95 already. I turn north onto 95 and take it to Oakland Park Blvd where I exit back east and figure I'll hit Federal sooner or later.

After seeing a terrible wreck scene lit up with police and rescue lights like a Christmas tree, I finally find Federal and turn left toward the neon signs. Pure Platinum looks okay, but Solid Gold looks even busier. I pull up and the valet guy lets me park on the sidewalk. After making sure they're serving dinner I head inside past the cutie checking ID's at the front. This is different. The restaurant is a separate part of the bar from where the strippers are dancing. I don't see a point in getting a table for just myself, so I grab a seat in the middle of the bar and get a cup of coffee to warm my insides. The waitress is a beautiful young girl with jet black hair, a pierced tongue and eyebrow, and an incredible body. There's nothing porn-resembling about her, no DD balloons, but just a great natural build that reminds me a lot of Sunshine's build. Like the rest of the waitresses, she's a present wrapped in a white corset, which really does a good job of showing off her upside-down heart-shaped ass. I notice that her corset has a slight rip in the side stitching, which regardless of how small, is an unwelcome distraction from an otherwise great view. It's easy to be forgiving when you see a girl at work or in a store that is attractive as a secondary function, but these girls are supposed to look perfect. Somehow that makes it an eyesore to see hail damage, wrinkles, or a clothing flaw. Wardrobe malfunction or not, she's still a doll.

While I'm waiting for my salad and bone-in ribeye to show up, I turn to the windows at the outer wall of the restaurant, where you can see the strippers on the main stage. I ask Jodi why the restaurant is separate, and she points at an older couple behind me that comes for dinner, but doesn't want to be right out there with the strippers. It seems bizarre to me that a couple that has an issue with strippers would come to Solid Gold for a nice dinner, but to each their own. I shoot the shit with a businessman from Boston who's going through a less-than-pleasant or cheap divorce. Eventually he decides to go out to the show bar area and donate some dollars. I will say there is some decent talent on the catwalk out there, but it's nice to be able to sit here and enjoy my dinner and the scenery behind the bar without having to deal with getting hassled by dancers for lap dances. Are they not even wearing bottoms out there? I ask if the place is full nude, and sure enough it is. Pink Pony in Atlanta was the only place I'd ever been where you could buy booze and the dancers were full nude. XTC in San Antonio was full nude, but you'd bring your own. Yes, I think I've officially found my new favorite strip club. It's a good thing I didn't have this place in San Antonio when I was drinking yet, as I think it would have been a frequent and expensive watering hole.

I ask Jodi if she ever dances, but she says she couldn't act that fake toward people. I can respect that she wants to be a genuine person, as that's admirable. I find it funny where girls draw their line in the moral sand as far as working at Hooters, bartending in a strip bar, dancing in a topless bar, being a full nude stripper, doing porn, hooking, or wherever. Everyone has their limits I guess. I see her pouring a sweet tea-flavored vodka shot, and ask how it tastes. She offers to make an extra shot for me to try, but I decline. She makes a little extra anyway and sets a shot in front of me, so as opposed to being rude or going into the whole heart surgery ramble, I thankfully accept. I admit it is pretty good, and it's just enough to put that warmth in my stomach in a way no amount of this coffee will do.

I have definitely changed over the last few years. Not so long ago at a time when I was single I would be sitting here doing shots with this girl, and doing my best to ensure that she and I were having breakfast in the morning. If Sunshine wasn't in my world, I can't say for sure that I wouldn't be trying to do that now, but perhaps without the shots. She's very attractive, seems fun, and even offers some feel of integrity with how she wants to be a genuine person, but likely brings her own bag of issues to the mattress as does everyone. I would never cheat on Sunshine, and really have no desire to do so. At this juncture I'm able to enjoy Jodi's service for the scenery and polite banter, pay my bill, wish her a happy new year, and head out the door without making any donations to her coworkers on the stage. I don't plan on ever seeing her again, and will simply register her as a pleasant image of beauty I appreciated today tucked away in my mind next to the palm trees in the setting sun and the charcoal Ferrari under the street light.

Sun 03 Jan 10

The lobby has a poor excuse for a continental breakfast, but if I wanted fancy I could've spent more money for a room. You get what you pay for. I choke down the half bagel and Hi-C, and clean out the hotel so I can hit the road. I notice a bottle opener with a fold-out corkscrew on the bathroom wall that's been painted over with the same white paint that was used to paint the door frame during the last rehabilitation to this room. The corkscrew is clearly necessary for the high-end clientele who splurged and stepped up from the spin-top wine for an occasion.

The sun's out, but it's fucking cold and there's no hiding from that chill in the air. I'm wearing all three T-shirts, both pairs of pants, and my balls are still retreating into my abdomen driving up A1A. I took the scenic route down here, but I just want to get home now. I take Sunrise over to 95 and head north at full throttle. Near West Palm Beach I slow down a little as I come up behind a sheriff. That's all I need is for them to add to their collection of speeding tickets issued to me. The bike sputters a little as I go up a hill, but I wouldn't think it'd be out of gas yet. I pull over and it only takes two gallons to fill up the tank, which means gas wasn't the problem for that hesitation. Fuck. Is the bike pissed because it thinks I'm going to sell it?

Holy shit, it's fucking cold out! These gloves are great, but I've got the throttle lock on full steam ahead and switch putting one hand between my legs to thaw it while I steer with the other hand. I'm definitely driving this thing hard and fast and just want to be home. I wonder if the sun's increasing warmth throughout the day will balance out the fact that I'm driving farther north at the same time.

The bike is cutting out, and it's definitely an electrical problem. Sonofabitch. Come on baby; get me home. I don't want to sell you. The bike is in its own special way saying, "Fuck you. This is for trying to get rid of me." The motor is officially shut down and I'm downshifting to neutral as I slowly coast over to the shoulder. The bike stops rolling at a guardrail, so at least I have a place to sit. About the time I pull over, so does a yellow Sexterra, but not the one driven by the guy who wanted to buy the bike. There are only three wires to the coil, and they're all tight. The guy tries to be helpful, but we both know there's nothing he can really do out here short of miracling my ass and the bike back to Jax.

This blows. I call Cousin Reno and Yoda, and neither of them answers. Finally Yoda calls and offers to come down with his trailer to pick me up. I'm in Vero Beach or so, which means it'll take him close to three hours to get here, but that beats pushing the bike that far. Normally I'd be beyond pissed at a time like this, but this isn't a cage fight, so getting mad doesn't help anything. The fact is I still had a great weekend, I'll eventually fix whatever's wrong, and I've got a good friend on the way down to help me get the bike and me back home. On a positive note, at least I won't have to spend the next three hours freezing my balls driving home either.

This feels like as good of a time and place as ever to end these memoirs. It seems a little incomplete to stop such a project at this point with so many unanswered questions in my mind, but I really don't know what lies ahead right now. The immediate fulcrum of my future is whether the Company in San Antonio offers me a position or not.

If they don't offer me the job, I'll probably still keep my eyes open for something. I just don't have confidence in the leadership at the Office. I'm the only person that sold anything last calendar year in the whole division, and I'm not even in sales. That's a major problem. If I can get back to Texas, have more stability, and make more money in a cheaper place to live, I have to take it. For right now I'm going to keep moving forward under the assumption that I'll be staying right where I am. I've got a nice little apartment, even with the little fucks next door that party until 1 am, but I'll eventually deal with them one way or another. I have an incredible girlfriend, who's happy selling art and just happy being happy. My parents have found renewed joy in their new grandchildren provided by Organisis and her husband. Vermin and her guy are doing well, just bought a house, and are getting married in the spring. I've got my Goat, my Anarchist, my Ape, and soon will have my chopper. I live in the sunshine state, even though I got soaked and freeze-dried two days ago, and I'm leaning against this guardrail freezing my ass right now. The beach is just minutes away, and hours away are everything from Lion Country Safari to Universal to Disney to Miami to Bike Week to Florabama Shores and everything in between. Most importantly I'm not only alive yet, but the healthiest I've been in years. I can run, lift, and fuck better than ever. I get really pissed off with the world around me sometimes, including the stupidity, unfairness, and downward spiral trends of the general population, but I try not to let it bring me down, and my perspectives are vastly improved overall. I appreciate skill exercised in performance of a craft, the two dimples in the lower back of a young girl in shape ironically called the whale tail, the flowing metal work of an exotic car, and the way the blue and orange melt into a sunset. The thrill of speed, growl of a throaty engine rumbling, and crunch of a distorted guitar all resonate through me and make my rebuilt heart race. There's no two ways about it. I've got a great life right now, and I don't take a fucking thing for granted anymore.

If they do offer me the job, my future will steer down a little different path, or maybe just the same path sooner. Sunshine and I will probably move into the Ventana and rent a two-bedroom apartment with two garages. I'll keep the Goat and one bike in one garage, and the shop stuff and other bike in the other garage. I'll dive into the new job balls-deep and do everything I can to not only maintain, but advance my career at the Company. The fact is they're going to be paying me a lot of money, more than I ever thought I'd make, and I don't want to waste a chance like this to make up for some of my lost years. Sunshine will look for a job in art sales, or whatever she can find that makes her happy. Maybe she can even start hiring herself out for cooking parties to teach groups of people to cook a meal in their home. Outside of the new job, I'll work on the chopper in the apartment garage while I look for a commercial place to rent so I can open Y Chrome back in San Antonio where it began back in August of 2002.

So much has happened since the last time I lived in Texas, but I don't look at it this potential move as a setback or even a reset. A change like this would instead be a significant advancement in my life. Over a decade ago I was a know-it-all, immortal kid finally graduating from ISU and excited about moving to San Antonio for a new career. I couldn't wait to live in Texas, make more money than I ever had before, and indulge in the sins of booze and hot young girls driving toward destruction with the accelerator through the floorboard. Now I'm still cautiously excited about the possibility of moving back to Texas. I'd be making more than I ever have before again, but I wouldn't be blowing fourteen-hundred bucks a month while drinking and banging everything in site this time. I'd probably save or invest some of the money, maybe get an MBA, and realistically probably spending way more than I should on vehicles. Much like last time, I'd still be disciplined in the gym, but I'd have traded the advantage of cock-strong youth for the advantages of wise sobriety and a new heart.

It's all just hopes and dreams until it happens. These balls aren't crystal, so all I can be sure of are experiences that have already happened, and even a large part of those are fuzzy at best. It doesn't really matter what comes next, because I do have a lot of experiences. I've red-lined a Ferrari, drove 160 mph in a 911 Turbo, tamed the Dragon's Tail on an Ape, and owned my own custom chopper shop. I've dead-lifted 590 lb, dipped with four plates hanging between my legs, had a screen door put in my abdomen for hernia repair, and had a cyborg valve put in my heart. I've graduated with honors in engineering, designed robots for the military, and been interviewed on the front page of the business section of the Times Union. I've been doing art since grade school, playing guitar since high school, and soon I'll have published a book.

It would be great if it sells and people enjoy it, but it doesn't matter if people buy it or like it or hate me for writing it. I did it for the experience of writing it, not for fame or fortune or acceptance. A real book written by a real author would probably have a more significant ending, but if this is the story of my life, then the story isn't really over until I die. I didn't set out to write an autobiography. I set out to write down whatever went through my head and help myself figure out what I could about my personal cartoon character in this little fucked up cartoon world. Axe the cartoon character has enjoyed his episodes of mischief over the years, but like the Coyote, he rarely hurt anyone but himself. Part of this rent-a-clown died in car wrecks, part of him drowned in a river in Illinois, and part of him never woke up from that slab in Colorado. Sometimes I miss the cartoon character, but I try to embrace the delayed maturation process too, and I'll always have those experiences that made me a better person today.

I find it rather poetic that I end this book standing here leaning against a guardrail. This trip may have not been the smoothest or most comfortable experience, but it was still a new adventure that I can add to my collection. As I think about the weekend, it's a fitting reflection of many aspects of my life in general. I came up with an idea, sort of planned ahead without committing, and decided to actually do it at the last minute. I got beat down by Mother Nature and my own vices, but I tested my limits, took the bad with the good, and still found a lot of enjoyment and beauty to appreciate along the way. I became impatient, went full throttle long and hard, and ended up breaking something causing myself more challenges. However, through the help of good people and my own resourcefulness, there's nothing I can't fix and I'll still come out unscathed.

I look down at the paralyzed engine in the Anarchist, and realize that these internal changes are all about evolution. Some things are still the same about me, some things I've consciously changed, and some things have changed despite my kicking and screaming. The old Shovelhead I used to drive was an old school V twin that leaked and broke down, but I miss it for what it was at that time in life, just like I miss the old Axe. I can't control the fact that I'm getting older and showing my age, but I accept that as a preferred alternative to being reduced to just another name carved in granite. Maybe I'm consciously living healthier because I really want to be a better person, and maybe it's just what I tell myself as opposed to admitting I can't live the way I used to. Self-induced brainwashing or not, I'm happy with the new Axe, and my renewed life. At first I resisted it, then I accepted it, and now I'm enjoying it even more than the last phase. Bouncing off this guardrail at high speed would have been more exciting and given me yet another story to tell, but slowly coasting up to it hurt a fuckload less, and better yet, it didn't scratch any paint on the bike, or any of the ink on me.

Afterword

The Denver landscape shrinks below us as our plane leaves for Texas. This weekend was one of the best trips I've taken to date. I wasn't surprised that somehow Cousin Reno and I failed to properly communicate and plan logistics when we arrived last Thursday, but eventually we all made it to Ronan's and still had time to grab a bite downtown. As we walked to the restaurant, it saddened me to see and hear a newscaster on the corner in such a nice area talking about a bunch of gang members that had been caged after numerous killings in that area. It sucks that even places like that aren't safe at night anymore. Where's Dexter when you need him?

Fortunately we didn't stay out too late Thursday, and we made it to Vermin's place Friday morning in plenty of time to join the convoy for whitewater rafting. Fat Uncle Slim stopped at her house too before he rode his rented Hawg to the mountains. I would've liked to have been able to ride with him too, but physics said I could only be in one place at once, and I'd never been whitewater rafting. The wet suits were more of a halter design compared to the ones I rent in San Diego for surfing, but they operate basically the same. Even though the guides bragged about how long it'd been since they showered, they were good entertainment and it's always good to see people happy with what they're doing. I was glad I'd listened to them and wore the splash jacket, as Reno and I caught the bulk of cold water blasts in the front of the raft. I wasn't nervous about drowning, but I just dreaded the thought of going over the side of the raft and ending up completely submerged in that frigid, freshly melted snow carrying us down the river. No wonder I thought I was in Colorado when I fell in that river in Illinois. I lost feeling in my feet from being in the water on the bottom of the raft, and my fingers closest to the water were like five little icicles hanging on to the paddle by the end of the trip. Besides a little coolness, it was a fucking blast though! The drops down a level into the next section of torrents usually resulted in a decrease in facial surface temperature, but an increase in adrenaline. It took Reno a few of those to learn not to yell at the river, so he'd quit getting a mouth full of cold water each time.

After seeing those mountain roads again, I got a major itch to get on two wheels and tear through those curves. Saturday we stopped by the Ape dealer in Ft. Collins to discuss the possibility of an RSV4. The Duc 1098 and 1198 are still badass V twins and engineering marvels, but I just didn't like how small they felt under me or the forward sloping seat that kept my balls against the tank and my head over the shield. The new BMW S1000RR is supposed to be one hell of a bike in performance, plus it's German engineered. I just don't like the idea of driving a straight four-cylinder in a bike or car, although I did enjoy both Candy and Caine and they were both German straight fours. There's just something about a V twin, or a V8 in cars, that gives that low end torque kick in the ass. I really don't even like the idea of the new Ape being a V4, but it's got the Italian styling and serious engineering performance. If I decide to buy anything, I think I'd buy it out here, carve through the mountains, leave it at one of the twisted sisters' places, come back in a month and ride it again, and eventually ship it back to Texas. It's too bad the dealer out here can't talk his owner into having one of each on the floor, so I can drive each one and decide which I like better. I could go to other dealerships to drive them, but I hate the idea of going to a dealer to drive a bike that I plan to buy somewhere else.

I was finally able to take my Spyderco and cut the calluses off the tips of my three middle fingers on my left hand yesterday. The last three months of constantly practicing was a little rough on the hand, but I completely fell in love with that new Martin acoustic I bought while playing it, and more importantly the practice paid off at Vermin's wedding on Saturday. Despite my amateur status, I felt like the music for the ceremony came out pretty well. It was starting to sprinkle before the ceremony while I was getting warmed up, and I jokingly asked Vermin if she wanted me to add "November Rain" to the play list. Because of the hesitation over the weather, I didn't even play "Beth" or "Patience." I went right from "Picture" to one verse of "Love Song," and then started playing and singing "Walk the Line" as Dad walked Vermin down the aisle. After the first verse, the guy that brought the PA looked back at me and notified me that the microphone wasn't on, so all they could hear was the music. How fucking embarrassing. At least I flipped the mic on and still got one good verse in before they got down the aisle. I decided to leave "More Than Words" as an instrumental since I still didn't feel 100% on the vocals for that. My favorite part was cranking out "All Shook Up" at the end as the wedding party and attendees exited. Performing Johnny Cash and Elvis in all black was rather fitting for my first public gig. The performance may not have been perfect, but I put my balls into it, added one more experience to my mental scrap book, and got to contribute something to my little sister's wedding day.

Thanks to the quick trip to a local music store for a mic sock, a genuine Les Paul Traditional will be accompanying my Martin back to Texas this week. I'd thought about getting one for the wedding, but chose the reduced dependency on electricity of the acoustic Martin. The BC Rich Class Axe I've had since college is about shot with the cracked body, broken whammy bar mount, failing tuning mechanisms, and poor connections, but I hadn't planned on getting a Les Paul anytime soon after just spending that much for the Martin. When I saw a Les Paul hanging on the wall marked from thirty-five hundred bucks down to twenty-three hundred and on sale for seventeen-fifty, I couldn't believe it considering the cheapest one I'd seen in San Antonio was twenty-eight hundred. Sunday we went back to the store so I could play it. I offered him fifteen-hundred for it, they called the owner, and I ended up getting it for sixteen-fifty. It's not that I really needed it, but for that price I couldn't pass it up. Ugh, I almost just shopped like a girl, but the fact is I would've eventually bought one anyway. Why not save over a grand? I can't fucking wait to get that Les Paul home and start making cool points with the neighbors. Between the two new guitars and the 12-string, I've got all the guitars I should ever need or even want. Done.

Tomorrow morning it'll be back to my new and improved life again. Every morning I wake up at 5 am to my alarm by Sixx AM telling me to open my eyes and reminding me that life is beautiful. I wake up next to the best girl in the world in a great little apartment in San Antonio, Texas. The Ape takes me less than three miles to work, unless there's heavy rain or I have to wear a suit, in which case I take the Goat. I drive the Anarchist on nights and weekends, but not to work. I have an incredible job at the Company, and I'm not going to jeopardize my career over a few naked devil chics. It was very flattering how hard the COO, Number three, and the President tried to keep me at the Office when I got the offer from the Company, but there are three things I learned from marriage: Never let yourself get talked into something, don't believe something bad will become perfect, and when you're done, you're done.

Not only was I able to meet Stu in Clearwater Beach before we left Florida, but I've already been to Houston with Cat to see Kramer when Ronan was in town for a Rugby tournament. It was a riot hanging with the rugby team, and Kramer's the same clown he was years ago, except with a few extra pounds. Houston had the usual selection of beauties decorating the clubs, but Austin is still tops, as we saw when Cartmanini visited. Sunshine and I took him to Austin to see Ronan in another rugby tournament. For a young single guy, I haven't found a better place than Austin to find the most beautiful girls around. At this age with a girl like Sunshine, those girls simply serve as beauty to be appreciated and reminders of the fun I used to have on 6th Street in my younger, immortal, more free spirited days.

As much fun as I used to have at the bars back then, I've probably enjoyed more memorable experiences in the San Antonio area in the last few months than I did in the whole six years of living here the first time. Sunshine and I have walked down the Riverwalk and through the Japanese Tea Gardens, climbed Enchanted Rock, and ridden the Ape through the hill country to Bandera. She and I have enjoyed meals at Altdorf Biergarten in Fredericksburg, Rudy's barbeque, Sushi Zushi, the lake-front Oasis and Hula Hut in Austin, Chuy's, and several other Mexican restaurants. We've gone to a tattoo convention, a couple concerts at the Scout Bar, a biker chili cook-off in New Braunfels, and a lowrider show, and I rode the Anarchist to meet Chip at a hot rod show in Austin. She and I each have a concealed weapon permit and a membership at Gold's Gym. Sunshine likes the people and terrain, as they remind her of Colorado. I like them because they remind me that once again I'm a Texan.

I do miss the beautiful ocean, beaches, and girls of Florida, Cousin Reno, and all the friends and coworkers back in the sunshine state, but I couldn't be happier in life than where I am right now. Sambo, Flanman, and others from the Institute all keep pretty busy with their wives and kids, so I don't get to see them as much as I'd like, but Chip's still around, lives just down the street, and still enjoys running around together when we can. Cat has a couple loin trophies, but he and the Mrs., Sunshine, and I still get together when schedules match. The people I work with are great, and a few of them even have a band. As much as I enjoy work and time with Sunshine or friends, I still love rocketing out 16 toward the hill country on the Ape, tearing around Scenic Loop Road in the Goat, and barreling down I10 on the Anarchist on the way home from downtown. For the first time since I left my parents' house in '92 to go to ISU, I feel like I have a home.

As part of my personal evolution, I've also tried to be a better person in general. If I see something I think someone in the family might like, I pick it up and send it to them. Sunshine and I are planning to visit Mom and Dad in the fall for the town festival when the Colorado crew will be home. I sent flowers to Hollywood's wife when her mother passed, took flowers to Sambo's house when his wife was in the hospital, and anonymously picked up the tab for a group of soldiers having lunch. People were very good to me when I went through surgery from the care packages from coworkers to all the cards from friends and family. Other people I don't even know that well like Alex, the cop whose tank I painted, and Nic, the calendar girl for the Stray Cat, called and graciously offered to help however they could when I was recovering on a couch. Now that I understand how those little gestures can be appreciated, I'm more apt to do those types of things for other people.

Y Chrome has been reduced to boxes of parts, a tool chest, and some other equipment that reside in the back of a rental garage at the apartment behind the Ape and Anarchist. Packing up that shop and six years of memories was probably the hardest part of moving, but one more reminder that nothing lasts forever. I gave it some thought, but even threw away the old Hardass gas tank that was to serve as my final resting place had things not gone in my favor. I hope to reopen Y Chrome again, but all my free time has been put toward practicing guitar since moving here. In addition I wanted to make sure I focused on getting established at the new career and make as great of an impression as possible. I checked into an MBA, but I'm having a hard time justifying the two years it'd take to get one. If I'm ever going to pursue it, now's the time. I'm sure after a few years, the salary gains would pay back the amount I'd have to pay to get it, above what the Company would contribute toward the degree. Even if I eventually recover the money it would cost, I'd never get back the time it would take to get an MBA, and that's more precious than money. Time can get a person money, but not vice versa.

I've got about eight and a half years before my contract comes up for renewal with the reaper, and I'm not going to waste a fucking second of that. Maybe I'll get more years after that, but I'm not taking anything for granted ever again. I want to make the most out of my career at the company, make as much dinero as I can while I'm there, but only to afford the ability to enjoy life outside of work. In the last two years I've done more reading, visiting friends and family, vacationing, guitar playing, relaxing, exercising, learning, and most importantly appreciating life than I had before. In that same period of time, I broke a lot of my cherries as I rode my Ape through the Smokey Mountains, entered one of my two-wheeled creations in the Rat's Hole bike show in Daytona Beach, rode a wave runner and a roller coaster, whitewater rafted, and performed my first live musical gig. Soon my Les Paul will be in Texas too, and I want to learn to play that and my Martin even better. Maybe I can find a couple bars and do an open-mic night or jam with the guys from work occasionally. I need to get back to the gun range and relax enough to focus on piercing a target with a couple hundred grains of lead at a time. Vermin bought me some German language books and a dvd, so I think I'll learn German, and then maybe get back to learning Spanish. I want to step up the workouts and eating habits even more and be the healthiest I can be, so I can milk every minute I can out of this heart and look my best while doing it. There's more art I'd like to do as well. I've got an empty canvas and full bottles of paint, both literally and figuratively.

Some things I'll do by myself, and other things I'll do with any combination of Sunshine, family, and friends, but I always want to be doing something. The grains of sand are falling from the bust to the hips of the hourglass and I want to enjoy and accomplish everything I can with as much passion as possible. When I'm sitting in a hospital in less than a decade, I'm going to look back, and say exactly what I said the last time. "It's been a wild fucking ride. I experienced life balls-deep, and those experiences are all I have right now to appreciate, because they're all I can take with me where I'm headed."

CPSIA information can be obtained at www.ICGtesting.com
Printed in the USA
LVOW10s1731040214

372314LV00001B/1/P